THE CALLING OF LAW

Emerging Legal Education

Series Editors:

Paul Maharg, *University of Northumbria, Newcastle upon Tyne, UK,*
Caroline Maughan, *University of the West of England, Bristol, UK* and
Elizabeth Mertz, *University of Wisconsin-Madison/American Bar Foundation, USA*

Emerging Legal Education is a forum for analysing the discourse of legal education and creating innovative ways of learning the law. The series focuses on research, theory and practice within legal education, drawing attention to historical, interdisciplinary and international characteristics, and is based upon imaginative and sophisticated educational thinking. The series takes a broad view of theory and practice. Series books are written for an international audience and are sensitive to the diversity of contexts in which law is taught, learned and practised.

Other titles in this series:

Law and Leadership
Integrating Leadership Studies into the Law School Curriculum
Edited by Paula Monopoli and Susan McCarty

The Arts and the Legal Academy
Beyond Text in Legal Education
Edited by Zenon Bańkowski, Maksymilian Del Mar and Paul Maharg

Affect and Legal Education
Emotion in Learning and Teaching the Law
Edited by Paul Maharg and Caroline Maughan

The Moral Imagination and the Legal Life
Beyond Text in Legal Education
Edited by Zenon Bankowski and Maksymilian Del Mar

The Calling of Law
The Pivotal Role of Vocational Legal Education

FIONA WESTWOOD
University of Glasgow, UK

AND

KAREN BARTON
University of Hertfordshire, UK

Routledge
Taylor & Francis Group

LONDON AND NEW YORK

First published 2014 by Ashgate Publishing

Published 2016 by Routledge
2 Park Square, Milton Park, Abingdon, Oxfordshire OX14 4RN
711 Third Avenue, New York, NY 10017, USA

First issued in paperback 2016

Routledge is an imprint of the Taylor & Francis Group, an informa business

British Library Cataloguing in Publication Data
A catalogue record for this book is available from the British Library

The Library of Congress has cataloged the printed edition as follows:
Westwood, Fiona, author.
The calling of law : the pivotal role of vocational legal education / by Fiona Westwood and Karen Barton.
   p. cm. – (Emerging legal education)
Includes bibliographical references and index.
ISBN 978-1-4094-5554-7 (hardback)
1. Law–Study and teaching. I. Barton, Karen, author. II. Title.
K100.W47 2014
340.071–dc23

2014003371

ISBN 13: 978-1-138-24780-2 (pbk)
ISBN 13: 978-1-4094-5554-7 (hbk)

Contents

PART I   CURIOSITY

PART II   CALLING

PART III   CHARACTER AND CONSCIENTIOUSNESS

PART IV   CONTRACT

PART V   CULTURE

List of Figures

List of Tables

Notes on Contributors and Editors

Editors

Karen Barton has had a long-term interest in teaching and learning, e-learning, professional learning and the use of IT within legal practice, and, as a result, has published widely and carried out a number of funded research projects in these areas. This includes the Standardised Client Initiative in interviewing skills for trainee lawyers; a JISC/HEA-funded e-Portfolio Project investigating the use of e-portfolios in professional legal education; and a JISC/HEA funded Open Education Resources project, *SimShare*. She has also carried out cross-disciplinary research in Professionalism and Professional Learning.

Her more general interest in professional education and training is reflected in her involvement in two leading edge projects: *The Standardised Client Project* and the e-*Portfolio Pilot Project* involving law students, trainees and trainers within a number of Scottish legal firms, and is author of a number of articles and book chapters in these areas. She has led a number of innovative teaching and learning projects involving transactional, web-based simulations as well as multimedia and webcast environments and is currently the Head of UH Online, the University of Hertfordshire's Centre for Online Distance Learning.

Fiona Westwood qualified as a solicitor in 1976 and practised for more than 20 years as a commercial lawyer, latterly as an equity partner of a large Glasgow and Edinburgh firm with particular responsibilities for business development across the whole business. Since 2000, she has been involved in postgraduate vocational skills development, initially as a part-time Tutor at Edinburgh and Strathclyde Universities and then Senior Lecturer in Legal Practice at Glasgow Graduate School of Law. She has also served on the Law Society of Scotland Working Parties on Education and Training, in particular as their CPD Project Leader, and on Professional Standards. Her particular areas of research, business and academic publications relate to practice leadership and management, professionalism and the development of professional judgement. In particular, she has researched and written three books on professionals, their organisations and their skill development. Her first two books, *Achieving Best Practice – Shaping Professionals for Success* and *Accelerated Best Practice – Implementing Success in Professional Firms* focus on the leadership and management of professional service organisations. Her third book, *Developing Resilience – the Key to Professional Success*, tackles personal and professional development from undergraduate to mastery. In addition to running her own management consultancy, Westwood Associates (www.westwood-associates.com), she is the Director of Continuing Professional Education, the School of Law, the University of Glasgow.

Contributors

Wilson Chow is Associate Professor of the Department of Professional Legal Education, Faculty of Law, The University of Hong Kong. He joined the Department in 1995 as the first full-time local teacher and acted as Head of Department between 2005 and 2011. He was responsible for the curriculum reform and development in the HKU Postgraduate Certificate in Laws programme and spearheaded major reform initiatives in legal education since 2001, was awarded a number of grants to develop innovative teaching tools and given the Faculty Outstanding Teaching Award in 2012. His key publications in the area of vocational legal education include: 'Too many "what's", too few "how's". *European Journal of Law and Technology*, 4.1, 2013 (with F. Tiba), 'Training the next generation of Hong Kong lawyers: new wine in a new bottle', in *Cross-Strait, Four-Region Law Developments in Taiwan, China, Hong Kong, and Macau – Legal Education for Lawyers and the Public*, edited by Dennis Tang and Chi Chung. Taipei: Institutum Jurisprudentiae, Academia Sinica, 2011 (in Chinese; with J. Jen, F. Chan and R. Wu); 'Developing active learning of skills in professional legal education – from theory to ethnography in Hong Kong'. *Asian Journal of Comparative Law*, 1.1, 2006 (with F. Chan and R. Wu); and 'The University of Hong Kong's New PCLL'. *Hong Kong Law Journal*, 32, 2002 (with S. Nathanson and F. Chan).

Craig Collins is Senior Lecturer in law at the Australian National University in Canberra, teaching into the Graduate Diploma of Legal Practice, LLB and JD programmes. He has worked as an academic lawyer for some 10 years and recently contracted as Lawyer Development Advisor with the Australian Government Solicitor. Previously, he worked for 12 years as a solicitor, including as a litigation partner developing particular expertise in commercial litigation, defamation and media law. Craig's research interests encompass legal history, legal education and the development of legal expertise, partly exemplified by the publication of a book chapter, 'Pericles was a Plumber: Towards Resolving the Liberal and Vocational Dichotomy in Legal Education', in *The Value of Knowledge: Illumination through Critical Prisms* (2008) (edited by Morley, I. and Crouch, M. New York: Rodopi).

Dr Richard L. Cruess graduated with a Bachelor of Arts from Princeton in 1951 and an MD from Columbia University in 1955. He is Professor of Orthopedic Surgery and a Member of the Centre for Medical Education at McGill University. An orthopaedic surgeon, he served as Chair of Orthopedics (1976–81), directing a basic science laboratory and publishing extensively in the field. He was Dean of the Faculty of Medicine at McGill University from 1981 to 1995. He was President of the Canadian Orthopedic Association (1977–78), the American Orthopedic Research Society (1975–76), and the Association of Canadian Medical Colleges (1992–94). He is an Officer of The Order of Canada and of *L'Ordre National du Québec*. Since 1995, with his wife Dr Sylvia Cruess, he has taught and carried out independent research on professionalism in medicine. They have published widely on the subject and been invited speakers at universities, hospitals and professional organizations throughout the world. In 2010 McGill University established the Richard and Sylvia Cruess Chair in Medical Education.

Dr Sylvia R. Cruess graduated from Vassar College with a Bachelor of Arts in 1951 and an MD from Columbia University in 1955. She is an Endocrinologist, Professor of Medicine and a Member of the Centre for Medical Education at McGill University. She previously served as Director of the Metabolic Day Centre (1968–78) and as Medical Director of the Royal Victoria Hospital (1978–95) in Montreal. She was a Member of the Deschamps Commission on Conduct of Research on Humans in Establishments. Since 1995, with her husband Dr Richard Cruess, she has taught and carried out research on professionalism in medicine. They have published extensively on the subject and been invited speakers at universities, hospitals, and professional organizations throughout the world. She is an Officer of the Order of Canada, and in 2011 McGill University established the Richard and Sylvia Cruess Chair in Medical Education.

Richard Devlin is Professor of Law at the Schulich School of Law and a University Research Professor at Dalhousie University. His areas of teaching include Contracts, Jurisprudence, Legal Ethics and Graduate Studies. He has published widely in various journals, nationally and internationally. Recent books include *Critical Disability Theory* and *Lawyers' Ethics and Professional Regulation* (2nd ed. 2012). In 2008 he was a recipient of the Canadian Association of Law Teachers Award for Academic Excellence. He has been involved in the design, development and delivery of Judicial Education programmes in Canada and abroad for more than 20 years. In 2012 he agreed to serve as the Founding President of the Canadian Association for Legal Ethics.

Jocelyn Downie is a Canada Research Chair in Health Law and Policy and a Professor in the Faculties of Law and Medicine at Dalhousie University. Her work in the area of legal ethics dates back to her law school days when she published a paper arguing for mandatory legal ethics education in Canadian law schools. She has taught the mandatory Legal Ethics and Professional Responsibility at Dalhousie University for over ten years. She has published papers on a variety of legal ethics topics, including professionalism, mandatory continuing legal ethics education and law societies as arbiters of mental fitness. She has also engaged in advocacy around legal ethics issues – in particular, challenging the Nova Scotia Barristers Society's policies and practices with respect to inquiries about applicants' mental health.

John Flood is Leverhulme Research Fellow studying the global consequences of the Legal Services Act 2007. He has researched and written extensively on legal profession and globalization of law. His articles have been published in *Modern Law Review, Law and Society Review, International Journal of the Legal Profession, Fordham Law Review* and *Boston College Law Review.* His book, *What Do Lawyers Do? An Ethnography of a Large Law Firm* (Quid Pro Books), is being published in 2013. He has an abiding interest in legal education and is a founding member of Law Without Walls. Flood is Professor of Law and Sociology at the University of Westminster and Visiting Professor of Law at UCL. His website is accessed at www.johnflood.com.

John Burwell Garvey is Professor of Law and Director of the Daniel Webster Scholar Honors Program at the University of New Hampshire School of Law, USA. He is the 2011 recipient of the New Hampshire Bar Association Award for Outstanding Professionalism, based upon his efforts with the Program. He has been named to the *National Jurist's* list of the 25 most influential people in legal education in the USA. In addition to his academic work, he has been repeatedly selected for inclusion in *Best Lawyers in America* for his expertise as an arbitrator and mediator.

Dr Sam Leinster graduated in medicine from the University of Edinburgh in 1971 and served for 5 years as a Surgical Specialist in the Royal Air Force. He then held clinical academic appointments at the Welsh National School of Medicine and the University of Liverpool, eventually becoming Professor of Surgery at the University of Liverpool with clinical and research interests in the treatment of cancer. In January 2001 he was appointed as Inaugural Dean of the new medical school at the University of East Anglia established in response to the government's decision to increase the number of medical students in the UK. Alongside his clinical career, he has established a reputation in medical education and developed expertise in curriculum design and methods of assessment which have been recognised by the award of a Senior Fellowship of the Higher Education Academy and a Fellowship of the Academy of Medical Educators. He has been an Educational Associate of the General Medical Council since 1996 and is currently involved with the GMC quality assurance processes for medical education at undergraduate and postgraduate level. His current academic interests are the meaning of medical professionalism and how it can be developed and assessed.

Michael Ng is Assistant Professor of the Department of Professional Legal Education, Faculty of Law, The University of Hong Kong. His research and teaching interests include corporate and investment transactions, professional legal education, comparative law and Chinese legal history. Author of *Foreign Direct Investment in China – Theories and Practices* (Routledge, 2013), he also published in *Journal of Comparative Law* (London), *International Journal of Asian Studies* (Cambridge) and *Hong Kong Law Journal* (Hong Kong), among others. Prior to joining the Faculty of Law in 2012, he has served in the legal and finance sectors for more than 15 years as commercial lawyer in private practice, finance director and chief investment officer at a listed multinational corporation and partner of private equity fund, focusing on mergers, acquisitions and direct investment transactions in Asia.

Donald Nicolson BA and LLB (University of Cape Town), Phd (Cantab) has taught law at the Universities of Cape Town, Warwick, Reading and Bristol, where he set up the University of Bristol Law Clinic. In 2000 he took up a chair at the University of Strathclyde Law School and in 2003 set up the University of Strathclyde Law Clinic. Donald currently teaches in the areas of evidence, legal methods and clinical legal practice. He has published numerous articles and a co-authored book on lawyers' ethics, various articles on clinical legal education, a co-edited book on affirmative action, articles on evidence theory, articles and a co-edited book on criminal law, and articles on law and gender, feminist legal theory and adjudication. His current research interests are in the areas of evidence and lawyers' ethics, with particular reference to moral development. He is on the editorial board of *Legal Ethics*, a trustee of the recently established LawWorks Scotland established to promote voluntary legal work and a member of Law Society of Scotland's Access to Justice Committee, and was awarded an OBE for services to the legal profession in 2011.

Moira Murray worked in private law firms and within government in the Australian Capital Territory until 2008. During that time she acted on behalf of and advised government departments and agencies, insurance companies and individuals in civil litigation matters in the Federal Court as well as various State Supreme and District Courts. Moira joined the Australian National University Legal Workshop in 2008. She convened the Professional Practice Core in 2012. She also convened Practice Management in 2010 and 2011, Civil Litigation in 2012 and regularly teaches in the Becoming A Practitioner course. Moira's research interests focus on teaching professionalism and reflective practice.

Margie Rowe is Senior Lecturer at the ANU College of Law, Australia, and Director of the College's professional legal education programme. Prior to becoming an academic, Margie was a practising lawyer for over 15 years, spanning private, community and government practice. Margie's research interests are legal education and the transition from student to practitioner, work-related learning and family law.

Suzanne Webbey was born in Sydney to post-war Lebanese immigrants. They grounded her in the value of education and the gift of living in a democratic society. She completed public schooling in Western Sydney, achieving high merit and entry to a combined Commerce/Law degree at the University of New South Wales at a time when the Whitlam Era free tuition policy remained in place. During

xvi   The Calling of Law

this time she worked as a volunteer at the Marrickville Legal Centre and with the Antioch Orthodox Church. Suzanne subsequently completed a Master of Laws at the University of Sydney. This reinforced her strong sense of justice and the importance of the rule of law in a stable democracy. Suzanne commenced practice in Sydney in 1989 and achieved partnership in 1999. Her expertise was developed in litigation and alternative dispute resolution after she completed training with the Australian Institute of Arbitrators and Mediators. Suzanne then worked as a sole practitioner until the firm merged with a commercial practice, allowing her to join the Australian National University from 2007 to 2012 as an Associate Lecturer, then Lecturer. During this time Suzanne continued to practice law and work as a volunteer with Legal Aid and continues to work in education.

Anne Zinkin, Senior Law Clerk to Chief Justice Linda S. Dalianis of the New Hampshire Supreme Court, is an attorney admitted to the California, New Hampshire and New York bars and has a BA with Honors in General Scholarship from Trinity College (1983) and a JD from New York University (1988), where she was an Arthur Garfield Hays Civil Liberties Fellow. She began her career as an employment litigator in San Francisco at Morrison & Foerster and Paul, Hastings, Janofsky & Walker, LLP. She was also a legal writing and research instructor at UC Berkeley School of Law and UC Hastings College of Law. She has worked at the New Hampshire Supreme Court since 2000.

PART I
Curiosity

Introduction

Karen Barton

Curiosity

In Carroll's Alice in Wonderland, it is curiosity that initially propels the young Alice into a confusing world where she is faced with a loss of confidence and a challenge to her identity as she struggles to find her way in this strange new environment. She is seldom given help or useful advice from the characters she meets and is invariably left to figure out how to solve the puzzles and problems she faces on her own. Her hesitant reply to the Caterpillar's question concerning her identity: 'I – I hardly know, sir, just at present – at least I know who I was when I got up this morning, but I think I must have been changed several times since then', reveals both vulnerability and at the same time a growing sense of her personal self along with the realisation that events had shaped her. As her curiosity leads her on, Alice learns from her experiences, the choices she makes and how she perceives the world. She grows. This wonderful depiction of the transition from childhood to adolescence, through periods of doubt, disequilibrium and self-realisation, reflects in many ways the journey from novice to professional. In a world of complex problems, competing demands and general erosion of professional status within society, when doubts and uncertainty abound, the reaffirmation of a 'calling' as a higher, core ideal of what it means to be a lawyer provides a sense of personal identity and self-actualisation that helps sustain individuals on their journey towards becoming a trusted, caring, empathetic and valued professional.

Preparation for any profession is a complex process of acquisition of knowledge, skills, experience and habits expressed as codes and values. As one of the 'learned' professions requiring advanced learning and high principles, law enjoys a special standing in society. In return for its status and rank, the legal profession is expected to exhibit the highest levels of honesty, trust and morality, the very values which underpin the legal system itself. In particular, the moral obligation placed upon lawyers to defend justice imposes upon them a reciprocal responsibility, which above all is based on upholding these values. This, in turn, entrusts to legal education a particular problem of addressing not only the substantive elements of the body of law, but a means through which the characteristics of the calling of law are imparted and instilled. As increased consumerism and regulation threatens the justification of its social contract and imposes external pressure on individual lawyers to exercise moral courage, there is a need to prepare the new generation of lawyers for these challenges by instilling in them qualities such as resilience, character, empathy and curiosity, traditionally honed through culture, constructive feedback, learning and practice. As a result, legal education plays a pivotal role in providing practical and active support to ensure the future viability of the legal profession.

The publication of this book is timely, coming at a time of disruptive change for the legal profession. With roots which can be traced back to the Clementi Report published in 2004, the Legal Services Acts in England (2007) and Scotland (2010) have introduced fundamental reform to the provision of legal services, the effects of which are still to be realised fully. Most recently the Legal Education and Training Review in England (LETR 2013) considered a range of environmental factors which will shape not only the sector but its education and training.

At a time when the very essence of the legal profession is under threat, this book calls for a realignment of the legal curriculum and pedagogies so as to emphasise the development of culture over industry, character over persuasion and calling over skill. In the context of the challenges outlined above and, as a result, we aim to provide an international resource for educationalists and other scholars, educators, practitioners, policymakers, technologists and students. Where Sullivan et al.'s *Educating Lawyers – Preparation for the Profession of Law* (2007) broke new ground in its advocacy of a new paradigm for improving the professional education of lawyers, this book aims to pick up this challenge and take it to the next stage of its realisation. Maharg (*Transforming Legal Education*, 2007) talks about four areas where the transformation of legal education might be rooted: experience, ethics, technology and collaboration. In each of these areas he uses words such as 'morals', 'creativity', 'culture' and 'collaboration' to describe the qualities that might emerge through this transformation. Adopting this approach, the chapters in this volume are grouped around the core content and four key themes of Curiosity, Calling, Character and Conscientiousness, Contract and Culture.

The book brings an international and cross-disciplinary perspective to the challenges ahead and presents alternative approaches aimed at tackling common issues, providing insight, and provoking debate. The proposals and solutions offered by the authors are rich in their variety and yet find common ground in the fundamental tenet of curriculum development and assessment, particularly in relation to the complexities of embedding ethics and ethical practice, professionalism and professional character. The legal jurisdictions represented in this volume, from the USA, to Canada, the United Kingdom, Hong Kong and Australia, face the same demands to address the globalisation and segmentation of the law. At the same time law schools are tasked with the responsibility of producing students who are 'ready to practice' while inculcating that sense of calling to their chosen profession. And so while individual chapters may emphasise a particular focus around one of the key themes as a response to these demands, there is a common thread running through which advocates instilling a commitment to the calling of law alongside a nurturing of the natural curiosity within as the bedrock of professionalism. The book, therefore, poses key questions about the purpose of vocational education and challenges readers to question current conventions and models with a view to transforming the system from within. In this respect it asks us to stimulate our own curiosity about what is possible and to imagine how that vision might be realized.

Structure and Outline of the Book

Calling

The book is arranged into Parts representing the key themes. In Part II we are asked to consider this notion of the 'Calling' of law and question to what extent it can survive in a climate of unprecedented change and reform. At the macro level, the forces to reduce the provision of legal services to a segmented and market-driven commodity appear overwhelming against a profession which is seriously under threat. John Flood and Fiona Westwood, in these opening chapters, set the scene for battle both eloquently and comprehensively.

John Flood's detailed review of the factors driving change in the provision of legal services globally and his comprehensive description of the resulting challenges for legal education in the face of such unprecedented and radical change is fascinating. Inevitably a chapter of this scope must be presented in context, but rather than focussing on its history, he concentrates instead on the changing nature of legal education in response to the challenges it faces across several key jurisdictions. His conclusion is that we are witnessing the Americanisation of legal education on a global scale and, while not necessarily advocating that particular route for the UK, he does urge us to take account of globalization and the role that professions play in society when reshaping legal education in order to maintain the reputation of the UK legal profession as a whole.

Fiona Westwood calls for vocational legal education to be re-established as a driver for change and force for 'self-actualisation'. Westwood's understanding of the current climate and the pressures driving change within the legal profession is perceptive. She presents the wide-ranging challenges the profession faces, and contends that vocational legal education's role is pivotal in maintaining the concept of a calling to the law; is crucial to the re-establishment of the social contract between the public and lawyers based on mutual respect and trust; and consequently enhances the protection of the profession's identity and role within society.

Character and Conscientiousness

In Part III, the notion of a calling is distilled into the concepts of 'Character' and 'Conscientiousness'. The chapters presented here are clearly rooted in the obligation placed on lawyers to provide the bedrock of a liberal, democratic society. For each of these authors the protection of access to justice for all and a moral duty to uphold the rights of individuals precedes all other considerations, and it is through development of conscientiousness and moral character that the public interest is served and professional identity formed.

Donald Nicholson presents an altru-ethical conception of professionalism which manifests itself as 'an obligation to contribute in some way to justice' and then goes on to suggest how legal education might instil a commitment to this ideal. Clearly Nicholson's intriguing definition strikes at the heart of the idea of a calling with its emphasis on professionalism grounded on ethics which in turn is grounded on altruism. He argues that these attributes are best developed in a culture which nurtures them and this, he contends, is not the culture which is prevalent in most law schools at present. He proposes instead a 'cradle to grave' Clinical Bachelor of Laws degree model as providing the foundation and ethos through which moral character, conscientiousness, ethics and altruism can be inculcated and provides a convincing argument to support his assertions.

Richard Devlin and Jocelyn Downie document the growing discontent with and criticism of the Canadian legal profession. They attribute this to a combination of factors including the failure to ensure access to justice; a general decline in professionalism and civility between lawyers; inadequate preparation of law students for practice; and the consequent erosion of public trust. Their proposition that 'Public Interest Vocationalism' might provide the means to respond to these issues is compelling not least in attempting to realign the aspirational aspects of a vocation or calling with the technical skills and competencies associated with the legal profession. Importantly, if taken to its logical conclusion, Public Interest Vocationalism facilitates a revision of the dominant models in the legal education system and serves as the catalyst for change. Devlin and Downie present some interesting examples of what this change might look like based on their own experiences as law teachers.

Contract

Part IV looks beyond the legal profession for insight into how the medical profession and medical education have dealt with the issues of self-perception and external relationships. Here the changing nature of a profession's 'Contract' with society is explored and how this, in turn, is altering the traditional notions of professionalism and, importantly, the professions' responses to this.

Sylvia and Richard Cruess focus on the concept of professional identity and the nature of the social contract within which professionals must function. They highlight the growing dichotomy between altruism and self-interest driven in large part by the changing nature of this contract; and argue that one way to resolve this is to develop a cognitive base of professionalism, based on a transformative process of acquiring personal identity, and to integrate this throughout the curriculum. They advocate ten general principles for achieving this, emphasising the importance of identity, role models and socialization, and which serve as a useful and welcome comparator for legal education.

Sam Leinster provides an interesting synopsis on the place and value of ethics and professionalism in medical education over time; the challenge to complacency that the profession faced in recent times; and how medical education responded to that challenge. The introduction of 'Fitness to Practice' processes in all UK medical schools, while not universally welcomed initially, is now generally accepted as an essential part of medical education and, he notes, is a good example of positive cultural change aimed at improving professional behaviour and re-establishing trust in the profession.

Culture

Part V is devoted to the theme of 'Culture' and brings further international perspective to the volume.

The first of two chapters from the Australian National University examine the challenges of facilitating common understandings and creating a collaborative culture in online communities of learners. Craig Collins and Suzanne Webbey focus on the relationship between legal culture and legal education and the historical tendency to favour individualistic approaches to learning how to be a lawyer over collaborative ones. They place Professional Legal Education at the focus of efforts directed towards reorientating and transforming engagement with the law among students, and describe recent innovations in their Graduate Diploma of Legal Practice programme aimed at doing just this. A model of simulated learning in 'virtual law firms' has been adapted to an entirely distance-learning approach and through this development they demonstrate how group work has been central to the effectiveness of the programme and argue that it is crucial in inculcating the language, customs, ethics and culture of the legal profession.

Simulation of a different sort, set within a different culture, is the focus of Wilson Chow and Michael Ng's chapter. Inspired by earlier work in the use of Standardised Clients in UK, USA and Australian law schools, Wilson and Ng describe how the approach was transferred to the Hong Kong jurisdiction and the challenges this posed. Their detailed account of the approach to selecting and training standardized clients provides evidence of how innovative approaches to legal education can cross cultures, institutions and professional backgrounds successfully, with some important insights on how this can be achieved. Like others, the issue of how communicative competence can be more authentically taught and assessed within the professional legal education curriculum has exercised their minds and the experience of adopting a methodology, which has been tried and tested in other cultural settings, has brought into focus the fact that 'it remains a highly contextualized discourse that is inevitably shaped by cultural and jurisdictional particularities'. This along with the challenges of language and institutional situations lead them to conclude that localised and indigenised schemes which effectively *de-standardise* some of the tools and processes is the way to spread the adoption of this approach globally.

Margie Rowe and Moira Murray discuss how they have integrated the teaching of concepts, practical skills and professionalism in their legal training programme at the Australian National University. They explore the challenges faced in teaching professionalism and communicating professional values in an online environment. By integrating online simulation with reality, structuring formative and summative assessment and identifying and dealing with individuals who negatively affect the learning of others they describe how they have dealt with the challenges of enabling distance-learning students to make the transition into practice. While technology can facilitate this transition, they also stress the importance of involving skilled practice mentors who are also working practitioners into this approach in a master-apprenticeship model.

Finally, John Garvey and Anne Zinkin's chapter present us with a vision of vocational legal education in the USA and a viable alternative to the State Bar Exam. In the Daniel Webster Scholar Honors Program at University of New Hampshire Law School, students are immersed in a two-year programme of practice-based, client-oriented education aimed at producing what they term 'client-ready' lawyers who, on successful completion, are certified as having passed the New Hampshire bar exam. While this concession in itself represents a significant change in culture for the legal profession in New Hampshire, the programme also provides a platform for reforming the culture of legal education as a whole. Garvey and Zinkin describe their programme in depth and spare no details in describing the challenges they faced. Evaluations of the programme have led to prominent legal scholars and organisations coming forward to endorse their method. They provide practical advice to law schools considering this type of reformation and conclude by affirming their adherence to Trujillo's (2007) assertion that '[l]aw schools have a moral obligation to society – and, to an even greater degree, to their students – to adequately prepare students to succeed as professionals'.

This seems to be a noble sentiment on which to conclude this introduction: with a call to act in the interests of society by placing students at the heart of vocational legal education reform.

References

Clementi, D. (2004), Review of the Regulatory Framework for Legal Services in England and Wales (http://webarchive.nationalarchives.gov.uk/ + http://www.legal-services-review.org.uk/content/report/index.htm) (accessed 2 August 2013).

LETR (Legal Education and Training Review) (2013), Setting Standards: Legal Services Education and Training regulation in England and Wales (accessed at http://letr.org.uk/wp-content/uploads/LETR-Report.pdf) (accessed 2 August 2013).

Maharg, P. (2007), *Transforming Legal Education: Learning and Teaching the Law in the Early Twenty-first Century.* Hampshire: Ashgate Publishing.

Sullivan, W.M., Colby, A., Wegner, J.W., Bond, L., Shulman, L.S. (2007), *Educating Lawyers – Preparation for the Profession of Law*. San Francisco: Jossey-Bass.

PART II
Calling

Chapter 1

The Global Contest for Legal Education[1]

John Flood

Introduction and Framework

Legal education is in a time of dramatic change throughout the world. In the US law schools are facing declines in numbers taking the LSAT and applications to law school where students fear the amount of debt they will incur and the lack of jobs that will let them pay off the debt. In England and Wales university tuition is rising and law jobs have also been declining. Elsewhere legal education is facing the demands of the market and is becoming more practice-oriented at the expense of its academic credibility. In China, for example, the ministries of education and justice have distinct ideas of what the composition of a law degree should be.

What is certain is that the academy has continuously gained control of the production of lawyers during the 20th century (Larson 1977). That control is now the subject of contestation between the state, regulators and the academy over content, form and product of legal education. My thesis in this chapter can be stated as follows. From an empirical point of view there is an inexorable move in the world towards the Americanization of legal education in the form of the widespread adoption of the JD degree over the LLB because of its perceived greater practice orientation. This shift is the result of three developments:

1. Globalization and the rise of technology;
2. The move from polycentric to monocentric modes of education and paths of entry into the legal profession; and
3. The re-professionalization of the legal profession as a result of the growth of the large law firm and new forms of regulation as in, for example, the UK and Australia.

Although globalization is located in element 1, it is in fact a pervasive feature of this chapter. To demonstrate the impact of globalization we only have to observe the figures for English-qualified lawyers, more precisely solicitors, working overseas. The Statistical Report for 2011 (Law Society 2012) informs us that

---

1   I am grateful to the Legal Services Board (LSB) for funding the research on which this chapter is based. The full report is available from the research website of the LSB at https://research.legalservicesboard.org.uk/. All the usual exclusions apply as these are my own opinions.

over 9,000 are practising outside their home jurisdiction[2] out of just over 160,000 solicitors on the Roll and nearly 122,000 with practising certificates. This makes us one of the largest exporters of legal talent, if not the biggest, in the world. From this two things of importance emerge: one is that the UK legal profession is global and that English-qualified lawyers are in demand outside the UK and the other is that UK-based legal education is respected elsewhere in the world. So at one level we can ask if there is anything amiss with English legal education? If not, is there any need to 'fix' it?

It has been 40 years since legal education was reviewed in England and Wales and set on its present course, with the subsequent addition of the Legal Practice Course. Since then, there has been massive change in the world, the professions, law and education. A review, therefore, is long overdue if our pedagogic model belongs to another age (Edmonds 2010). But underlying Edmonds' hypothesis is not a desire for some updating as that occurs all the time, but rather a question about the configuration of legal education within a changing regulatory structure that will bring about radical change to the legal profession. Should legal education undergo analogous radical change?

The UK is not the only country facing this question. Canada, France, India, Australia, China and the US, for example, are contemplating or instituting change in their legal education sectors. Would the UK be left behind if it failed to change? Does it matter if the UK lawyer is accepted globally? It does if the UK wishes to retain its hegemonic position alongside the US attorney.

This chapter is not so much concerned with the history of legal education although some mention of it will occur, but rather with more 'horizontal' dimensions that are geographical and technological in character.

1. English Legal Education

Legal education has maintained an *ad hoc* character for most of its existence in that it has never focused on a systematic theoretical approach to the study of law as civil law has, instead preferring a craft approach. It has long been tied to the fortunes of the legal profession. The distinction between civil and common law was exaggerated by the former having a privileged place in the universities with its connections to the church whereas common law was mostly confined to the Inns of Court (Boon and Webb 2008). The fortunes of legal education waxed and waned until the turn of the 19th and 20th centuries when both the Law Society and the Bar introduced examinations for intending lawyers. Apprenticeships were still the norm and actual teaching was carried out mostly by practitioners. University law schools were small in number and size, carried little intellectual weight and competed with the legal profession as conduits into the profession. Not until 1971 did solicitors have to possess a degree for entry. The Bar adopted a similar route in 1979.

---

2   Includes lawyers working in private practice and in-house legal departments.

The consequence of the move towards the academy becoming the main route of entry to the profession was a divergence of interests between academic and professional lawyers. The profession was not wholehearted in its support that a degree was necessary to be a professional lawyer. Solicitors especially viewed themselves as 'men of business' who needed experience of life rather than knowledge from books. Nevertheless with control of legal education divided between the academy and the profession, an uneasy alliance held. Law schools subscribed to core subjects prescribed by joint statements on qualifying law degrees while academic law became embedded in universities with the concomitant evolution of research and a proliferation of postgraduate law degrees, most notably LLMs and the PhD.

The profession focussed instead on vocational education, the Legal Practice Course and the Bar Vocational Course. Over these, considerable control was exercised by the Bar Council and Law Society and they laid the emphasis on practical skills required by lawyers in practice. Despite the Lord Chancellor's Advisory Committee on Legal Education and Conduct's (ACLEC) attempt to have the Bar and Law Society consider joint training, neither was prepared to take the step and each retained separate paths in their vocational training (Boon 2003). As a result, legal education has mostly been tinkered with rather than face a substantial overhaul in light of the changes to the legal services market wrought by the Legal Services Act 2007 (LSA).

In addition to the academic and vocational stages of English legal education there have been various interstitial steps of the common professional examination (CPE), later reincarnated as the Graduate Diploma in Law (GDL), enabling non-law graduates to convert their degrees over the span of a year into basic requirements to undertake the vocational stage. Some universities have also created a form of top-up degree taking two years. The CPE route has been a surprisingly popular one for entrants and also for employers.

The final part is the role of continuing legal education or continuing professional development. This is the requirement that training is part of a life-long learning process and that knowledge requires updating and expanding (Boon 2011). The academy probably plays a lesser role in the delivery of continuing legal education than private providers although some scholars are imagining 'cradle to grave' legal development models (Wilkins et al. 2011).

We can make two fundamental distinctions about legal education in the abstract. They are important as we consider the effects of changes on English legal education and the legal services market and their global repercussions. The first is that England has traditionally pursued education from the perspective of the profession rather than as an abstract body of knowledge. According to Weber's analysis of the emergence of legal professions and types of legal thought, England's development centred on the courts and the lawyers that grew up around them (Weber 1978). The courts and lawyers embodied the law in a series of precedents that were contested in future cases. Thus learning law was essentially an empirical matter based on craft principles which were augmented by the guild character of lawyers' practice which reserved certain activities to them alone (Epstein 1998; Krause 1998; Ogilvie 2008). Craft with its associated apprenticeship was not taught in universities but through practice. This has given English law (and consequently US law) a form which we term 'substantive rationality', that is the procedure follows formal rules but the system is not closed in that, for example, 'policy interventions' can be introduced. Although the academy has become the main route into the legal profession, Twining (1994) still felt that English legal education was an uncomfortable compromise between the academy and the profession.

The second distinction is based on the scientific approach to law as found in canon or Roman law and hence in a number of civil law systems. This approach starts from either sacred texts or codes such as the Napoleonic codes – law is imbued with abstraction and is viewed as a system of norms which are interpreted through highly formal and rational means. Scientific approaches to law are located with the university as the sole mode of entry although some apprenticeship is necessary to impart some practical skills. Lawyers were not therefore the carriers and makers of law, as were English lawyers, but rather engaged in restating the formally rational aspects of law. Thus, for example, notaries in Italy were, and are, one of the most important strata of the legal profession who, through their alliance with the universities, promoted the scientific approach to law in their drafting and construction of legal documents. In the UK and US notaries are perceived as guarantors of oaths. Similarities to the Italian example are apparent within the French and German systems.

The results of these distinctions, which have ramifications for modern legal education, have been posed as academy versus profession. Which is to dominate the reproduction of the legal profession? Clearly both sides, civil and common law, have compromised: both embrace the academy and both use some element of craft training. Yet the distinction remains and has consequences for how those outside the UK perceive the quality of legal education and training here. Despite this characterization this polarization of academy and profession is not inevitable: indeed, we could envisage a collaborative model that engages both sides with mutual respect. Institutionally, within the UK there is a beginning of cooperation but more is needed if collaboration is to be a working reality.

2. Globalization, the Rise of Technology, and the Legal Services Act

(a) Globalization

In the period since the end of the Second World War there have been fundamental changes to the economy which have spurred further developments elsewhere. We can briefly characterize them as the rise of the neo-liberal agenda (Held et al. 1999). They include the emergence of supra-national institutions such as the United Nations, World Bank and International Monetary Fund, the World Trade

Organization and the European Community. These have been further bolstered by the hybrid institutions including the G8, G20 and others such as the Organization of European Cooperation and Development (OECD).

If the international community was trying to reshape the global agenda by establishing a range of institutions that aimed to conserve international comity and stability, private initiatives in this direction were not to be excluded. These came about through the intercession of foundations and other NGOs such as the Ford Foundation's law and modernization movement in conjunction with the World Bank. These projects sought to bring new legal education and liberal justice systems to third world countries (Ford Foundation 2000; Krishnan 2004).

Institutions of commerce and business played a significant role in developing private ordering in the world. Three are notable in this context, namely investment banks, accounting firms and law firms. All three were largely Anglo-Saxon creations and reflected this outlook in their approaches even though they became global in reach. They were natural allies of the neo-liberal agenda and promoted the 'Washington Consensus' (Williamson 2002). These institutions were and are small in number and have generally established long-term relationships that have made it difficult for those outside the club to join (Flood 2002, 2007). This is particularly the case in areas such as mergers and acquisitions and capital markets. The result is that their impact is out of proportion to their number.

Taking law firms, for example, a report by McKinsey (Becker et al. 2001), the consulting firm, showed that big law firms were arranged along a spectrum from those firms with global reach (for example, Baker and McKenzie and Clifford Chance) to those which were highly selective about the numbers of offices they maintained, generally preferring to depend on a 'best friends network' of correspondent firms (for example, Wachtell Lipton and Slaughter and May) (Beaverstock et al. 1999; 2000). The crucial aspect of these big law firms is that they were capable of articulating normative orders based around the construction of agreements and contracts that were accepted throughout the world (Morgan and Quack 2006; Faulconbridge and Muzio 2008; Flood and Sosa 2008; Gessner 2009). Indeed, they were central to the formation of international standards through organizations such as the International Swaps and Derivatives Association.

The large law firms that grew rapidly throughout the second half of the 20th century and into the 21st promoted the paramountcy of Western common law or, more accurately, that of New York state law and English law. Western common law relied on the contract as its core constituent and large law firm lawyers were masters at drafting it. Complex, detailed and comprehensive, the Anglo-American contract was drafted to respond to every eventuality. Such contracts run to hundreds and thousands of pages: they were effectively self-sufficient. Unlike the continental European contract which spanned a few pages relying on the Civil Codes to provide the rationale for its interpretation, they were the antithesis of the common law style. Globalized capital was driven by the capital markets of New York and London and therefore employed the legal technology it was used to. Paris and Amsterdam had long lost their pre-eminent positions in global capital (Cassis 2006). Despite the recession, the large law firms have maintained their dominant positions within the global economy (Sahl 2010; Fordham Law Review 2010).

The preceding is not meant to create the impression that law serves only corporate ends, although much of the analysis of legal services and the legal profession tends to focus on this sector. For heuristic purposes it is worth adopting the analysis proposed by Heinz and Laumann (1982) that law practice is separated into hemispheres, namely the corporate and the individual. The distinction here is dependent on client and work. For example, securitization work is performed for corporate clients and only rarely for individual clients unless of high worth. Divorce, however, is individual client work. The two hemispheres are characterized by lawyers from different backgrounds and legal training. Generally, the corporate hemisphere is dominated by elites while the individual is populated by lower status lawyers, both in terms of perceived quality of law school and level of qualifications. There are overlaps and crossovers when corporate lawyers might undertake some individual-type work such as obtaining immigration permits for corporate executives, but on the whole the hemispheres are separate and the two mingle little. Recent research on legal careers suggests that, because of the growing 'lateral move' market in law practice, this kind of distinction is being attenuated (Dinovitzer et al. 2004).

From the perspective of globalization we might think that the individual hemisphere is fundamentally local in its jurisdiction, for example, crime, family, employment, but there has been a growing amount of individual-type work in the global arena. Sousa Santos[3] and his colleagues demonstrated how land movements and struggles for cheaper medicines among others have moved onto the global stage enlisting the help of NGOs to transport strategies and tactics across national borders. For example, the challenges to WIPO and the big pharmaceutical companies' control of HIV drugs in South Africa led to sweeping changes in the pricing and distribution of these medicines across the globe (Klug 2005). These movements combine the political and the legal, but as Levine and Pearce (2009) argue, legal education and entry requirements to practice do have an impact on the rule of law and human rights, especially in countries where such things are still nascent.

From the perspective of legal education, globalization is an ineluctable movement which it must contend with in order to stay ahead (Davis 2006). Aggressive moves are being made by the US, Australia and even some continental European countries alongside China towards building a bigger share of the graduate legal market. Terry's tour through global educational initiatives shows how strong this has become: the percentage increases in mobility are stark. For example, Terry (2011: 3) reproduces WTO statistics to show that global mobility of students between 1999 and 2007 from North America rose by 50 per cent and from Latin America and the Caribbean by 70 per cent.

---

3 See for example http://www.bbk.ac.uk/law/our-research/leverhulme-lectures-professor-boaventura-de-sousa-santos.

(b) Rise of Technology

The second major shift in this period has been the rise of technology and its impact on the practice of law. Futurologists such as Richard Susskind have prophesied, Jeremiah-like, that the end of lawyers is nigh (2008). While this is speculative, certain fundamental changes are taking place. The clearest evidence is in the rise of commoditization and outsourcing of legal services to countries like India where the legal process outsourcing industry has grown enormously in the 21st century (see Daly and Silver 2007). And, if we take on board Thomas Friedman's ideas about the world becoming flatter and therefore potentially more intricately linked, then all lawyers are affected as their worlds become virtually tied together and substantively convergent (Terry 2008b). Terry states that the effects are felt by small firm lawyers as much as big law firms. According to her, because of offshoring and supply chaining, clients are constantly having to seek legal advice from around the world. Not all wish to hire big law firms and look for lawyers with local ties but global appreciation.

The underpinning for this move can be seen in a speech given by Mark Chandler, general counsel of Cisco, in 2007 (Earnhardt 2007). He argued that his company's motivations and that of law firms are 'orthogonal' to each other, that is, they diverge. Cisco reduces costs while law firms raise theirs. Much of law firm work – routine document production, for example – can be slotted into technological knowledge management systems thus reducing law firm spend. For Chandler lawyers' addiction to maximizing revenue per partner has to be reined in to become a 'normalized' business model. Increasing use of outsourcing and paralegal work leaving highly trained lawyers to concentrate on difficult legal issues is, to Chandler's mind, a better use of scarce professional resources. The answer is for lawyers to use more technology in their law practices.

The rise of technology goes hand in hand with specialization. Legal practice has become highly fragmented and disparate. The difference between criminal and civil work is almost unbridgeable in a modern legal practice, except for a few areas such as white collar crime which represents corporate interests primarily. Not only is the content radically different but the administrative facilities required to conduct these practices are dissimilar. Taking corporate legal practice as an example, the compartmentalization of practice and law firms is such that departments within firms are tantamount to a species of firm themselves with often low levels of communication between them (Flood 1996; Mayson 1997; Heinz et al. 2001; Faulconbridge and Muzio 2008). Compartmentalization requires efficient intra-departmental communication and inter-departmental communication through means such as email and instant messaging. Maximizing utility of lawyers in departments requires a sustained level of standardization through the use of boilerplate documents (for example, ISDA and LMA) and knowledge management systems. Increasingly firms are attempting to counter hyper-specialization by organizing themselves on a matrix which includes legal specialisms and sectoral divisions: for example, Antitrust, Telecommunications, Media and Technology.

Outsourcing, which depends on technology for its success, is already having an impact on legal practice and will eventually reach legal education. Although outsourcing is usually associated with offshoring to India, depending on economic circumstances and the changing economy of the legal market, it is beginning to signify more onshoring than otherwise. Companies that have begun in India or employed Indian lawyers are setting up offices in the UK and the US, for example, Pangea3, recently bought by Thomson Reuters and Integreon which has opened an office in Bristol. Two forces are impelling this move: one is the uncertain regulatory environment for outsourcing and offshoring, especially in the US, which is persuading both lawyers and clients that domestic inshoring companies could be preferable to offshoring; the other is the recession which has made legal labour much less expensive than it used to be. It has brought into focus Henderson's (2009) depiction of the binomial distribution of starting salaries for lawyers out of law school where there is a spike around the $50,000 point and another at the $160,000 point (see NALP 2008). Onshore outsourcers are offering salaries at the lower end of the scale and finding ample demand from applicants (Timmons 2011).

Others have repeated and amplified this message countless times since. Perhaps the one part of the system that has not heard the message is legal education. It still lives in the Gutenberg age where the book reigns supreme. Computers are used in class but mostly as note-taking adjuncts rather than serious accompaniments to education. The two most graphic demonstrations of the use of technology are the creation of a legal game by a Dutch law firm called 'The Game', and the running of new approach to legal education called 'Law Without Walls' (LWOW) designed at the University of Miami School of Law. The former provides a simulated environment of a takeover by a foreign company and includes real documents, interviews with characters and a context that encourages real-time participation. LWOW brought together a number of students from different law schools in different countries and time zones through the medium interactive video-conferencing. In addition, the faculty were interdisciplinary which stretched the students outside the normal limits of legal study (Padgett 2011). In both cases the technology reaches well outside the classroom, but at great expense and it is unlikely that most law schools could sustain these types of instruction given the high human capital costs.[4]

At a simpler level, some law teachers have brought experiential learning into the classroom in a way that requires a high level of correlative thinking on the part of the students. Using simulations, students establish law offices, deal with witnesses and document production, as well as researching the law. Maharg (2007, 2011) argues that games and simulations encourage interdisciplinarity and

---

4   It is unclear which way this might go. As the programme expands (for 2011 and 2012 it has added another four law schools) there will come critical limits to the current pedagogical techniques. There are alternatives such as the Open University model which has successfully placed distance learning on the global map since its inception in the 1960s.

interaction with other students, which among other things enables values and ethics to be brought into the situation something that is otherwise excluded. The new law school at York University has introduced elements of this in its curriculum.[5]

(c) The Legal Services Act

The Legal Services Act (LSA) envisages a legal services market in which lawyers are only one significant element. Since a range of differently skilled people will be populating the legal services market it is worth asking what distinguishes them from each other in order to understand what forms of legal education are being highlighted. I shall return to this discussion later in the third section of the chapter when looking at the production of producers by producers. The key distinction to be drawn is between the proportions of theoretical education and practical training.

Professional work is fundamentally made up of two components: indeterminacy and technicality (Jamous and Peloille 1970). The balance between the two creates an ideal environment for the professional ethos. Technicality refers to the instrumental aspects of work, for example, how to fill in a document correctly or knowing when to file an instrument at court. Every occupation has a technical component to its work. Not every occupation has indeterminacy, especially not in the way professions claim. For example, a clergyman has to be able to carry out certain rites such as marriage or a christening, but the ability to do them does not fully demarcate the role. In order for a clergyman to be accepted by parishioners and the church as a clergyman, he (or she) must express a commitment to his (or her) 'vocation' by a declaration of faith. Without this the role is valueless.

So it is for lawyers. While they do not claim faith as their raison d'être, they adhere to principles of free access to justice and the rule of law. These are philosophical and moral positions which are considered essential to the proper functioning of a legal system. We have enshrined these values in part in the regulatory objectives in Part One of the LSA. These ethical values are inculcated in the theoretical element of legal education most often in the universities. In addition we can include the imparting of knowledge of the substantive elements of law – the nature of contract; distinguishing between rights *in rem* and *in personam*; and so forth. One unfortunate aspect of professionalization is that it inevitably produces information asymmetries that are potentially deleterious to the client (Decker and Yarrow 2010).

The market 'predicted' by the LSA will be diverse and so will require a range of skills from the full professional education to the limited technical training. It is possible to argue that the former – full professional education – is living on borrowed time as the main model of legal education. Webb (1999) argued that commodification of legal education in England and Wales has already arrived with a number of potentially adverse consequences. He analyses the impact of the flexibilisation of legal education allowing students 'to jump on and off the

---

5   See Studying Law at York Law School http://www.york.ac.uk/law/ugrad/llb/index.htm.

conveyor belt at various points in the process'. For many students, Webb says, this could be a false hope because legal employers would not be convinced by bureaucratic recruitment policies partly because of credential inflation and so instead search for packages of 'credentials, technical skills and charismatic qualities' (Brown 1995: 42). The result is a stratified market for skills in legal services. This probably would not sit well, for example, with how the Council of European Bars (CCBE) would expect to see legal education harmonized across Europe (Gout 1998), nor how indeed legal education has fared, that is, as there has been no such harmonization of academic cores (Ladrup-Pedersen 2007). This led Colin Tyre, president of the CCBE in 2007 to say that what is essential for 'day one outcomes' 'is an understanding of what it is to be a lawyer rather than merely having the knowledge of what the law is' (Tyre 2007: 3).

What we can draw from this is that the possibility of the success of the disaggregation of legal education and training is dependent on two factors. One is the quantity and quality of training required to deliver particular services in the legal services market. The other is the reception of such training by a legal market that is imbued with a conservative culture when it comes to innovation. The LSA then has two challenges with respect to legal education and training. One is to ensure enough lawyers or legally trained personnel are in the market to satisfy need; the other is to remove some of the barriers to this end that are harder to perceive because their visibility is murky at best. The struggle in the balance of indeterminacy and technicality rages in many forms and will continue to assert itself most probably in the guise of upholding the public interest.

In the next section I will consider the various pathways taken into law in different countries and their consequences. As the CCBE discovered, harmonization is not a realistic goal for legal education and there are some fundamental differences in systems. The most stark is between the US and the UK.

3. Monocentric and Polycentric Modes of Legal Education

(a) UK Legal Education

To date, the UK has adopted a multi-path entry way into the legal services market for those who wish to work in it. In describing this I have deliberately avoided using the words lawyer or legal profession, which other systems would most likely insist on. Julian Lonbay (2007: 10) sets out the paths as if they were train lines with crossing points. Using admission to the Roll of solicitors as his end point, he identifies three main lines to that terminus.[6] The shortest and least complicated is for applicants to take A levels to enter university and then take a law degree which is followed by a one-year Legal Practice Course (LPC) and a two-year Training Contract (TC), including a Professional Skills Course (PSC), leading to admission.

---

6   Dixon (2011) identifies four routes to admission for solicitors.

In general this takes about six years without break and excluding A levels. The second shortest route is again to take A levels then a degree in any subject and follow this with a one-year Common Professional Examination (or Graduate Diploma in Law), then join line one with an LPC and TC to admission. This adds one year to the duration, making seven years in total. The third route is much more variable and elastic over time taken. Indeed route three might not lead to admission but halt along the journey. Lonbay's starting point is either a student with GCSEs[7] or a mature student who enters some kind of unspecified legal employment. This student joins the Institute of Legal Executives (ILEX) and takes ILEX part one and two examinations to become a legal executive. After a further two years of legal experience the student can enrol on the LPC, take the PSC and be admitted. This route allows for broken journeys and rest stops or even premature halts. After taking these journeys an admitted solicitor should be capable of demonstrating the expected SRA day one outcomes (Boon and Webb 2008: 119). There is no explicit regulation of the law degree (LLB) by the legal profession apart from the joint statements on the qualifying aspects of the degree and, of course, review by the Quality Assurance Agency for Higher Education which examines all degree courses including law. With respect to the Legal Practice Course and Bar Professional Training Course there is closer supervision involving audits and inspections by their respective regulators, the Solicitors' Regulation Authority and the Bar Standards Board. For LLMs and research degrees in law there is no professional review.

The UK therefore currently falls within the *polycentric* model of legal education and training as do a number of other countries and legal systems. But many do not.

(b) US Legal Education

I contrast the US system of legal education and training in order to examine a *monocentric* system. The American Bar Association is granted the power to accredit and approve law schools and regulate them by the US Department of Education.[8] The result of this accreditation is that a student graduating with a Juris Doctor (JD) degree can sit the bar examination of any state in the US.[9] There are approximately 200 ABA accredited law schools in the US. Law schools which

---

7   GCSEs are examinations taken generally at the age of 15 or 16 to test competency in a range of basic subjects.

8   The National Advisory Committee on Institutional Quality and Integrity advises the Secretary for Education on accreditation issues. At a recent review the ABA was found to be out of compliance with 17 regulations and although its accreditation was renewed, it was given one year to remedy the problems (http://taxprof.typepad.com/taxprof_blog/2011/06/aba-is.html).

9   Some states still permit reading for the bar but this type of route is not significantly used. While there may some elements of polycentrism in the US bar admissions process, it remains essentially monocentric.

are not accredited may be permitted by their state to confer eligibility on students to take the state's bar examination. The number of unaccredited US law schools is not fully known. For example, California recognizes three categories of law schools: ABA accredited; state-accredited law schools; and unaccredited law schools. The latter two have varying degrees of regulation (unaccredited does not mean unregulated). California has the largest number of state-accredited and unaccredited law schools in the US, 18 and 28 respectively. Graduates from these latter two types can take only the California Bar examination and those of others if the other state will permit it.

Law schools in the US are categorized as 'professional schools' along with medical, journalism and business schools. They are distinguished from graduate schools which confer advanced degrees on research students (PhDs). Admission to professional school normally requires the completion of an undergraduate degree which for law can be in any discipline. The ABA requirements say that at least three-fourths of a first degree must be completed for entry to law school. However, this partial requirement applies more to the unaccredited law schools. For example, California requires 60 hours of undergraduate credit for entry to state-accredited and unaccredited law schools. In addition to a first degree entrants need to take an admissions test which is usually the Law Schools Admissions Test (LSAT), and in many cases write a personal statement.

US ABA-accredited law schools meet quite rigorous standards in delivering legal education. A law degree involves 58,000 minutes of instruction via an academic year of 130 days. Each credit is equated to 700 minutes of tuition. Most full-time JD programs take three years although there are some programs that reduce the time to two years. Satisfactory completion of law school enables a graduate to sit the state's bar examination although this is typically prefaced by a two-month bar review course which prepares students for the actual examination. Bar examinations, though state-based, have almost become nationwide through their adoption of the Multistate Bar Examination (MBE) developed by the National Conference of Bar Examiners (NCBE). The MBE covers contracts, torts, constitutional law, crime, evidence and civil procedure and for some states a passing grade in this exam is sufficient for admission to the state bar. Indeed, the NCBE has developed the Uniform Bar Examination which is designed to test all the requirements for admission, but can be supplemented with additional tests if individual states so determine. So far five states have adopted the uniform approach. The NCBE also administers the MPRE which is the professional responsibility examination that every applicant must pass.[10] Following admission to the state bar a lawyer commences practice immediately without articles or training contracts.[11]

---

10   The state of Wisconsin still applies diploma privilege which means that graduates of the state's law schools are automatically admitted to the Bar without sitting an examination (Wisconsin Supreme Court Rules, Chapter 40).

11   A very small number of US states require some kind of clerkship as a condition of admission, for example, Delaware requires a clerkship of five months,

The ABA may seem to exercise considerable sway over law schools but the academy, as in the UK, is generally free to organize the content of legal education in its own way. However, its freedom is being challenged by the ABA's proposal to reform law school accreditation standards. The Standards Review Committee has put forward a series of changes to liberalize legal education by permitting more online instruction, less security for faculty and various other changes.[12] These have been challenged by the American Association of Law Schools (AALS) which sees the proposals as deleterious for legal education as a whole and, instead, has requested the ABA restart its review.[13] The ABA has refused to do this (Hansen 2011).

(c) Canadian and Australian Legal Education

If the US and UK forms of legal education represent the extremes on the polycentric to monocentric scale, others are located more towards the middle combining aspects of both. The Canadian and Australian systems of legal education are situated here. Both countries have elements of the UK and the US. This is understandable in the context of Australia having been a transit point for lawyers who wanted to requalify in either the US or the UK. In the case of Canada, it is almost inevitable because of its proximity to the US and the American demand for its graduates.

(i) Canada

Canadian law schools were long viewed as 'trade' schools under the authority of the law societies and in the period following the Second World War its grip was loosened with legal education becoming academic (Boyd 2005). The Arthurs report of 1983 showed that Canadian legal education was insular, inward looking and illiberal and argued that it should embrace contextualization and learn from the social sciences (Arthurs 1983). While this happened to an extent with the rise of socio-legal studies and clinical legal education, some commentators believe there has been a retrenchment as legal education has become 'commodified' (Boyd 2005; Martin 2009). In part this has come about because the University of Toronto Faculty of Law decided to compete head to head with the best US law schools. This involved raising tuition costs significantly in order to increase faculty salaries and target the big law firms throughout North America as potential employers of its students.

Canadian legal education mainly adopts the US model. There are 17 law schools where a four-year bachelor's degree is followed by a three-year law degree. This can either be in a common law or civil law faculty. In Quebec the civil law faculties do not require a preliminary degree for entry. After law school a graduate joins a

---

http://courts.delaware.gov/bbe/docs/ClerkshipRequirements2011memo.pdf.

12   See ABA Standards Review Committee at http://www.americanbar.org/groups/legal_education/committees/standards_review.html.

13   See AALS letter to ABA at http://www.aals.org/advocacy/Olivas.pdf.

law society in one of the provinces (Ontario is the largest) and articles for a period in a law firm then takes the society's licensing examination.[14] As it stands there is no national standard for legal education in Canada (unlike in the US with the ABA) as befits the looser federal structure in this part of North America. The Federation of Law Societies of Canada set up a Task Force on the Canadian Common Law Degree which reported in 2009 and which has recommended a set of standards be introduced by 2015. These cover competencies, skills, problem-solving, oral and written communications, along with awareness of ethics and professionalism, as well as substantive legal knowledge. It is worth pointing out that in some respects Canada is the spiritual home for the English Legal Practice Course as it was Canadian academic thinking that informed the framers of the LPC.

A number of Canadian law schools now use the JD degree in favour of the LLB, and some faculties have joint ventures with US law schools for their graduates to complete their studies with both Canadian and US law degrees. The key one is the joint venture between Osgoode Hall Law School of York University and New York University Law School where over four years students take two sets of two-year courses at Osgoode and NYU to earn a Canadian LLB and an ABA-approved JD (De Brennan 2008). Two other Canadian law schools have linked with US schools for joint degrees: Windsor with the University of Detroit Mercy and Ottawa with Michigan State University and American University in Washington. For De Brennan (2008) the combined effects of the Canada-US Free Trade Agreement of 1989 and the North American Free Trade Agreement of the 1990s increased the levels of cross-border trade between Canada and the US which concomitantly required raised awareness of the legal aspects of cross-border trade issues.

Two results flow from these developments: one is that the 'Americanization' of legal education is taking hold, and two is that, it is argued, students may be 'self-censoring' themselves to ensure they only take courses in law school (business law, commercial paper) that will appeal to law firms. Some have suggested this can be analogous to 'dumbing down' or de-liberalizing the curriculum as it restricts intellectual challenge and diminishes diversity (Thornton 2001; cf. Webb 1999; James 2009). Certainly Canada's legal education is in transition.

(ii) Australia
Australia has also been changing and rationalizing its legal education system in not dissimilar ways to Canada. There are 32 accredited university law schools,[15] of which 28 are public and two are private institutions (Douglas and Nottage 2009: 5). Accreditation of universities is carried out on a national basis whereas law school accreditation is state by state. Higher education bodies can be set up under federal or state authority but in order for them to receive grants or their students to obtain assistance they must be recognized by the Australian Minister for Education, Science and Training. Quality standards for universities are managed through the

---

14   For details see http://rc.lsuc.on.ca/jsp/licensingprocesslawyer/exams.jsp.
15   See Council of Australian Law Deans at http://www.cald.asn.au/schools.htm.

Australian Qualifications Framework.[16] The accreditation, content and quality of law degrees is supervised at state level. So, for example, in New South Wales, law degrees are accredited by the Legal Professions Admissions Board under the Legal Profession Act and the Legal Profession Admission Rules (Douglas and Nottage 2009: 4–5).

There is, however, an equivalent of the ABA which is the Law Council of Australia. The Law Council has been active in working with the United States Conference of Chief Justices (CCJ) and the ABA to improve access for Australian lawyers to the US legal market. Australia is reasonably liberal in permitting qualified American lawyers to be admitted without further study. And the CCJ has passed resolutions calling on states to reciprocate, which Delaware has done (Terry 2008a: 198: Hawkins 2008). This bilateral action has raised the level of Australian-American interaction as Hawkins (2008: 11) notes: 'Australia and the United States have much in common in terms of their legal systems'.

Australian legal education has similarities with both the Canadian and the US. The typical Australian route is via study in another discipline which is then combined with study in law. Law is a three-year degree so that a full study period is around five years. Although law is classified as an undergraduate degree, because of the combined nature of the degree, a number of US law schools have recognized the equivalence of Australian and US law degrees which allows for the exchange of students and also reinforces the action taken by the CCJ. The University of Melbourne has taken this a step further by transforming its law degree into a graduate JD which requires prior undergraduate study and taking the LSAT (Pollak 2008). Subjects and duration of the law degree fall under the authority of the Law Admissions Consultative Committee, an advisory body of the Australian Council of Chief Justices. Practical legal training is compulsory and is often done as a postgraduate element or through clinical legal education. Unlike other jurisdictions, Australian states do not examine their entrants but evaluate them on the basis of their academic and practical training in addition to character and fitness requirements. However, new lawyers are only given a restricted practising certificate for their first two years that necessitates supervision.

Australia is now in the process of establishing a national legal services market. The National Legal Profession Reform Project initiated by the Council of Australian Governments is attempting, through a taskforce set up in 2009, to harmonize regulation of the profession across states. This has been consulting although it is thought it will take some time to implement the proposals, especially as Western Australia and South Australia are reluctant to join in.[17]

From a globalizing perspective the US has the lead over the UK in exporting ideas and technologies of legal education. The general flow is towards graduate degrees with an eye on their links to practice. There are clear similarities of difficulty over content in the US and the UK. That aspect does not seem to be

---

16 See http://www.aqf.edu.au.
17 See http://www.ag.gov.au/legalprofession.

overwhelmingly influenced by the level at which education takes place, however there is an expectation that graduate level degrees will resonate better with more mature students than undergraduates. However, it is worth flagging up one area of caution. Pearce and Levine (2009) argue that moving towards more selective American-style models of legal education will deny the opportunity to become legally trained to many with adverse consequences for the rule of law, access to justice and human rights. Elite lawyers will focus on the commercial side of law at the expense of the social and humane. But access to justice for the majority will become harder and more remote as a result.

Conclusion

Legal education in the UK cannot be viewed in isolation from the rest of the world. Laurel Terry's research into the global aspects of the removal of trade barriers and their effects on legal service providers shows how deeply imbricated legal professions are in globalization (Terry 2008a, 2008b, 2010). The UK legal profession has enjoyed immense status and popularity in the globalization of law. English and New York law have long dominated the international economy and so benefited their legal professions. However UK legal education is at a crossroads. The undergraduate legal degree combined with apprenticeship is losing attraction in the world. The US appears to be more advanced in exporting its model of legal education, especially to emergent markets such as China and India. Even former adherents to the British model (Australia and Canada) are adopting American ways.

There are critics who argue that moving to graduate legal education restricts access to the profession and is damaging to human rights and access to justice while others say that undergraduates are too immature to understand the entirety of legal education. Parts of Europe, however, seem to find the undergraduate model congenial for its legal services market while there is significant movement towards US-style graduate degrees. The UK itself has not been immune from a form of creeping Americanization of legal education. Dixon's study (2011) of entry into the legal profession shows that the attractiveness of the qualifying law degree as the main mode of entry to admission has fallen since the 1980s while the CPE/GDL route has risen in popularity to the extent that since 1996–97, 22 per cent of admitted solicitors followed this route.[18] There is no equivalence between the CPE and the JD but in terms of timing and career selection it shows an interesting trend that might suggest later legal training is desirable, at least from the perspective of the employer if not the student. What this does indicate is that the connection between education and practice is getting stronger so that the idea of law as a liberal education is fading and no longer an ideal in itself (cf. Bradney 1995, 2003).

---

18 Note the New York State Board of Examiners demand proof of a qualifying law degree from foreign applicants which the CPE and LPC combination does not yet satisfy.

The cost of education is another factor driving this tendency, as the debates between the ABA and the AALS demonstrate. In all countries the expense of education is rising rapidly and expectations are not always met by success in the job market and law has suffered in this respect. This is not to say that innovation is not being sought. The 2011 Future Ed3 conference in New York placed the business model of legal education at the centre of its programme.[19] For example, Wilkins et al. (2011) proposed a four-phase model of legal education and development that moves from 'cradle to grave' realizing that education is not a finite activity.

Any changes in the way legal education is delivered need to take account of globalization and the role that professions play in society. Denying their effects could cause serious damage to the reputation of the UK legal profession.

References

Arthurs, Harry (1983), *Law and Learning: Report to the Social Sciences and Humanities Research Council of Canada*. Consultative Group on Research and Education in Law. Minister of Supply and Services: Ottawa.

Beaverstock, J., Smith, R. and Taylor, P. (1999), 'The Long Arm of the Law: London's Law Firms in a Globalizing World Economy', *Environment and Planning A*, 31 (10): 1857–76.

Beaverstock, J., Smith, R. and Taylor, P. (2000), 'Geographies of Globalization: United States Law Firms in World Cities', *Urban Geography*, 21 (2): 95–120.

Becker, Wendy, Herman, Miriam, Samuelson, Peter and Webb, Allen (2001), *Lawyers Get Down to Business*. McKinsey: New York.

Boon, Andrew (2003), 'Ethics in Legal Education and Training: Four Reports, Three Jurisdictions and a Prospectus', *Legal Ethics*, 5 (1): 34–67.

Boon, Andrew (2011), *Continuing Professional Development in Ethics and Professional Conduct for Solicitors*. Solicitors' Regulation Authority.

Boon, Andrew and Webb, Julian (2008), 'Legal Education and Training in England and Wales: Back to the Future?' *Journal of Legal Education*, 58 (1): 79–121.

Boyd, Susan (2005), 'Corporatism and Legal Education in Canada', *Social and Legal Studies*, 14 (2): 287–97.

Bradney, Anthony (1995), 'Raising the Drawbridge: Defending University Law Schools', *Web Journal of Current Legal Issues*, http://webjcli.ncl.ac.uk/articles1/bradney1.html.

Bradney, Anthony (2003), *Conversations, Choices and Chances: The Liberal Law School in the Twenty-First Century*. Hart Publishing: Oxford.

Brown, Phillip (1995), 'Cultural Capital and Social Exclusion: Some Observations on Recent Trends in Education, Employment and the Labour Market', *Work, Employment and Society*, 9 (1): 29–51.

---

19 See Future Ed3 at http://www.nyls.edu/centers/harlan_scholar_centers/institute_for_information_law_and_policy/events/future_ed/fe3_program.

Cassis, Youssef (2006), *Capitals of Capital: A History of International Financial Centres, 1780–2005*. Cambridge University Press: Cambridge.

Daly, Mary and Silver, Carole (2007), 'Flattening the World of Legal Services? The Ethical and Liability Minefields of Offshoring Legal and Law-Related Services', *Georgetown Journal of International Law*, 38: 401–47.

Davis, Kenneth (2006), 'Six Uneasy Pieces', *Wisconsin International Law Journal*, 14 (1): 31–40.

De Brennan, Sebastian (2008), 'Legal Education in Australia – Is It Time to Take a (Maple) Leaf Out of Canada's Book?', http://www.asialink.unimelb.edu. au/__data/assets/pdf_file/0003/8157/SDBrennan.pdf.

Decker, Christopher and Yarrow, George (2010), *Understanding the Economic Rationale for Legal Services Regulation*. Legal Services Board: London.

Dinovitzer, Ronit et al. (2004), *After the JD: The First Results of a National Study of Legal Careers*. http://www.americanbarfoundation.org/uploads/cms/documents/ajd.pdf.

Dixon, David (2011), *Entry to the Solicitors' Profession: 1980–2010*. Law Society: London.

Douglas, James and Nottage, Luke (2009), 'The Role of Practice in Legal Education: National Report for Australia', 18th International Congress on Comparative Law, Topic 1D, Legal Education, Washington, 25 July–1 August, 2010.

Earnhardt, John (2007), 'Cisco General Counsel on State of Technology in the Law', http://blogs.cisco.com/news/cisco_general_counsel_on_state_of_technology_in_the_law/.

Edmonds, David (2010), 'Training the Lawyers of the Future – A Regulator's View', Lord Upjohn Lecture, 19 November, Legal Services Board.

Epstein, Stephan (1998), 'Craft Guilds, Apprenticeship, and Technological Change in Preindustrial Europe', *Journal of Economic History*, 58 (3): 684–713.

Faulconbridge, James and Muzio, Daniel (2008), 'Organizational Professionalism in Globalizing Law Firms', *Work, Employment and Society*, 22 (1): 7–25.

Flood, John (1996), 'Megalawyering in the Global Order: The Cultural, Social and Economic Transformation of Global Legal Practice', *International Journal of the Legal Profession*, 3 (1–2): 169–214.

Flood, John (2002), 'Capital Markets, Globalisation and Global Elites', in Michael Likosky (ed.) *Transnational Legal Processes: Globalisation and Power Disparities*. Cambridge University Press: Cambridge.

Flood, John (2007), 'Lawyers as Sanctifiers of Value Creation', *Indiana Journal of Global Legal Studies*, 14 (1): 35–66.

Flood, John and Sosa, Fabian (2008), 'Lawyers, Law Firms and the Stabilization of Transnational Business', *Northwestern Journal of International Law and Business*, 28 (3): 489–525.

Ford Foundation (2000), *Many Roads to Justice: The Law-Related Work of the Ford Foundation Grantees Around the World*, M. McClymont and S. Golub (eds). Ford Foundation: New York.

Fordham Law Review (2010), 'Symposium: The Economic Downturn And The Legal Profession', *Fordham Law Review*, 78 (5): 2051–450.

Gessner, Volkmar (ed.) (2009), *Contractual Certainty in International Trade: Empirical Studies and Theoretical Debates on Institutional Support for Global Economic Exchanges*. Hart Publishing: Oxford.

Gout, M. (1998), *Quality Harmonization: The Current Situation and the Ways Forward*, CCBE: Brussels.

Hansen, Mark (2011), 'ABA Committee Members Show No Inclination to Start Over on Accreditation Standards Review', *ABA Journal*, April 2, http://www.abajournal.com/news/article/aba_committee_members_show_no_inclination_to_start_over_on_accreditiation_s/.

Hawkins, Murray (2008), 'Questions and Answers: Australian Legal Education and Bar Admissions', *The Bar Examiner*, February: 11–22.

Heinz, John and Laumann, Edward (1982), *Chicago Lawyers: The Social Structure of the Bar*. Russell Sage Foundation and American Bar Foundation: New York and Chicago.

Heinz, John, Nelson, Robert and Laumann, Edward (2001), 'The Scale of Justice: Observations on the Transformation of Urban Law Practice', *Annual Review of Sociology*, 27: 337–62.

Held, David, McGrew, Anthony, Goldblatt, David and Perraton, Jonathon (1999), *Global Transformations: Politics, Economics and Culture*. Polity Press: Cambridge.

Henderson, William (2009), 'The Bursting of the Pedigree Bubble', *NALP Bulletin*, 21 (7): 12–14.

James, Nickolas (2009), 'Australian Legal Education and the Instability of Critique', TC Beirne School of Law, University of Queensland, http://ssrn.com/abstract=1490780.

Jamous, H and Peloille, B. (1970), 'Professions or Self-Perpetuating Systems? Changes in the French University-Hospital System', in J.A. Jackson (ed.), *Professions and Professionalization*. Cambridge University Press: Cambridge.

Klug, Heinz (2005), 'Campaigning for Life: Building a New Transnational Solidarity in the Face of HIV/AIDS and TRIPS', in Boaventura de Sousa Santos and Cesar Rodriguez-Garavito (eds), *Law and Globalization from Below: Towards a Cosmopolitan Legality*. Cambridge University Press: Cambridge.

Krause, Elliott (1998), *Death of the Guilds: Professions, States, and the Advance of Capitalism, 1930 to the Present*. Yale University Press: New Haven.

Krishnan, Jayanth (2004), 'Professor Kingsfield Goes to Delhi: American Academics, the Ford Foundation, and the Development of Legal Education in India', *American Journal of Legal History*, 46 (4): 447–99.

Ladrup-Pedersen, Tom (2007), 'Tuning Legal Studies in Europe: Preliminary Results', CCBE Conference on Improving Legal Education and Training in a Converging Europe.

Larson, Magali (1977), *The Rise of Professionalism: A Sociological Analysis*. University of California Press: Berkeley.

Law Society (2012), *Trends in the Solicitors' Profession: Annual Statistical Report 2011*. London: Law Society.

Levine, Samuel and Pearce, Russell (2009), 'Rethinking the Legal Reform Agenda: Will Raising the Standards for Bar Admission Promote or Undermine Democracy, Human Rights, and the Rule of Law?', *Fordham Law Review*, 77 (4): 1635–63.

Lonbay, Julian (2007), 'Training Outcomes for European Lawyers', CCBE Conference on Improving Legal Education and Training in a Converging Europe.

Maharg, Paul (2007), *Transforming Legal Education: Learning and Teaching the Law in the Early Twenty-first Century*. Ashgate: Aldershot.

Maharg, Paul (2011), 'Sea-change', http://www.slideshare.net/paulmaharg/bileta-2011-slideshare-version.

Martin, Robert (2009), 'University Legal Education is Corrupt Beyond Repair' (paper on file with author).

Mayson, Stephen (1997), *Making Sense of Law Firms: Strategy, Structures and Ownership*. Blackstone Press: London.

Morgan, Glenn and Quack, Sigrid (2006), 'Global Networks or Global Firms? The Organizational Implications of the Internationalisation of Law Firms', in A. Ferner, J. Quintanilla and C. Sanchez-Runde (eds), *Multinationals and the Construction of Transnational Practices: Convergence and Diversity in the Global Economy*. Palgrave Macmillan: LondonNALP, 2008, 'Another Picture Worth 1,000 Words', http://www.nalp.org/anotherpicture.

Olgilvie, Sheilagh (2008), 'Rehabilitating the Guilds: A Reply', *Economic History Review*, 61 (1): 175–82.

Padgett, Tim (2011), 'Amid Changes, Law School Tries to Get Real', *Time*, 23 May.

Pearce, Russell and Levine, Samuel (2009), 'Rethinking the Legal Reform Agenda: Will Raising the Standards for Bar Admission Promote or Undermine Democracy, Human Rights, and Rule of Law?', *Fordham Law Review*, 77 (4): 1635–63.

Pollak, Michael (2008), 'Revolutionary Changes to Legal Education', *The Australian*, 19 September, http://www.theaustralian.com.au/business/legal-affairs/revolution-in-legal-education/story-e6frg97x-1111117523930.

Sahl, Jack (2010), 'Foreword: The New Era – Quo Vadis?' *Akron Law Review*, 43 (3): 641–76.

Susskind, Richard (2008), *The End of Lawyers?: Rethinking the Nature of Legal Services*. Oxford University Press: Oxford.

Terry, Laurel (2006), 'Living with the Bologna Process: Recommendations to the German Legal Education Community from a U.S. Perspective', *German Law Journal*, 7 (11): 863–905.

Terry, Laurel (2007), 'A 'How To' Guide for Incorporating Global and Comparative Perspectives into the Required Professional Responsibility Course', *Saint Louis University Law Journal*, 51 (3): 1135–59.

Terry, Laurel (2008a), 'The Future Regulation of the Legal Profession: The Impact of Treating the Legal Profession as "Service Providers"', *Journal of the Professional Lawyer*, 189–211.

Terry, Laurel (2008b), 'The Legal World is Flat: Globalization and its Effects on Lawyers Practicing in Non-Global Law Firms', *Northwestern Journal of International Law and Business*, 28 (3): 527–59.

Terry, Laurel (2008c), 'The Bologna Process and its Impact in Europe: It's So Much More than Degree Changes', *Vanderbilt Journal of Transnational Law*, 41 (1): 107–228.

Terry, Laurel (2010), 'From GATS to APEC: The Impact of Trade Agreements on Legal Services', *Akron Law Review*, 43 (3): 875–984.

Terry, Laurel (forthcoming 2011), 'International Initiatives that Facilitate Global Mobility in Higher Education', 2011 *Michigan State Law Review*, 1–54.

Thornton, Margaret (2001), 'Among the Ruins: Law in the Neo-Liberal Academy', *Windsor Yearbook of Access to Justice*, 20: 3–23.

Timmons, Heather (2011), 'Legal Outsourcing Firms Creating Jobs for American Lawyers', *New York Times*, 2 June.

Tyre, Colin (2007), 'The Contribution of Education and Training to the Identity of the Legal Profession', CCBE Conference on Improving Legal Education and Training in a Converging Europe.

Twining, William (1994), *Blackstone's Tower: The English Law School*. Sweet and Maxwell: London.

Webb, Julian (1999), 'Post-Fordism and the Reformation of Liberal Legal Education, in Fiona Cownie (ed.) *The Law School: Global Issues, Local Questions*. Ashgate: Aldershot.

Weber, Max (1978), 'The Legal Honoratiores and the Types of Legal Thought', *Economy and Society*, G. Roth and C. Wittich (eds), Volume 2: 784–802. Berkeley: University of California Press.

Wilkins, David, Way, Cory and Westfahl, Scott (2011), '" Cradle to Grave" Legal Professional Development', Future Ed3, New York Law School, 15–16 April, http://dotank.nyls.edu/futureed/2011proposals/13ctg.pdf.

Williamson, Jeffrey (2002), 'Winners and Losers over Two Centuries of Globalization', Working Paper 9161, Cambridge, MA: National Bureau of Economic Research.

Chapter 2

Vocational Legal Education – Its Pivotal Role in the Future of the Legal Profession

Fiona Westwood

Introduction

This chapter argues the importance of vocational education in allowing the UK legal profession to respond positively to the challenges that stem from a number of marketplace trends that are directly impacting on how legal services are provided.

The profession is facing considerable and disruptive change (Schumpeter 1950). Neo-liberalisation and the introduction of external regulation have reduced the power and influence of the professional bodies to effect independent reform. The LETR report (2013) has considered in detail how to sustain the competency of the legal profession as it copes with the impact of globalisation and increasing fragmentation and specialism, as well as how to reform it to meet future needs in a market that is difficult to predict (Boon et al. 2005). As job certainty erodes and career structures weaken, it is essential to look at the impact of this on experiential learning and the transition from novice to expert (Cheetham and Chivers 2005; Raelin 2008). And, perhaps most importantly, it is essential to reflect upon the effect of commoditisation and information technology on the nature of the job of being a lawyer and its 'calling', with its emphasis on personal responsibility and service to society (Kronman 1995; Boon et al. 2001).

The first section of this chapter will look at the effect of these influencers of change. It will argue that the UK legal profession's identity is threatened by globalisation, external regulation, client demands and new entrants into their core market and services and, as with any profession, its survival is predicated on the viability of its perceived value to society. Its unique role and sustainability lies in relation to protecting access to justice by ensuring the continued provision of legal practitioners who are able to defend their clients' rights and who are trusted, caring, empathic and valued.

The second section will consider the implications of this for UK legal education and using one model of professionalism will describe the ways that education can help sustain the future of the legal profession as a whole. Sullivan et al. (2007: 22) describe the six tasks of professional education as:

1. developing fundamental knowledge and skill,
2. providing the capacity to engage in complex practice,
3. enabling learning to make judgments under conditions of uncertainty,
4. teaching how to learn from experience,
5. introducing the disciplines of creating and participating in a responsible and effective professional community and
6. forming the ability and willingness to join an enterprise of public service.

While it is accepted that current UK higher and vocation deliverers address most of these, they tend to 'teach' them individually with few longitudinal linkages (Re 1994; Westwood 2010). It seems likely that globalisation and alternative business structures will increase specialisation of functions and limit the traditional methods of the development of practitioners through exposure to more experienced people. Vocational legal education, with its historical ability to deliver lawyers 'fit to practice' has endeavoured to be the bridge between the law degree with the 'swamp' of early practice (Maughan and Webb 2005). Therefore, it has the potential to play a pivotal role in developing new delivery mechanisms so as to ensure the provision of contemporary practitioners and the future viability of the legal profession as an independent and distinct entity.

Finally, this chapter will consider what has been demonstrated by these earlier sections in the context of the individual lawyer. Regardless of the external drivers to increase commoditisation and reduce the need for input from 'qualified' lawyers (Susskind 2008), clients need expert professionals who are skilled in making complex decisions in the circumstances of particular situations (Maister 1997; Rhode 2000; Empson 2007; Galanter 2011). This expertise is predicated by a passion to be a lawyer that harnesses commitment and energy in a way that is personally fulfilling (Kronman 1995). The role as educators is to encourage students who have that calling to acquire the knowledge, skills and attitudes needed to achieve 'self-actualisation' that provides personal satisfaction and sense of worth (Maslow 1968).

As a result, it will consider the inherent value of having a vocation, learning a 'craft' and achieving mastery. It will look at the importance of building character, imbuing ethical behaviour and developing professionalism. It will consider the context of professional learning and the pressures on resilience, of conscientiousness, of forming good judgement and confidence and the role of experience. It will reflect on the importance of culture and potential 'loss' of collaboration and communities of practice that have been the traditional building blocks of professional learning and development, individually and collectively. It will demonstrate the essential value of vocational legal education in re-establishing the social contract between the public and lawyers 'whose basic tenets include service to others and the responsibility to conduct themselves in a morally appropriate way in situations of complexity and uncertainty' (Mann 2006: 147).

Section 1: Effect of External Drivers for Change

This section analyses the impact of the current external drivers for change in the context of the UK legal services market and the profession's position in society.

To précis what is well established, the rationale for distinguishing a profession from an occupation is based on a number of core elements (Sullivan 2005: 36) that include:

1. applying specialist knowledge and skills gained through formal training under more experienced practitioners to a specific area of professional practice (Larson 1977; Abbott 1988),
2. providing a service to society that is recognised and valued (Cheetham and Chivers 2005) and
3. self-regulating through limiting membership to entrants who meet a qualifying standard and ensuring that its members comply with prescribed rules and codes of conduct (Collins 1990).

Earlier commentators, in their consideration of how well the legal 'profession' meets these criteria, illustrate evidence of tensions in relation to its social contract. For instance, some saw it as a self-sustaining monopoly (Larson 1977; Abel 1988, 2003) that creates the 'maze of legal procedures, codes and precedents' which results in the need for lawyers (Collins 1990: 20) and limits both the 'production by producers' and the 'production of producers' (Abel 1988). Freidson's (1986) and Abbott's (1988) interpretations argued that the development of specialist knowledge allowed each profession to retain exclusivity over its particular 'jurisdictions' (Abbott 1988: 136).

The functionalist approach adopted by Parsons (1968) considered their 'professionalism' in the context of lawyers' role in society, especially as it relates to their self-regulation. He argued that their autonomy and independence would be paramount if they are to be able to use their specialist knowledge to provide access to justice and mediate between individuals and society. Their self-control is therefore permitted as long as they provide a service that meets the demands of the public and merits the recognition of providing that needed service by society in general. This internal control is 'grounded in a long socialization process' (Rueschemeyer 1969: 267) and as a result, is dependent upon having established norms and values that reflect that their members have a 'calling' (Neighbour 1992).

Nelson and Trubeck's (1992(a)) interpretative approach highlights the importance of considering the inter-relationship between this professional ideology and structural change (Gray 1999). This is of particular relevance given the current structural changes impacting on the UK legal profession that have stemmed from the political, economic, sociological and technological trends (Johnson et al. 2007) affecting the whole professional services marketplace (Cheetham and Chivers 2005). These include:

- increased consumerism with clients more likely to question the quality of advice and services provided,
- the impact of technology on how clients access professionals and how professional services are delivered,
- growth in neo-liberalism with the professions' monopolies and self-regulation being eroded and
- increased segmentation and globalisation.

(a) Increased Consumerism and the Impact of Technology

Increased consumerism and the impact of the Internet in relation to the public's access to previously protected areas of professional knowledge (Susskind 1996) have led to a demystification of the law and shift in the balance of dependency between lawyers and their clients (Paterson 1996; Hilton and Midgal 2005; Westwood 2001, 2008, 2010). Dolliver (1990: 271) outlines that the loss of its distinctive knowledge and increasing recourse by individuals to the law to provide recompense for alleged wrongs is resulting in 'lowered public esteem and the cry for accountability'. Commentators argue that this shift requires a response from the profession that leads to an adjustment of its social contract to re-establish trust. Paterson (1996: 140) suggests that there is 'an enduring tension between service orientation and self-interest' and, as a result, proposes a variety of futures for the legal profession, including its disappearance, fragmentation and transition into 'little different from businessmen' (157). Westwood (2011(a), 2011(b)) offers both worse and best case scenarios based on extrapolations of current market trends.

Commoditisation of legal work through the use of technology and pressures from clients to provide a better service (Hilton and Migdal 2005) have changed the way law firms are organised (Susskind 1996, 2000, 2008), moving away from the traditional trading and reward structures of partnerships based on collegiality and equity (Hinings et al. 1999) to more specialist firms and business models that reward individual performance (Galanter and Palay 1992). This trend of 'commercialisation' of the profession was seen by many as an erosion of 'professionalism' particularly in relation to ethical conduct as illustrated by the ABA Report (1986) and the State Bar Codes that flowed from it. Senior judges commented on the decline in the behaviour of the lawyers (Burger 1993: 3, 7) with 'the standing of the legal profession ... at its lowest ebb in the history of our country', and concluded that 'we must remember that we are a profession, but we will remain a profession only if our standards command it'.

(b) Neo-liberalism

Successive UK governments responded to the consumer lobby by seeking to make improvements to access to justice and in the quality of legal services in a number of ways (Paterson 1990; Goriely 1994; Sherr et al. 1994; LSB 2011(a), 2011(b); Sullivan 2011). This move towards neo-liberalism in relation to the legal profession culminated most strategically in the loss of its established monopolies and self-regulation as the result of the implementation of the recommendations of Sir David Clementi (2004). The driver behind these is to improve access to justice and the overall quality of legal services by seeking to alter the way they were provided at both the macro and micro level. The Legal Services Act 2007 in England introduced eight approved regulators (Boon 2010) overseen by the Legal Services Board and the Legal Ombudsman in 2010, mirrored in Scotland with the establishment of the Scottish Legal Complaints Commission in 2008 and passing of the Legal Services (Scotland) Act 2010. From 2012, the legal services market is open to new entrants with a variety of alternative business structures available for authorisation.

These changes and their prior consultations and responses have taken up a considerable amount of the focus of the professional bodies and their members and have resulted in difficult dialogues with UK and national governments. As argued by Webb (2004: 95), the complexities of the interactions and relative weight of the interests seeking to influence the outcomes were considerable and the legal profession attempts to retain both market control and its own autonomy by relying on 'monopoly power and the discourses of collegiality, independence, self-regulation' failed to recognise this. As advocated by Irvine (2009: 186) in relation to the medical profession's response to similar challenges, success 'will depend on the extent to which the [medical] profession demonstrates that it can be trusted to deliver its part of the bargain' and the legal profession seemed to be found falling short in relation to this (Abel 1988, 2003).

(c) Segmentation and Globalisation

Market pressures in traditional areas of fee income such as conveyancing and increased complexity of the law led to a bifurcation of law firms into the two client markets of commercial and individual clients with different drivers and structures (Galanter 1983; Kelly 1996; Gray 1999; Galanter and Roberts 2008). With the growth in the numbers of women and people of mixed ethnic background entering the profession (Galanter 2011), the profession became more diverse. This, coupled with increasing specialism, increased recruitment of in-house counsel and a variety of trading structures has led to segmentation (LSB 2011(a), 2011(b)) to the extent that the professional bodies find it difficult to argue that they continue to be able to represent their membership collectively (Abel 1989, 2003; Webb 2004).

Developing 'knowledge workers' by harnessing their improvisation, intelligence and autonomy to meet the changing needs of clients is seen as an important strategic response to the impact of global markets (Hammer 1988; Westwood, 2006; Leitch 2006; Brown, et al. 2008) and has impacted on the structure, operations and culture of large law firms (Flood 1996; Faulconbridge and Muzio 2008; Cook et al. 2012). With the ease of document retrieval and transfer through the Internet (Susskind 1996), widening recognition of the transfer of professional qualifications and the demand from clients for services to support their trans-national commercial dealings (Rose and Hinings 1999), these firms sought to position themselves and model their structures in a similar way to global accountancy firms (Empson 2007). This has caused 'partners ... to resemble other capitalists, with firms resembling closely held corporations rather than true partnerships' (Sechooler 2008: 243), and the 'dramatic conjunction of specialisation and globalisation ... will fundamentally change the values of the lawyers in these firms' (Boon et al. 2001: 592).

The legal profession's attempts to respond to these external drivers for change have led to cultural and ideological tensions (Nelson and Trubeck 1992(a)) and challenges to all three elements of its right to call itself a profession. As long ago as 1999, Kritzer (1999: 740) concluded that changes in the underlying assumptions of legal practice were inevitable and, as a result, argued the need for a 'new professionalism (that) will be more dynamic, reflecting the rapidity of change in the workplace and the accompanying demands of the market'. The move away from collegiality and partnership trading structures, the increase in partner defection to competitors (Kronman 1995) and working more as in-house counsel, coupled with redundancies of lawyers and changes in work levels and specialities, resulted in 'concrete evidence of a marked change from the traditional notion of the solicitors' profession as providing a job for life' (Moorhead and Boyle 1995: 246). Pressures to become more commercial are challenging the altruistic values of having individual commitment to 'a calling' (Neighbour 1992) and 'meaningful work' (Raelin 1985). Yet the fiduciary nature of the solicitor/ client relationship is based on trust (Maister 1997; Westwood 2002, 2008, 2010) and confidence in professional judgements (Schon 1987; Svensson 1990; Maister et al. 2000) that are founded on 'who we are as moral persons' (Webb 2002: 133). Sullivan (2005: 169) offers that the current readjustment of the proper role of lawyers is the basis for this crisis as 'in the absence of social confidence in the value of the work done, ambition must become paranoid and even self destructive'.

The inter-relation between what the profession considers appropriate, what the marketplace demands of it and the resources available determines its range of responses (Johnson et al. 2007; Westwood 2002, 2008) and results in strategic choices that 'will ... "remake" the dispositions of the group for future action at the same time that strategic actions contribute to ongoing trends and developments within the legal profession' (Nelson and Trubeck 1992(b): 22). The trend towards segmentation that inhabits distinct cultures (Galanter 1983; Kelly 1996; Gray 1999; Galanter and Roberts 2008) will result in 'character ... shap(ing) these institutions, but these institutions also will shape character' (Regan 1999: 3; cf. Mather 2011).

The impact of the new commercial entrants to the legal services market is currently uncertain and may meet Clementi's (2004) stated aim of providing a cost-effective legal service in a consumer-friendly way. Market forces are driving some lawyers to align themselves more closely with commercial values of differentiation and loyalty to their employer rather than their professional body. High street practitioners are experiencing an erosion of their core areas of fee income to such an extent that they are focussed on their immediate survival. Others are moving to work in-house rather than have to deal with the pressures of running a business in a competitive and consumer-driven environment. The larger law firms see themselves more as commercial entities (Flood 1996; Galanter and Roberts 2008) and limit their dealings with the relevant professional bodies to achieving their particular strategic and/or operational objectives.

Regan (2002: 162) describes three professional values of lawyers: devotion to client, craft autonomy (the ability to exercise discretion and judgement in performing one's work) and 'seeing themselves stewards of the legal system'. While the first two fall within the accepted generic definitions of a profession, the latter is unique to law. Rueschemeyer (1969: 271) illustrates this point in his comparison between medicine and law when he argues that lawyers must be grounded in the values of their society because it is their role to develop law in *that context*. Unlike medicine where knowledge is based on science, legal knowledge is predicated on legislation and judicial decisions, both of which are 'significantly influenced by members of the legal profession'. As a result, the values of the legal profession itself are an important determinant of how the law develops. Yet commentators including Higgenbotham (1987), Kronman (1995), Sullivan (2005) and Argyris and Schon (1974) argue that there has been an historical shift away from social trusteeship to becoming technical experts with loyalty only to themselves and from being a craft towards the creation of replicable standards in a commercial industry. 'Priority of profits and the resulting sweatshop schedules have squeezed out time for public service and family life' (Rhodes 2000: 208) and poses the question whether the role of 'stewards of the legal system' is being and indeed can be maintained.

With so many of their underlying assumptions being challenged, lawyers 'may find it difficult or impossible to recognize the limits of their ability to predict new professional role demands' (Argyris and Schon 1974: 153), and with the continued fragmentation of the profession itself, and the reduction in the power and influence of their professional bodies (Abel 2003, Westwood 2010), the unique essence of the role of lawyers itself may well become dissipated to such an extent that it loses its identity because (Lewis and Maude 1952: 1) 'other and greater possessions are at stake' including 'a valued culture; complicated or subtle techniques ... self-examining integrity and self-forgetful service'.

Argyris and Schon (1974: 30–31) propose that, in relation to professional effectiveness, theory-building and learning arise out of dilemmas and offer illustrations of the types of dilemmas that challenge the continuing currency of the theories-in-use ('what we do') adopted by each profession. These include dilemmas of:

1. incongruity arising out of tensions between them and espoused theories ('what we say'),
2. inconsistency where their governing variables become increasingly incompatible with the reality of practice,

3. effectiveness where they become less and less achievable,
4. beliefs where to sustain them requires an individual to act against his or her personal values and
5. testability, where they actively undermine people's ability to function properly.

Following Schon (1987, 1991), it is possible to employ behaviour to illustrate someone's theory-in-use and, as a result, there is evidence that:

-   some lawyers are prepared to put self-interest above that of their clients (Kronman 1995),
-   pressure to achieve chargeable hours is at variance with a professional's duty to achieve the best result for each client (Higgenbotham 1987) and
-   sharing expertise and spending time training the next generation is undermined by 'tournament' reward processes (Galanter and Palay 1991; Galanter and Roberts 2008).

In addition, new business structures will introduce 'competing scripts' that offer the 'opportunities for entrepreneurs, moral or economic, to reshape professional organization' (Nelson and Trubeck 1992b: 24). Given all of this, it may become necessary to consider how new theory building will occur in a profession which is increasingly fragmented and globalised (Hutchinson 1998).

The scale of these disruptive changes (Schumpeter 1950) results in it being difficult to extrapolate what the UK legal services marketplace will look like five years from now. There are a number of futures that can be suggested based on the current trends ranging from the demise of the profession as a separate and independent entity to a repositioning to become the recognised protectors of society (Paterson 1996; Westwood 2011(a), 2011(b)). One option following the premise that flexibility and innovation will be the drivers of future success (Faulconbridge and Muzio 2010) is that lawyers become technical experts 'traveling light psychologically, with few loyalties or other encumbering ties expect economic ambition' (Sullivan 2005: 7). Freidson (2001) offers a move away from the 'third logic' of the professional structure based on collegiality to either the entrepreneurial or the bureaucratic structures, the former limiting the sharing of expertise and the latter inhibiting individual judgement, both of which run counter to professional cultures and norms (Chivers and Cheetham 2005; Raelin 2008).

Section 2: Implications for UK Legal Education

The LETR report (2013: Chapter 3) indicates that fragmentation is likely to continue as individual elements of the profession respond differently to the opening up of the marketplace, competition and globalisation. The increasing recognition of the status of paralegals and licensed conveyancers may result in a number of formal job options, leading to a hierarchy of qualification and career choices (Cheetham and Chivers 2005). It may be that new entrants to the legal services marketplace concentrate on low-risk, high-volume work, offering limited employment for accredited solicitors. Large law firms may select alternative structures that reduce the need for practicing certificates and their involvement with legal regulators and professional bodies. As a result, the range of functions and resulting influence of the law societies will continue to decline. As external regulators seek consistency of competence and service standards and with continued pressures on work-life balance from 24-hour access by clients and demands on chargeable and recoverable times (Moorhead and Boyle 1995), lawyers may prefer to focus on the immediate job in hand, losing the 'opportunity for pro-bono service, civic involvement and breadth of experience that build professional judgement and sustain a professional culture' (Rhodes 2000: 10).

The increasing direct costs of higher education may inhibit equality and diversity of access and put more emphasis on the future employability of graduates. The provision of legal education is itself becoming more commercialised and globalised with, for example, BPP in July 2010 becoming an accredited university college and the College of Law being acquired in April 2012 by Montagu Evans Private and Equity. Formal training places are limited and dominated by the larger firms, resulting in their growing influence on legal education (Boon et al. 2001) and law graduates not finding it easy to secure an entry route into the profession.

Despite the challenges to its 'production by producers and of producers' (Abel 1988), society will continue to need independent lawyers (Galanter 2011), whether to provide protection for individuals from government, enable access to justice and/or help to regulate individual dealings. Regardless of pressures to commoditise and routinise much of the daily work that used to be carried out by lawyers (Susskind 1996, 2000, 2008) because 'no longer does legal services rely on highly credentialised workers' (Sullivan 2005: 12; cf. Cheetham and Chivers 2005), the law will continue to become more complex and society more diverse. It will need lawyers who have 'engaged expertise' (Sullivan et al. 2007: 115) and who are able to interpret the law as it applies to particular client situations; and even with a major part of the service delivery becoming routinised and undertaken by paralegals, experienced practitioners will have to be involved in developing the contents of such systems and supervising its production. While information technology may reduce the drudgery of routine practice, expert professionals will continue to make judgement calls in the most complex and high-risk areas (Schon 1987), determined by the needs of each particular client grounded on trust, and underpinned by ethics and wisdom (Webb 1998).

External regulation and growing consumerism of clients is leading to lawyers being asked to defend their judgement calls to third parties in a complex and globalised world at the same time as information technology is reducing the routine work that allowed novices to learn incrementally and through practice (Neighbour 1992; Raelin 2008). This is putting pressure on formal legal education to provide students who are 'fit to practice', illustrating the 'crisis of confidence'

(Schon 1991: 14) that results when 'professional knowledge is mismatched to the changing characteristics of the situations of practice – complexity, uncertainty, instability, uniqueness, and value conflicts'(Schon 1991: 14).

As employers place more emphasis on inter-personal skills and the ability to work effectively in teams (Maister 1997; Westwood 2003; Empson 2007), learning needs to be 'collaborative, outward looking and goal oriented rather than an end in itself' (Boon et al. 2005: 481). Traditionally, the undergraduate experience concentrated on teaching knowledge of the law and less on the skills and attitude needed to succeed in practice (Cook 1992; Re 1994; Webb 1995, 1998) with the effect that 'practical and the experiential have been undervalued as conceptions of legal knowledge' (Webb 1995: 191). In the UK, this balance was adjusted to include transferable skills (Bell and Johnstone 1998; Stuckey 2007) and management skills (Sherr 2000), with these added to the Legal Practice Course (LPC) and the Diploma in Legal Practice (DLP), as well as offering students the opportunity to work in simulated learning environments (Maharg 2007), blended degrees and law clinics (Nicolson 2008). The large law firms have used their increasing influence in the trainee employment market to form alliances with LPC deliverers and direct the content of these courses to their particular specialisms as well as more closely reflect their culture and values (Boon et al. 2001; Faulconbridge et al. 2010).

In addition to the innovative developments of 'virtual simulations' and law clinic work, students need to acquire competence by embedding knowledge and skills in actual practice and making the transition from novice to master (Farren 2000). To do this, trainees need to be able to practise under the supervision of and by being able to observe more experienced exemplars (Schon 1987). This predicates the importance of experiential and work-based learning as the main influence on the development of professionals (Raelin 1998; Cheetham and Chivers 2005). These communities of practice are powerful socialising mechanisms (Wenger 1998) and form identity and norms and influence behaviours and values (Cheetham and Chivers 2005). This creates challenges when associated with continued fragmentation and loss of a composite identity of the legal profession.

Social learning theory (Wenger 2009: 211) argues that people learn through the interconnected elements of:

- Identity – learning as becoming
- Meaning – learning as experience
- Practice – learning as doing
- Community – learning as belonging.

This supports Abel's view (1989: 245) that 'the increasing specialization of both legal knowledge and role expectations has magnified the importance of first employers are socializing agents'. Regan (1999: 74) suggests that it is essential to be aware of the individual drivers of these firms as 'their 'character and leadership' will determine how different firms respond. Given the inter-dependence between values, identitfy, communities of practice, organisational norms and structural change (Gray 1999; Cook et al. 2012; Westwood 2002, 2008, 2010), it is necessary to match the aspirations of the leaders and owners of these businesses with the people who provide services to their clients. It is also important to understand the patterns of influences that occur within law firms and their inter-relationship with powerful professional behaviour to frustrate or achieve successful change (Gray 1999; Westwood 2002, 2008, 2010).

Sullivan (2005: 27) suggests that there are three apprenticeships of professional education that allow novices to learn how 'to think, to perform and to conduct themselves like professionals'. The structural and operational changes introduced by law firms to respond to market conditions has resulted in a move away from the traditional model of professional training and development based on the 'master-apprentice' relationship (Neighbour 1992; Raelin 2008) that provides the scaffolding for the experiential learning in the 'swamp' of professional practice (Schon 1987; Maughan and Webb 2005; Raelin 2008). This has been particularly the case in the large law firms (Faulconbridge and Muzio 2010), using the 'tournament' reward system (Galanter and Palay 1991), with its emphasis on fee earning and levels of hierarchy between trainee and equity partner (Galanter and Roberts 2008). This has shifted the responsibility onto the universities to deliver students 'ready to practice' (ACLEC 1996; McCrate Report 1992; Pearce 1987) in line with the general demands being made on higher education to consider what it teaches and how it teaches it (Leitch 2006; Brown et al. 2008).

As a result, education must emphasise the importance of life-long learning through the 'volitional and affective dimensions' that shape how individuals learn (Webb 2002: 150; Maughan 2011). In addition, given the increased fragmentation within the profession and the impact of culture on future identity (Cook et al. 2012), vocational education is pivotal both in relation to the formation of identity and professional character (Mann 2006; Barton and Westwood 2011(a), 2011(b)) and in matching the aspirations of students to the reality of their future practice (Rhodes 2000).

Commentators, mirroring the 'communities of practice' that underpin professional development (Wenger 1998; Raelin, 2008), illustrate that account should be taken of the socialisation effect of law firms on culture and values of their professionals (Kelly 1996; Regan 1999; Boon et al. 2001; Sullivan et al. 2007; Sechooler 2008; Flood 2011; Mather 2011). For example, Barton and Westwood (2011(a), 2011(b)) outline how the development of professional character (cf. Webb 2002) can be encouraged through simulated working in virtual law firms (Maharg 2007). Webb (1998) advocates the need to embed ethics through using it to develop a sense of community, to consider the importance of one's function or role, to enhance integrity, to value connections with others and personal responsibility and to develop the capacity for judgement (cf. Nicolson 2005; Duncan 2011). Maughan and Webb (2005: 27) argue that 'to be a competent practitioner … Requires … the ability to develop your own sense of ethics and social responsibility and to make decisions consistent with those values'. To do this requires moral courage (Higginbotham 1987; Duncan 2011) underpinned by 'values of honour, integrity and altruism' (Webb 2002:150).

Given the perceived impact of increasing commercialisation of the profession, one important element is the inclusion of the formal teaching of ethics (Webb 1998; Economides and Rogers 2009). ACLEC (1996) argues that personal and professional values and standards must be internalised from the earliest stages of education and training (cf. McCrate 1992; Sullivan et al. 2007). In addition, despite increased commoditisation, practicing as a lawyer cannot be 'duplicated, mass-produced, imprinted or assigned ... It is rather a social process that ... individuals must achieve through personal apprehension, thoughtful reflection and most importantly mindful action' (George et al. 2006: 65).

Vocational legal education is positioned between theory and practice and seeks to transform students into trainee practitioners in a restrictive time frame and with limited direct exposure to the practicalities of working as a lawyer as 'it is expert practice that is the source of formal knowledge about practice, not the other way round' (Sullivan 2005: 250). Students come to law school with the 'hope to find a professional identity and with that a measure of personal fulfillment in their work' (Kronman 1995: 374) and their early experience of practice often disappoints them (Rhode 2000). As a result, the next section will look at why, if trainees are to make a successful progression to masters, professional judgement must be enabled and professional character preserved.

Section 3: Learning a Craft, Judgement and Character

Nelson et al. (1992b: 5) describe professionalism as 'the set of norms, traditions and practices that lawyers have constructed to establish and maintain their identities as professionals and their jurisdiction over legal work'. The foregoing analysis illustrates how fragmented these norms, traditions and practices have become with the resulting threat to their identity and jurisdiction. The past two sections have concentrated on the macro level influences on the profession and legal education. This section will concentrate on the micro level challenges impacting on individual lawyers and how vocational education can provide both context and support.

With external regulation and increased consumerism, individual professionals are being called upon to defend decisions (Irvine 2009; Bolton 2010) that involve the transformation of formal knowledge to meet the particular demands of individual clients (Svensson 1990; Westwood 2010). This requires both practical experience and 'the reflective type of knowledge ... which can better explain how professional proficiency is embedded in practice itself, with the contextual conditions that are tied to specific situations' (Svensson 1990: 69–70). As described in the first section of this chapter, the existence of professionals stemmed from a basic need of society to be able to source expert help and be able to trust the judgement of individuals who will put their clients' and patients' interests first as well have the necessary expertise based on currency of the relevant knowledge and high standards of practice (Collins 1990; Cheetham and Chivers 2005; Sullivan 2005).

Yet at the same time as commoditisation and information technology are limiting the exercise of individual judgement (Susskind 2008), clients continue to seek out professionals able to make decisions that blend 'careful analysis, intuition, and wisdom and judgement distilled from experience' (Dreyfus and Dreyfus 1986: 8).

Paraphrasing Schon (1987: 309), the historical gap that has been created by the academy and practice operating separately from each other (Re 1994) has to be filled by placing a reflective practicum at the centre. This must recognise and allow for 'artistry' that is based on the ability to make decisions through combining increasing uncertainty and complexity (Mezirow et al. 1990) underpinned by moral development (King and Kitchener 1994; Epstein 2006). This demonstrates the importance of developing individual character that is founded in the ethics and values of the relevant profession (Webb 1998; Mather 2011) whose members 'require courage, judgment, and self-knowledge as well as a prodigious amount of discipline-specific knowledge and skills' (Mann 2006: 147).

A related problem to the challenge to identity described before is the erosion of job satisfaction resulting from 'the more routine and unchallenging legal work becomes, the less likely a lawyer is to see it as anything but a means of making a living' (Kronman 1995: 373). With jobs and work roles an inherent part of individual's 'personae' and well-being (Cheney et al 2010), without personal satisfaction and a sense of achievement, it is difficult to meet the demands of professional practice (Westwood 2010). However, the importance of having a vocation goes beyond personal altruism and links directly into one of the core elements of professionalism (Sullivan 2005) that recognises the value of having a belief in the intrinsic value of work that benefits others (Freidson 2001). As discussed earlier, it provides a sense of community and identity (Wenger 1998) underpinned by the 'three clusters of values – values of the academy, of professional practice and ethical-social values of professional identity' (Sullivan 2005: 28).

As a result, it provides the underpinning necessary to practice successfully as it establishes 'an enduring set of normative and behavioural expectations' (Moore 1970: 5) and offers a 'feeling of identity, collegiate loyalty and shared values' (Cain 1983: 147). Individual practice has to be grounded in the context of accepted and established norms to ensure that he or she is 'acting competently to serve responsibly' (Sullivan et al. 2007: 23). Balancing at times the conflicting demands of clients, our professional Rules and Codes of Conduct and of our businesses and/or employers requires 'empathy' and 'moral courage' (Webb 1998; Duncan 2011) and to be able to access the ethical framework of a recognised and independent body. In the unique context of the legal profession in providing access to justice, 'each lawyer must consciously and constantly assess his or her values and goals in forging rules of law for the future' (Higgenbotham 1987: 815).

This structure allows professionals to be able to develop 'considerable individual discernment and capacity for initiative and judgment' (Sullivan 2005: 15).

Professionals have to exercise these capacities 'in the real world of uncertainty, dynamism and time pressures' (Sadler-Smith 2008: 53–4; cf. Schon 1987, 1991) and where 'the rules for reaching an answer or evaluating it rightness are unclear perhaps because two goods or two evils are involved and there is no established way of quantifying them for direct comparison' (Ozarak 2005: 149).

Expertise is developed through years of practice 'by becoming a person of good judgment and not just an expert in the law' Kronman (1995: 2–3) and by acquiring wisdom 'which is far more than knowledge for it characterises what you are rather than what you have' Raelin (2008: 38). Experts operate at the leading edge of their practices, 'acting not on guesses but on perceptual grasp and the ability to make qualitative distinctions gained through experiential learning' (Sullivan 2005: 249; cf. Martin 2002).

Experiential learning is by definition practice-based and 'inherently complex, underdetermined and emergent' (Cooke et al. 2010: 41; cf. Maughan and Webb). As a result, progression from novice to master is achieved by 'exposure and immersion' (Schon (1987: 38) and through an apprenticeship 'well grounded in the subtleties of experienced distinctions and analogical reasoning' (Sullivan 2005: 249). By definition, an apprentice works under a master, observing and modelling himself or herself on an aspirational 'role model' that exemplifies and motivates (Svensson 1990). Given the impact of 'communities of practice' on identity, meaning, purpose and belonging (Wenger 2009), there is a risk that segmentation leads to multiple identities.

Kronman (1995: 16) in his call for the return to his 'lawyer-statesman' argues that 'real excellence can only be achieved by acquiring certain valued traits of character'. Barton and Westwood (2011a: 236) offer that 'common examples include self-reliance in independent work; co-operation in group activities; professional commitment to ethical practice; and an ability to value others as individuals'.

Earlier sections have identified the current pressures on the identity and jurisdiction of the legal profession and it is important to respond constructively to these. To maintain its identity by readjusting the social contract as suggested above will help go some way to rekindle individual lawyers' sense of doing a job that has intrinsic value. However, the profession has also to find a way to succeed commercially so as to sustain its long-term professional viability and its responsibility for ensuring access to justice. Rather than treat the aims of being commercially and professionally successful as irreconcilable they are 'in fact are intertwined in complex ways' (Regan 1999: 18; cf. Westwood 2002, 2004, 2008). To succeed in an increasingly competitive market, a professional service provider must deliver a quality service and value as the client defines and measures it (Westwood 2002, 2008; Greenwood 2007), with the result that its competitive advantage lies in the ability of its experts to make good judgement calls, to refine and hone its existing products as well as develop new ones (Maister 1997; Johnson et al. 2007).

Pearce (1995: 1276) suggests that rather than 'lamenting the decline of professionalism' it is better to focus on 'the more important work of improving the delivery of legal services and promoting justice'. The Model II paradigm advocated by Argyris and Schon (1974: 154–5) accepts that clients and other 'externals' have the right to determine how services are provided and how quality is defined, that lawyers must demonstrate not only competence but also a willingness to help others, to devise new solutions and expect and welcome challenges (cf. Westwood 2001, 2008, 2010). It highlights the importance of the need to develop a common culture and ways of operating by 'recruiting, developing, educating, and mainly maintaining the loyalty of the professionals who will be supplying the services' (Aharoni 1999: 38).

The legal profession as a distinct entity has a duty to ensure that society will always have access to justice serviced by lawyers who continue to have a vocation and the requisite knowledge, skills and character (Kronman 1995; Rhode 2000) to provide 'effective practice. founded upon (1) sufficiency of knowledge and (2) artistry of application' (Sadler-Smith 2008: 53–4; cf. Webb 1998; Westwood 2010).

As a result, it is necessary for students and trainees to acquire 'the complex ensemble of analytical thinking, skilful practice and wise judgment on which each profession rests ... thinking, performing and behaving' and apply their acquired knowledge in the 'uncertain conditions of practice and identify themselves with the best standards and in a manner consistent with the purposes of their chosen profession' (Sullivan et al. 2007: 27). In order to progress to mastery they need to develop the capacity for judgement 'developed through experience, and grounded in our ability to deal not just rationally but relationally with others' (Webb 1998: 144).

Conclusion

This chapter argues the case for the pivotal role of vocational education in supporting the UK legal profession sustain its future identity founded on shared norms and values. One potential future is that the fragmentation that has already occurred and the weakened role and influence of its professional bodies has fractured its identity so fundamentally that the bifurcation into corporate and private client delivery models cannot be rejoined (Westwood 2011(a)). Another and more hopeful scenario also exists founded on the premise that society will continue to need lawyers who have a high level of expertise and skills and are able to operate in areas of complexity and importance with ease, based on experience and mastery, gained through years of exercising good judgement in professional practice (Westwood 2011(b)). This must be grounded in working with others, discussing and sharing knowledge based on mutual trust and respect. The element that underpins any continuing definition of professionals is that they care about the work they do and the quality of service they provide to their clients and patients (Schon 1987, 1991; Hammer 1998; Neighbour 1992; Mann 2006).

Argyris and Schon (1974: 134–46) offer five central questions to provide a structure to analyse discontent within a profession:

1. Who does the profession serve?
2. Are professionals competent?
3. Does cumulative learning influence practitioners?
4. Is reform possible?
5. Can self-actualization occur?

It is necessary to consider the first question in the context of the current external pressures of change and in relation to its continued identity and its primary role as the providers of access to justice. New commercial entrants are unlikely to see this role as their main driver resulting in increasing the need for the profession to supply this role, underpinned by its values and ethics (Hutchinson 1998).

In relation to question two the currency of this competence is vital and legal education and training has an absolute duty to deliver new entrants who are 'ready to practice'. To allow the legal profession to continue to provide a valuable service to society, it has to sustain an orientation and a mechanism to maintain its currency of expertise to achieve quality of service delivery (Boon et al. 2005; Westwood 2002, 2008, 2010), inherently committed to 'life long learning' (Schein 1972). In addition, progression to mastery is an important element of personal satisfaction and self-actualisation (Maslow 1968), artistry (Schon 1987) and wisdom (Raelin 2008). This places education and training in a central position in relation to its macro and micro success, confirming that 'it is no exaggeration to say that education remains a dominant feature of professional life, even long after the formal phase of training' (Sullivan 2005: 25).

Question three considers whether cumulative learning influences practitioners. As discussed above, 'communities of practice' are an inherent part of practicing a craft, allowing novices to learn from masters and masters to share their knowledge and skills (Wenger 1998, 2009; Raelin 2008). However, they offer more than individual development as they create mechanisms that allow themselves to learn to adapt in order to survive in a changing environment (Wenger et al. 2002; Wenger 2009).

This provides an answer to the fourth question of whether reform is possible. At both the macro and micro level, the legal profession must be able to adapt and learn (Senge 1990; Schon 1991; Argyris and Schon 1974). As outlined above, the profession as a whole must find a way to respond to the external changes being imposed upon it and can do so by maintaining its identity and jurisdiction through 'moving towards the goal of social and legal justice for all' (Higgenbotham 1987: 815). At the micro level, practitioners must maintain the currency of their knowledge and skills so as to be able to provide complex and specialised services that are subject to external regulation (Irvine 2009; Westwood 2002, 2008, 2010). Trainees in particular need to work in an environment where they are able to learn and improve (Neighbour 1992; Raelin 2008) and where exemplars and masters are visible and articulate the context and the tacit elements of how they make decisions (Svensson 1990; Westwood 2010) as 'having intellectual knowledge without practical experience can be extremely jarring' (Farren 2000: 99). In addition, it provides them with the opportunity to discover 'what kind of person one must become in order to be accepted as a competent member of the community' (Raelin 2008: 101).

The final question asks whether self-actualisation can occur. The answer to this has to be 'yes' as otherwise professional work becomes merely an occupation (Martin 2000; cf. Sullivan 2005). One of the core elements of a profession is operating in a field of complexity and service. Its masters (by definition) operate at a high level of personal achievement and satisfaction with confidence to manage constant dichotomies (Maslow 1968), act consistent with their values (Mezirow et al 1990) and push out the boundaries of accepted practice. As a result they achieve 'via a commitment to an important job and to worthwhile work ... the path to human happiness' (Maslow 2000: 12).

Argyris and Schon (1974: 145) ask 'where are the professionals who will reform professional education?' and offer, referencing Schein (1972: 53), that the professions need 'innovators to improve practice and to clarify the profession's role in society'. Vocational education sits within the context of professional practice and allows students to observe masters in action. As a result, it can inspire them, enable them to recognise their calling and build confidence and personal resilience (Westwood 2010). It establishes strong foundations grounded in the ethics and values of their chosen profession that will support them throughout their careers. Given the challenges facing the UK legal profession in particular, it sustains its community and identity. And because of all of this, it plays a pivotal role in the profession's ability to respond constructively.

References

ABA. (1986), *In the Spirit of Public Service: A Blueprint for the Rekindling of Lawyer Professionalism*. Report New York: American Bar Association.

Abbott, A. (1988), *The System of Professions*. New York: Oxford University Press.

Abel, R. (1988), *The Legal Profession in England and Wales*. Basil Blackwell: Oxford.

Abel, R. (1989), 'Comparative Sociology of Legal Professions', in Abel, R. and Lewis, P. (eds), *Lawyers in Society: Comparative Theories*. Berkeley: University of California Press.

Abel, R. (2003), *English Lawyers between Market and State*. Oxford: Oxford University Press.

ACLEC. (1996), *First Report on Legal Education and Training*. London: Advisory Committee on Legal Education.

Aharoni, Y. (1999), 'Internationalization of Professional Services: Implications for Accounting Firms', in Brock, D., Powell, M. and Hinings, C.R. (eds), *Restructuring the Professional Organization*. London: Routledge, 20–40.

Argyris, C. and Schon, D.A. (1974), *Theory in Practice – Increasing Professional Effectiveness*. Jossey Bass: San Francisco.

Barton, K. and Westwood, F. (2011(a)), 'Developing Professional Character – Trust, Values and Learning', in Maharg, P. and Maughan, C. (eds), *Affect and Legal Education – Emotion and Learning in the Teaching of Law*. Farnham: Ashgate, 235–56.

Barton, K. and Westwood, F. (2011(b)), *Developing Professional Values and behaviours in the Context of Virtual Learning Environments BMAF HEA Enhancing Graduate Impact in Business and Management, Hospitality, Leisure, Sport and Tourism*. Newbury: Threshold Press.

Bell, J. and Johnstone, J. (1998), General Transferable Skills in the Law Curriculum. London: Department for Education and Employment.

Bolton, G. (2010), *Reflective Practice – Writing and Professional Development*. London: Sage.

Boon, A. (2010), 'Professionalism under the Legal Services Act 2007', *International Journal of the Legal Profession*, 17(3): 195–232.

Boon, A., Duff, L. and Shiner, M. (2001), 'Career Choices and Choices in a Highly Differentiated Profession: The Position of Newly Qualified Solicitors', *Modern Law Review*, 64: 563–94.

Boon, A., Flood, J. and Webb, J. (2005), 'Postmodern Professions? The Fragmentation of Legal Education and the Legal Profession', *Journal of Law and Society*, 32(3): 473–92.

Brown, P., Lauder, H. and Ashton, D. (2008), *Education, Globalisation and the Knowledge Economy London: Economic and Social Research Council Report*.

Burger, W. (1993), 'The Decline of Professionalism', *Tennessee Law Review*, 63: 1–7.

Cain, M. (1983), 'The General Practice Lawyer and the Client: Towards a Radical Conception', in Dingwall, R. and Lewis, P. (eds), *The Sociology of the Professions*. London: Macmillan, 152–76.

Cheetham, G. and Chivers, G. (2005), *Professions, Competence and Informal Learning*. Cheltenham: Edward Edgar Publishing.

Cheney, G., Lair, D.J., Ritz, D. and Kendall, B.E. (2010), *Just a Job? Communication, Ethics and Professional Life*. Oxford: Oxford University Press.

Clementi, D. (2004), Review of the Regulatory Framework for Legal Services in England and Wales (http://webarchive.nationalarchives.gov.uk/ + http://www.legal-services-review.org.uk/content/report/index.htm) (accessed 2 August 2013).

Collins, R. (1990), 'Changing Conceptions in the Sociology of the Professions', in Torstendahl, R. and Burrage, M. (eds), *The Formation of the Professions – Knowledge State and Strategy*. London: Sage Publications, 11–23.

Cook, A., Faulconbridge, J. and Muzio, D.A. (2012), 'London's Legal Elite: Recruitment through Cultural Capital and the Reproduction of Social Exclusivity', *City Professional Service Fields Environment and Planning A*, 44(7): 1744–62.

Cook, E.A. (1992), 'Professionalism and the Practice of Law', *Texas Tech Law Review*, 23: 955–1009.

Cooke, M., Irby, D.M. and O'Brien, B.C. (2010), *Educating Physicians: A Call for Reform of Medical School and Residency*. San Francisco: Jossey-Bass.

Dolliver, J.M. (1990), 'Law as a Profession; Will it Survive?' *Gonzaga Law Review*, 26(2): 267–75.

Dreyfus, H.L. and Dreyfus, S.E. (1986), *Mind over Machine: The Power of Human Intuition and Expertise in the Era of the Computer*. New York: Free Press.

Duncan, N. (2011), 'Addressing Emotion in Preparing Ethical Lawyers', in Maharg, P. and Maughan, C. (eds), *Affect and Legal Education – emotion and learning in the teaching of law*. Farnham: Ashgate, 257–82.

Economides, K. and Rogers, J. (2009), *Preparatory Ethics training for Future Solicitors*. London: The Law Society.

Empson, L. (2007), 'Your Partnership', in Empson, L. (ed.), *Managing the Modern Law Firm*. Oxford: Oxford University Press, 10–36.

Epstein, R.M. (2006), 'Mindful Practice and the Tacit Ethics of the Moment', in Kelly, N. and Shelton, W. (eds), *Lost Virtue: Professional Character Development in Medical Education*. Kidlington: Elsivier, 115–44.

Farren, C. (2000), 'Mastery: The Critical Advantage', in Chowdhury, S. (ed.), *Management 21C*. Harlow: Pearson Education, 99–105.

Faulconbridge, J. and Muzio, D. (2008), 'Organizational Professionalism in Global Law Firms', *Work, Employment and Society*, 22(1): 7–25.

Faulconbridge, J. and Muzio, D. (2010), Legal education, globalization, and cultures of professional practice UK Economic and Social Research Council funded project Ref RES-000-22-2957.

Flood, J. (1996), 'Megalawyering in the Global Order: The Cultural, Social, Economic Transformation of Global Law Practice', *International Journal of the Legal Profession*, 3: 169–214.

Flood, J. (2011), Legal Education in the Global Context: Challenges from Globalization, Technology and Changes in Government Regulation Report. London: Legal Services Board.

Freidson, E. (1986), *Professional Powers: A Study of the Institutionalization of Formal Knowledge*. Chicago: University of Chicago Press.

Freidson, E. (2001), *Professionalism: The Third Logic*. Chicago: University of Chicago Press.

Galanter, M. (1983), 'Mega-law and Mega-lawyering in the Contemporary United States', in Dingwall, R. and Lewis, P. (eds), *The Sociology of the Professions*. London: Macmillan, 152–76.

Galanter, M. (2011), 'More Lawyers than People: The Global Multiplication of Legal Professionals', in Cummings, S.L. (ed.), *The Paradox of Professionalism*

– *Lawyers and the Possibility of Justice*. New York: Cambridge University Press, 68–79.

Galanter, M. and Palay, T. (1992), 'The Transformation of the Big Law Firm', in Nelson, R.L., Trubek D.M. and Solomon, R.L. (eds), *Lawyers' Ideals/Lawyers' Practices – Transformations in the American Legal Profession*. New York: Cornell University Press, 31–62.

Galanter, M. and Roberts, S. (2008), 'From Kinship to Magic Circle: The London Commercial Law Firm in the Twentieth Century', *International Journal of the Legal Profession*, 15(3): 143–78.

George, D., Gosenhauser, I. and Whitehouse, P. (2006), 'Medical Professionalism: The Nature of Story and the Story of Nature', in Wear, D. and Aultman, J.M. (eds), *Professionalism in Medicine: Critical Perspectives*. New York: Springer, 87–102.

Goriely, T. (1994), 'Debating the Quality of Legal Services: Differing Models of a Good Lawyer', *International Journal of the Legal Profession*, 1(2): 159–71.

Gray, J.T. (1999), 'Restructuring Law Firms – Reflexivity and Emerging Forms', in Brock, D., Powell, M. and Hinings, C.R. (eds), *Restructuring the Professional Organization*. London: Routledge, 87–104.

Greenwood, R. (2007), 'Redefining Professionalism? The Impact of Management Change', in Empson, L. (ed.), *Managing the Modern Law Firm*. Oxford: Oxford University Press, 186–95.

Hammer, M. (1998), *Beyond Re-engineering*. London: Harper Collins.

Higgenbotham, A.L. (1987), 'The Life of Law: Values, Commitment and Craftsmanship', *Harvard Law Review*, 100: 795–816.

Hilton, T. and Migdal, S. (2005), 'Why Clients Need, Rather than Want, Lawyers', *International Journal of the Legal Profession*, 12(1): 145–63.

Hinings, C.R., Greenwood, R. and Cooper, D. (1999), 'The Dynamics of Change in Large Accountancy Firms', in Brock, D. Powell, M. and Hinings, C.R. (eds), *Restructuring the Professional Organization*. London: Routledge, 131–53.

Hutchinson, A.C. (1998), 'Legal Ethics for a Fragmented Society: Between Professional and Personal', *International Journal of the Legal Profession*, 5(2–3): 175–92.

Irvine, D. (2009), 'The Relationship between Teaching Professionalism and Licensing and Accrediting Bodies', in Cruess, R.L, Cruess, S.R. and Steinert, Y. (eds), *Teaching Medical Professionalism*. New York: Cambridge University Press, 185–99.

Johnson, G., Scholes, K. and Whittington, R. (2007), *Exploring Corporate Strategy*. 8th edition. London: Prentice Hall.

Kelly, M.J. (1996), *Lives of Lawyers – Journeys in the Organizations of Practice*. Michigan: University of Michigan Press.

King, P.M. and Kitchener, K.S. (1994), *Developing Reflective Judgment – Understanding and Promoting Intellectual Growth and Critical Thinking in Adolescents and Adults*. San Francisco: Jossey-Bass.

Kritzer, H.M. (1999), 'The Professions are Dead, Long Live the Professions: Legal Practice in a Post Professional World', *Law and Society Review*, 33(3): 713–59.

Kronman, A.T. (1995), *The Lost Lawyer: Failing Ideals of the Legal Profession*. Cambridge, Massachusetts: Harvard University Press.

Kronman, A. (1999), 'Our Beleaguered Public World', *Journal of Legal Education*, 49: 50–57.

Larson, M.S. (1977), *The Rise of Professionalism*. Berkeley: University of California Press.

LETR (Legal Education and Training Review) (2013), Setting Standards: Legal Services Education and Training regulation in England and Wales (accessed at http://letr.org.uk/wp-content/uploads/LETR-Report.pdf) (accessed 2 August 2013).

LSB (2011(a)), A Framework to Monitor the Legal Services Sector. London: Legal Services Board.

LSB (2011(b)), Research Note. London: Legal Services Board.

Leitch, A. (2006), *Prosperity for all in the Global Economy – World Class Skills*. Norwich: HMSO.

Lewis, R. and Maude, A. (1952), *Professional People*. London: Phoenix.

McCrate, R. (1992), *Legal Education and Professional Development – an Educational Continuum*. New York: American Bar Association.

Maharg, P. (2007), *Transforming Legal Education: Learning and Teaching the Law in the Early Twenty-First Century*. London: Ashgate.

Maister, D.H. (1997), *True Professionalism – The Courage to Care about your People, your Clients and your Career*. New York: The Free Press.

Maister, D., Green, C. and Galford, R. (2000), *The Trusted Advisor*. New York: Free Press.

Mann, K.V. (2006), 'Learning and Teaching in Professional Character Development, in Lost Virtue: Professional Character Development', in Kelly, N. and Shelton, W. (eds), *Medical Education*. Kidlington: Elsivier, 145–83.

Martin, M.W. (2000), *Meaningful Work – Rethinking Professional Ethics*. New York: Oxford University Press.

Maslow, A.H. (1968), *Towards a Psychology of Being*. New York: John Wiley & Sons.

Maslow, A.H. (2000), *The Maslow Business Reader*, edited by Stephens, D.C. New York: John Wiley and Sons.

Mather, L. (2011), 'How and Why do Lawyers Misbehave? Lawyers, Discipline and Collegial Control', in Cummings, S.L. (ed.), *The Paradox of Professionalism – Lawyers and the Possibility of Justice*. New York: Cambridge University Press, 109–31.

Maughan, C. (2011), 'Why Study Emotion?', in Maharg, P. and Maughan, C. (eds), *Affect and Legal Education – Emotion and Learning in the Teaching of Law*. Farnham: Ashgate, 11–44.

Maughan, C. and Webb, J. (2005), *Lawyering Skills and the Legal Process*. 2nd edition. Cambridge: Cambridge University Press.

Mezirow, J. and Associates. (1990), *Fostering Critical Reflection in Adulthood – a Guide to Transformative and Emancipatory Learning*. San Francisco: Jossey-Bass.

Moore, W.E. (1970), *The Professions: Roles and Rules*. London: Sage.

Moorhead, R., and Boyle, F. (1995), 'Quality of Life and Trainee Solicitors: A Survey', *International Journal of the Legal Profession*, 2(2/3): 217–51.

Neighbour, R. (1992), *The Inner Apprentice – an Awareness-centred Approach to Vocational Training for General Practice*. Newbury: Petroc Press.

Nelson, R. and Trubek, D.M. (1992(a)), 'Arenas of Professionalism', in Nelson, R.L., Trubek, D.M. and Solomon, R.L. (eds), *Lawyers' Ideals/Lawyers' Practices – Transformations in the American Legal Profession*. New York: Cornell University Press, 177–214.

Nelson, R. and Trubek D.M. (1992(b)), 'Introduction', in Nelson, R.L., Trubek D.M. and Solomon, R.L. (eds), *Lawyers' Ideals/Lawyers' Practices – Transformations in the American Legal Profession*. New York: Cornell University Press, 1–27.

Nicolson, D. (2005), 'Making Lawyers Moral? Ethical Codes and Moral Character', *Legal Studies*, 25(4): 601–26.

Nicolson, D. (2008), 'Education Education Education: Legal, Moral and Clinical', *The Law Teacher*, 42: 145–73.

Ozarak, E. (2005), '"Wisdom Cries Aloud in the Street": Using Service-Learning to Teach Ethics Across the Curriculum', in Strain, J. and Robinson, S. (eds), *The Teaching and Practice of Professional Ethics*. Leicester: Troubador, 147–54.

Parsons, T. (1968), *The Structure of Social Action*. New York: The Free Press.

Paterson, A. (1990), *Professional Competence in Legal Services Report*. London: National Consumer Council.

Paterson, A. (1996), 'Professionalism and the Legal Services Market', *International Journal of the Legal Profession*, 3(1/2): 137–68.

Pearce, D. (1987), *Australian Law Schools: A Discipline Assessment for the Commonwealth Tertiary Education Commission*. Canberra; Commonwealth Tertiary Education Commission.

Pearce, R.G. (1995). 'The Professionalism Paradigm Shift: Why Discarding Professional Ideology will Improve the Conduct and Reputation of the Bar', *New York University Law Review*, 70: 1229–76.

Raelin, J.A. (1985), *The Clash of Cultures – Managers Managing Professionals*. Boston: Harvard Business School Press.

Raelin, J.A. (2008), *Work-based Learning – Bridging Knowledge and Action in the Workplace*. San Francisco: John Wiley and Sons.

Re, E.D. (1994), 'The Causes of Popular Dissatisfaction with the Legal Profession', *St John's Law Review*, 68: 85–136.

Regan, M.C. (1999), 'Law Firms, Competition Penalties and the Values of Professionalism', *Georgetown Journal of Legal Ethics*, 13(1): 1–74.

Regan, M.C. (2002), 'Taking Law Firms Seriously', *Georgetown Journal of Legal Ethics*, 16: 155–72.

Rhode, D.L. (2000), *In the Interests of Justice – Reforming the Legal Profession*. New York: Oxford University Press.

Rose, T. and Hinings, C.R. (1999), 'Internationalization of Professional Services: Implications for Accounting Firms', in Brock, D., Powell, M. and Hinings, C.R. (eds), *Restructuring the Professional Organization*. London: Routledge, 41–67.

Rueschemeyer, D. (1969), *Lawyers and Doctors: A Comparison of Two Professions in Sociology of Law*, edited by Aubert, V. London: Penguin Education.

Sadler-Smith, E. (2008), *Inside Intuition*. Abingdon: Routledge.

Schein, E.H. (1972), *Professional Education: Some New Directions*. New York: McGraw-Hill.

Schon, D.A. (1987), *Educating the Reflective Practitioner*. San Francisco: Jossey-Bass.

Schon, D.A. (1991), *The Reflective Practitioner – How Professionals Think in Action*. Aldershot: Ashgate.

Schumpeter, J. (1950), *Capitalism, Socialism and Democracy*. New York: HarperCollins.

Sechooler, A. (2008), 'Globalization, Inequality and the Legal Services Industry', *International Journal of the Legal Profession*, 15(3): 231–48.

Senge, P. (1990), *The Fifth Discipline*. London: Random.

Sherr, A. (2000), 'Professional Work, Professional Careers and Legal Education; Educating the Lawyer for 2010', *International Journal of the Legal Profession*, 7(3): 325–42.

Sherr, A., Moorehead, R. and Paterson, A. (1994), 'Assessing the Quality of Legal Work: Measuring Process', *International Journal of the Legal Profession*, 1(2): 135–58.

Stuckey, R. (2007), *Best Practice for Legal Education: A Vision and Road Map*. Columbia: Clinical Legal Education Organization.

Sullivan, R. (2011), *Quality in Legal Services: A Literature Review*. London: Legal Services Board.

Sullivan, W.M. (2005), *Work and Integrity – The Crisis and Promise of Professionalism in America*. San Francisco: Jossey-Bass.

Sullivan, W.M., Colby, A., Wegner, J.W., Bond, L. and Shulman, L.S. (2007), *Educating Lawyers: Preparation for the Profession of Law*. San Francisco: Jossey-Bass.

Susskind, R. (1996), *The Future of Law – Facing the Challenges of Information Technology*. Oxford: Clarendon Press.

Susskind, R. (2000), *Transforming the Law: Essays on Technology, Justice and the Legal Marketplace*. Oxford: Oxford University Press.

Susskind, R. (2008), *The End of Lawyers – Rethinking the Nature of Legal Services*. Oxford: Oxford University Press.

Svensson, L.G. (1990), 'Knowledge as a Professional Resource: Case Studies of Architects and Psychologists at Work', in Torstendahl, R. and Burrage, M.

(eds), *The Formation of Professions – Knowledge State and Strategy*. London: Sage Publications, 51–70.

Webb, J. (1995), 'Where the Action is: Developing Artistry in Legal Education', *International Journal of the Legal Profession*, 2(2/3): 187–216.

Webb, J. (1998), 'Ethics for Lawyers or Ethics for Citizens? New Directions for Legal Education', *Journal of Law and Society*, 25(1): 134–50.

Webb, J. (2002), 'Being a Lawyer/Being a Human Being', *Legal Studies*, 5(1 and 2): 130–151.

Webb, J. (2004), 'Turf Wars and Market Control: Competition and Complexity in the Market for Legal Services', *International Journal of the Legal Profession*, 11(1 and 2): 81–102.

Wenger, E. (1998), *Communities of Practice – Learning, Meaning and identity*. New York: Cambridge University Press.

Wenger, E. (2009), 'A Social Theory of Learning', in Illeris, K. (ed.), *Contemporary Theories of Learning*. Abingdon: Routledge, 209–18.

Wenger, E., McDermott, R. and Snyder, W.M. (2002), *Cultivating Communities of Practice*. Boston: Harvard Business School Press.

Westwood, F. (2001), *Achieving Best Practice – Shaping Professionals for Success*. Maidenhead: McGraw-Hill.

Westwood, F. (2003), *Diploma in Legal Practice Research Report*. Edinburgh: The Law Society of Scotland.

Westwood, F. (2006), 'Moving Towards the Knowledge Economy – do Professionals Provide Models for the Development of Knowledge Workers and what this Means for Management Education?' *International Journal of Management*, 41(17–27).

Westwood, F. (2008), *Accelerated Best Practice – Implementing Success in Professional Firms*. Leicester: Troubador.

Westwood, F. (2010), *Developing Resilience – the Key to Professional Success*. Leicester: Troubador.

Westwood, F. (2011(a)), 'The Demise of the Legal Profession?' *Law Business Review*, August: 24–28.

Westwood, F. (2011(b)), 'Survival of the Fittest', *Law Business Review*, October: 36–39.

PART III
Character and Conscientiousness

Chapter 3

Calling, Character and Clinical Legal Education: Inculcating a Love for Justice from Cradle to Grave

Donald Nicolson[1,2]

Introduction

To be a true professional, one needs to be an amateur! This statement becomes less paradoxical, though not necessarily less controversial, if one ignores the more modern association of 'professional' with those who are paid to provide skilled work and recalls the Latin roots of 'amateur' and its association with conduct performed for the love of it, rather than the pejorative notion of unpaid and unskilled, if not incompetent, services. This chapter states the case for a return to an older ideal of professionalism, in which professionals were regarded as experiencing a calling to exercise their skills and some at least were willing to do so irrespective of whether they were paid. However, instead of reviving a patrician *noblesse oblige* ideal (Luban 1988) or relying as others do on arguments addressed to the profession as a whole, I will seek to ground this sense of professionalism in the personal ethics duties of practitioners and argue that individual lawyers have moral duties to ensure that legal services are not confined to those who can pay or qualify for legal aid. In other words, law involves a calling to devote one's training, skills and privileges to the benefit of those who require law's benefits or protections, and hence that a true legal professional is a lover of justice.

Previously, I have argued that a core element of professionalism is the maintenance of ethical standards – what I called 'ethical professionalism' (Nicolson 2008). Here I will use the neologism 'altru-ethical professionalism' to argue that, just as ethics are a core aspect of professionalism, so is altruism[3] a core aspect of ethics. After seeking to justify this admittedly idealistic view

1   This chapter is based on an article by the author with the same title found at *Legal Ethics* 2013 Volume 16, pp. 36–56.

2   I would like to thank Nicola Zoumidou for conducting two of the student surveys referred to in section 3.3, Monica Barry for helping with a third and Kristina Moodie for analysing the resulting data.

3   By altruism is meant 'actions that not only benefit others, but are also primarily motivated by the desire to benefit others' (Carlo et al. 2009: 272).

of professionalism, I will explore how legal education might seek to inculcate this ideal. Again drawing on previous work (Nicolson 2008, 2010), I will argue that to be effective legal education needs to start a process whereby altru-ethical professionalism becomes part of what I have called professional moral character, namely those permanent character traits which are exercised in the context of professional life (Nicolson 2005), and that the most effective means of doing so is through lengthy involvement in a voluntary law clinic. Finally, I will outline an innovative new clinical law degree which seeks to integrate a focus on ethics and justice throughout legal education in order to start this process of inculcating altruism as part of professional moral character.

Law as a Calling to Justice

Before justifying the altru-ethical conception of professionalism, it is worth clarifying that I do not see altruism solely in terms of performing *pro bono* legal services, but more broadly as an obligation to contribute in some way to access to justice. This, in turn, I understand as a contribution to redressing unmet legal need, rather than simply providing legal services without payment. For instance, those who forego the higher salaries of corporate or other lucrative legal work to work in law centres or as legal aid lawyers (whether out of a sense of calling or otherwise), who waive or reduce fees when needy clients run out of money to pay or who support others who provide services to those in need such as through providing training or financial resources all contribute to access to justice.

But why can it be said that a duty of altruism exists? One argument rests on the idea that there exists an implied social contract between the profession and society, in terms of which society accords lawyers high status, financial rewards, protection from competition and independence from state control in return for expert knowledge, quality legal services, ethical behaviour and, crucially, altruism and access to justice (for example Paterson 2011: ch. 2). Such an argument provides useful leverage in the hands of the state and other groups campaigning to ensure that professionalism involves less of 'a conspiracy against the laity' as George Bernard Shaw's famous line from *The Doctor's Dilemma* puts it, and more of a benefit to society as whole. But it is far less likely to be effective as an aspirational ideal that inspires incoming and existing lawyers to devote at least some of their time or income to assisting those in need of legal services. For one thing, lawyers have managed for years to retain the benefits of professional status without being overly concerned about access to justice. Perhaps more importantly, obligations which derive from the enlightened self-interest of a contract (albeit a fictional one), like other forms of extrinsic motivation, are less likely to have a lasting and robust effect than those which develop out of more intrinsic and personally felt motivations (Carr 1991: 150–155; Lapsley and Power 2005).

Prima facie, a more promising route to developing altruism appeals to the notions of professionalism as a calling. Here one can argue that the essential difference between professionals and even the most skilled members of other occupations is the idea that professional skills are exercised and services provided, not merely for financial reward, but out of a calling and a love for the job. Otherwise, there is little to distinguish those who we regard as professionals from those who perform occupations because they provide a means to make a living which reflects their aptitude, training and contextual circumstances. It may obviously occur, but it seems unlikely, that many become plumbers out of the love of unclogging drains or sell insurance because of a desire to protect others against risk. There are obviously other attributes to being a professional – autonomy, the maintenance of high ethical standards, knowledge and skill developed through education and training and accredited by some external body and the guarantee of indemnity for any harm caused to clients. But many of these are also found or could easily be developed in other occupations.

However the idea of a calling only takes us so far towards altru-ethical professionalism. Some might argue that, as long as law is practised, not just for extrinsic reasons like money and prestige, but for the intrinsic reward of a career which is stimulating and challenging, lawyers qualify as professionals. One problem with this 'intrinsic reward' notion of a calling is that over time it may degenerate into a focus on extrinsic reward because of the sort of things lawyers are required to do on behalf of clients (cf. Nicolson and Webb, 1999: 175–8). It seems difficult to maintain satisfaction in a job well done when the consequences involve harm to others, the public interest or the law itself. Treating legal practice merely as a well-paid job avoids such cognitive dissonance, but possibly at the expense of amoral cynicism leaking into one's personal life.

In event, even those like Kronman (1993) who have eloquently argued for the importance of this sense of calling have gone further to combine it with a concern for ensuring that legal arguments best serve the public good. Others with a similar liberal persuasion see the guaranteeing of access to justice as promoting the public interest. This is because the law itself is a public good and this in turn is because it ensures that society operates in an ordered and fair fashion by protecting the autonomy and dignity of all citizens through the provision of rights to liberty and protection from others (for example Pepper 1986; Paterson, 2011: 68–70). However, as many citizens do not have the knowledge and skills to vindicate the rights which protect their freedom and dignity, lawyers who provide legal services contribute not only to protecting their clients, but also to peaceful social flourishing. Moreover, limiting services to those who can afford them can be said to contravene the idea of equality before the law which is a core aspect of both the rule of law and liberal society. Accordingly, it can be argued that lawyers who ensure access to justice promote both liberty and equality and thereby fraternity.

On the other hand, some are sceptical about the sort of equality, dignity, autonomy and fraternity espoused in liberal societies, though not necessarily of these values in themselves (see for example Nicolson and Webb 1999: 197–205). For them, an alternative source for an obligation to contribute to access to justice can be sought in ethical theory alone (Nicolson and Webb 1999: ch. 2). Utilitarianism, for instance, might support a duty on lawyers to promote the greatest good for all by giving up some of their privileges to help others. The postmodernist ethic of alterity would require the lawyer to reach out to give succour to the 'other' in need of legal services, as possibly would also the feminist ethic of care. But a more specific, and probably more persuasive, argument relies on a moral duty of reciprocity, or even that of gratitude, towards the citizen as taxpayer.

The argument starts from the recognition that through their taxes citizens pay for school education and, still in Scotland, for much of the cost of legal education. This investment enables law students to go on to enjoy substantial financial rewards. Taxpayers are thus paying for lawyers to make money, presumably because it is thought that this education benefits society. However, only those who can afford a lawyer or who are fortunate enough to qualify for legal aid benefit from this public investment in the education of lawyers. Put bluntly: the reason why so many people lack access to legal services is because so many lawyers price them out of the market by the fees they charge for their services. Consequently, it can be argued that lawyers have a moral duty to take some remedial action to repay those who helped put them in their privileged position, but who do not benefit from this investment.

As regards the large number of lawyers who work for large law firms, there is an additional moral reason supporting a duty to extend legal services beyond their clients. Many of these clients are large commercial institutions providing goods or services to the public, who pass on the high cost of legal services to their consumers. Consumers thus subsidise high legal fees, yet many cannot themselves afford legal services. Indeed, the link between the behaviour of law firms and the justice of the legal system is even more direct, given that those without legal representation often face law firms using all the skills and resources at their disposal to protect clients from, for example, paying compensation for unfair dismissal, unlawful discrimination and unlawful evictions. One response to such power imbalances is for firms to adopt a less adversarial stance towards unrepresented clients. However, given that lawyers owe clients a duty of zeal, a far more plausible response is for them to take steps to ensure that no one goes unrepresented. Admittedly, this might lead some to engage in what has been called 'schizoid lawyering' (Gordon 1988: 22–3), whereby they seek to resolve the sort of problems after work to which they have contributed during office hours, but this seems a necessary price to pay if such lawyers are to enhance access to justice.

If accepted, the argument about the link between professional status and repaying a debt of gratitude to society can go a long way to founding a duty of altruism. This is because not only does the ethical duty or virtue of gratitude avoid some of the problems of alternative foundations for such a duty, but research suggests that gratitude is in fact linked to altruism, in that those who have knowingly received benefits from others are often spurred to general acts of altruism generally rather than merely to help those who have helped them (Emmons 2009).

Altru-ethical Professionalism and Legal Education

1: Clinics, Character and Calling: The Argument

We thus see that if law is currently not conceived of as a calling, lawyers have good reason to stress this dimension of professionalism in order to distinguish themselves from the many occupations currently competing for equivalent status. Indeed, this argument has added resonance in the current climate of a growing commercialisation of legal practice (Francis 2005; Paterson 2011: ch. 2). Moreover, if professionalism is currently not seen as extending a duty to ensure access to justice, there are powerful arguments to support such a case. The question then is what role can law schools play, not just in making the case for, but also in instilling a commitment to, altru-ethical professionalism?

An obvious first, and relatively easy, step is to introduce students to problems of access to justice. However, it is doubtful whether a few lectures and possibly a tutorial on the issue will engage student interest especially when swamped by endless hours devoted to learning substantive law. By contrast, bringing in practitioners to discuss their successes and satisfaction gained from helping those in need and/or by using literature and films with similar messages may act to spark student interest and concern (for example Johnston and Treuthart 1991, 100-101; Menkel-Meadow 1999: 61, 64–6; Menkel-Meadow 2000). Such narratives can also be linked to discussions of professional ethics. However, at present, legal ethics currently plays a very marginal role in undergraduate legal education.

Although this may be about to change in England and Wales as the Legal Education and Training Review (LETR 2013) has recommended a greater role for legal ethics in the academic stage of training, an even bigger problem flows from what is variously called the law school's 'hidden' (Cramton 1977–78), 'latent' (Pipkin 1979), 'implicit' (Lesnick 1986: 634) or 'informal' (Economides 1998, xvii) curriculum. This is said to be likely to undermine any focus on access to justice as part of legal ethics and indeed any underlying commitment incoming law students might have to seeing legal practice as a calling. This hidden curriculum is contained in the unarticulated value assumptions, which supplement and may be as powerful as those contained in the formal curriculum. It is communicated to students by example, teaching methods, curriculum design, student culture and contacts with the legal profession. According to the commentators, it conveys the message that issues of ethics and justice are of little relevance to the real business of law, and that a legal career is largely a means to success and financial rewards rather than one in which legal heroes seek justice and help those in need (cf. Goldsmith 1996; Sherr 1995) .

Numerous studies in the US (summarised in Chapman 2002: 73–9) show that the hidden curriculum engenders moral and political cynicism, and undermines any idealism students might have about using law to promote justice. This finding has yet to be replicated in the UK, though Sherr and Webb (1989) found that Warwick Law School left untouched the overwhelming conservative political orientation of incoming law students. A recent unpublished study by Nicola Zoumidou and myself (Nicolson 2011) offers a less pessimistic picture of University of Strathclyde law students, while also failing to detect any obvious negative effect of legal education on attitudes within the first three terms of study. Given the scarcity of information on this issue in the UK, it is worth setting out the results in a little detail.

In September 2009, incoming law students were asked various questions designed to gauge their motivation in pursuing a legal career and then re-surveyed three months and then again another 16 months later. When asked before they began studying, 70 per cent of those surveyed declared an intention to practice law, with 26 per cent still undecided and 4 per cent set against a legal career, but 16 months later the figures had altered to 61 per cent, 34 per cent and 5 per cent, respectively[4] – findings which are broadly consistent with similar studies in England and Wales.[5]

As a way of indirectly exploring their sense of calling, the students surveyed were asked to rate a number of specific reasons for studying (and later for continuing to study) law on a Likert scale of one to five, with one representing 'not important' and five 'very important'. The responses for incoming students was as follows:

Table 3.1   Reasons for choosing to study law

Reasons for choosing to study law	N	Mean
Interesting subject to study.	132	4.50
Leads to a good career in terms of being interesting/stimulating.	132	4.38
To work with and help people.	131	3.97
Leads to a good career in terms of salary.	131	3.96
Desire to ensure social justice.	132	3.65
Status given by having a law degree.	128	3.63
To serve the underprivileged.	128	3.56
Leads to a good career in terms of prestige/status.	130	3.36
Uncertain what else to study so chose law.	129	1.63
Family tradition/pressure/expectation.	130	1.38

4   Though here attempts at a statistically reliable longitudinal study were scuppered by the fact that only 38 students provided their student number on each of the three survey responses and hence at best we could only compare three different cohorts, albeit ones whose membership largely overlapped, with regard to the 39 students, however, those still intending to study law dropped from 75 per cent to 58 per cent.

5   Thus those intending to enter practice constituted 58 per cent of incoming students in McDonald's study (1982), 62 per cent across all three undergraduate years in that of Sherr and Webb (1989) and 60 per cent of second year students in Rees et al. (2000).

Ignoring the last two more neutral answers, if we group these reasons into those that are largely altruistic (3, 5 and 7), those which reflect material self-interest (4 and 8) and those which reflect a more enlightened self-interest (1 and 2), altruism rates marginally higher than material self-interest (combined mean score of 3.72 as compared to 3.65) – a picture which differed only marginally between students intending to practice law and those unsure or set against doing so. In other words, what the students surveyed seem most to want is an interesting and stimulating career. They might see law as a calling, but not necessarily a calling to do justice.

Obviously these results are indicative only. Not only do the questions combine reasons for studying law with practising law, but as with earlier studies which produced similar results (Sherr and Webb 1989),[6] it is possible that some respondents were reflecting the answers they thought they should give rather than their real reasons. Perhaps more reliable are the reasons students gave for wanting to join the University of Strathclyde Law Clinic (USLC), which operates on a largely extra-curricular basis:

Table 3.2   Reasons for wanting to join the Law Clinic

Reasons for wanting to join the Law Clinic	N	Mean Intending to join, Sept 2009	N	Mean Admitted, Feb 2011
To gain useful skills.	111	4.71	36	4.31
To put into practice theoretical knowledge.	111	4.59	36	4.35
To help others.	111	4.25	36	4.50
To improve my CV.	110	4.15	36	3.73
To increase access to justice.	109	3.95	36	4.26

What these tables reveal is that, while students understandably have mixed motives for studying and wanting to practice law, even those who wanted to become involved in providing voluntary legal help were as much, if not more motivated, by the benefits to themselves rather to those in need. On the other hand, as the second column in Table 3.2 shows, those who successfully completed the rigorous USLC selection process had much higher scores for altruistic reasons for wanting to join. Moreover, as the comparison in Table 3.3 of the student responses on entry with those 16 months later suggests,[7] legal education at the University of Strathclyde Law School did not have a noticeable negative (nor indeed positive)

---

6   Though Strathclyde students did seem to be more altruistic and more intrinsically motivated to study law and less motivated by material self-interest.

7   Here again the caveat raised in footnote 3, above, applies.

impact on student attitudes, except that, as we have seen, it seems to put some students off practising law:

Table 3.3   Reasons for choosing to study law (2)

Reasons for choosing to study law	Sept 2009	Jan 2011	t	s
Interesting subject to study.	4.50	4.10	2.63	<0.05 sig
Leads to a good career in terms of being interesting/ stimulating.	4.38	4.04	2.21	<0.05 sig
To work with and help people.	3.97	3.94	0.62	>0.05
Leads to a good career in terms of salary.	3.96	3.75	1.26	>0.05
Desire to ensure social justice.	3.65	3.61	0.40	>0.05
Status given by having a law degree.	3.63	3.41	1.41	>0.05
To serve the underprivileged.	3.56	3.40	0.94	>0.05
Leads to a good career in terms of prestige/status.	3.36	3.11	1.84	>0.05
Uncertain what else to study so chose law.	1.63	2.13	-4.07	<0.001
Family tradition/pressure/expectation.	1.38	1.61	-1.17	>0.05

In other words, at least at Strathclyde there is some potential to work with in seeking to develop altruism in law graduates and no evidence that such efforts have to work against the impact of legal education. In fact, attention to moral psychology suggests that law schools might be better focusing their efforts on fostering altruism in a relatively small group of students rather than spreading its efforts amongst all.

This realisation starts with an understanding of the psychology of moral behaviour. Following Rest, it has become accepted that moral behaviour (whatever its content) requires the engagement, though not necessarily consciously or chronologically, of four psychological components (for example Rest 1984; Rest et al. 1999; Rest and Narvaez 1994: esp. ch. 1). *Moral sensitivity* is required to enable students and lawyers to recognise particular ethical problems, such as that of unmet legal need. Having done so, *moral judgment* is required to enable individuals to recognise a duty to respond to the problem and to select and justify their response to it. However, empirical research repeatedly confirms that knowing what is morally right by no means guarantees moral behaviour (Rest 1984: 21–2; Rest 1988). Thus, thirdly, *moral motivation* is required to ensure that individuals want to put into effect the solution selected and elevate it over competing considerations like self-interest or organisational and institutional values. Finally, even if individuals care about ensuring access to justice, they require the *moral courage* to be able to resist temptations to compromise moral standards.

Crucial here are moral fibre, steadfastness, perseverance, 'backbone and what psychologists call ego-strength' (Blasi 1995: 74).

This suggests that law schools are unlikely to have much impact on encouraging altruism via traditional forms of teaching even if issues of access to justice and legal ethics are made more central. By contrast, a growing consensus amongst moral psychologists, educationalists and legal scholars (see for example Peters 1981; Condlin 1983; Eisele 1987; Nucci 1989; Luban and Millemann 1995; Carr 1991; Webb 1998a, 1998b, 1999) draws on a much older tradition of moral philosophy to argue that the most effective means of ensuring the development of all four psychological components is through a process of character development. According to Aristotle (Aristotle 1987) and other virtue ethicists (for example Dreyfus and Dreyfus 1990; Kupperman 2005: 203; Narvaez and Lapsley 2005), education should be aimed at gradually developing relatively stable character dispositions, or habits of perception, thinking, feeling and behaviour, through actual engagement with moral issues in a way similar to how expertise is developed in other walks of life. By emulating others, by trial and error, by instruction and feedback from authoritative others, by experiencing and reflecting on the appropriate pride or regret at the outcome of one's actions, moral habits or dispositions are said to gradually develop to the point that appropriate moral behaviour and feelings become embedded in the individual's character. In other words, character formation results not so much from direct teaching but from the experience of frequent immersion in real-life problems, exercise of one's moral muscles and learning from mistakes and successes.

Applied to the context of inculcating altru-ethical professionalism, actual involvement with those most in need of legal services would hopefully not only provide students with a better appreciation of the depth of the problem of access to justice and the need for lawyers to respond to it, but also help develop their motivation to play a role despite competing demands on their time and the courage to resist workplace and other pressures to concentrate on making money and other material rewards. Where all four moral components are developed to the extent that virtue becomes a way of life, altruism is far more likely to ensue. Indeed, empirical studies suggest that moral behaviour is more likely when moral considerations are central to one's personal identity and sense of self (see Blasi 1995; Power 1997; Lapsley and Power 2005; Narvaez and Lapsley 2009). Indeed, where moral motivations are central to the individual's self-identity, relevant moral behaviour is thought to flow from a kind of 'spontaneous necessity' without the need for willpower or moral courage to overcome temptations or pressures to eschew altruism, and there is empirical evidence to suggest that this applies to altruism (Aquino and Reed 2002; Carlo et al. 2009).

While research has yet to be done on whether and to what extent universities can positively influence character development, there are reasons for optimism (Davidson 2005: 223; Rhodes and Smith 2006). Certainly, as we have seen, law schools can have a negative impact, whereas research does show that, particularly if accompanied by ethical instruction and involvement in community projects, universities can have a lasting effect on moral judgment (for example Abramson 1993; Boss 1994; Rest and Narvaez 1994 *passim*; Bebeau 2006, 55–6), and on moral sensitivity and the related capacity for moral imagination (see Bebeau 1994, 2006: 51–3; Brandenberger 2005). Admittedly, as already noted, moral reasoning does not necessarily translate into behaviour. However, there is some, albeit weak, connection between the two (Blasi 1980; Thoma 1994; Rest et al. 1999: 80ff) and if universities can affect moral reasoning and sensitivity, why not other psychological components? Admittedly, also, students come to university with fairly well-formed moral characters. However, given that such character has been developed in response to ethical issues raised by everyday life rather than legal practice and as law students might be prepared to learn from those who seem to have expertise in law, there is an opportunity to help adapt what can be called personal moral character to the moral demands of practice by creating *professional* moral character and moral self-identity in which altruism has a central place.

Nevertheless, it has to be recognised that radical changes to moral character are likely to be rare, and hence there is probably little that universities can do to inculcate the habits of altru-ethical professionalism in those who enter university with, or quickly develop, cynical attitudes to legal practice. Such inculcation requires a lengthy immersion in real-life experiences and a supportive context in which students are given guidance and examples to follow. Thus, rather than spreading effort and resources across all students,[8] it seems more sensible to concentrate on reinforcing the orientation of those who enter university with an existing calling to do justice and, more ambitiously, on seeking to influence those without predispositions towards either cynicism or altruistic professionalism to choose the latter path. And while it might be possible for other aspects of ethical professionalism to be developed by role plays and simulations, whereas placements with outside bodies might go some way to strengthen and/or inculcate a sense of law as a calling to justice, by far the most likely means of doing so is involvement in live-client law clinics, especially if combined with opportunities to reflect on these experiences and learn from relevant academic literature.

Like all forms of active learning, involvement in live-client law clinics has many advantages over traditional forms of learning (see for example Brayne, Duncan and Grimes 1998). By engaging the interest and emotions of students, it has more potential to develop moral commitment (Richards 1981; Sprinthall 1994). Learning is more profound where student experiences are more personal, immediate and realistic, and relate to the fulfilment of their future social roles (Bloch 1982), and when prior assumptions and settled values jar with experienced reality causing

8   On the other hand, given that 1 in 2 applicants to the USLC are unsuccessful and that these are likely to include some with a potential for developing a calling for justice, there are plans to establish a Community Engagement Class designed to teach issues relating to access to justice and facilitate reflection on student placements in community legal service organisation.

'disorienting moments' involving moral crises, cognitive dissonance and, when others challenge one's own moral views, social disequilibrium (Haan 1985; Quigley 1995; Webb 1996: 282). By encouraging students to see issues from the side of clients, clinics may also encourage the development of empathy and other emotional sentiments (Goldsmith 1996: 13), which virtue ethicists and others see as so important to morality (Rest 1994: 389).

However, it is generally accepted that clinics have important advantages over other forms of active learning (Condlin 1983: 80, 320–324; Jewell 1984: 507–10; Aiken 1997: 47; Boon 2002: 60; Webb 1998b: 296; Rhode 1995: 141; Duncan 2002; Luban and Millemann 1995; Glennon 1992). By engaging with flesh-and-blood clients with actual problems students are far more likely to develop empathy for their plight. Lessons learnt are likely to go deeper when students bear responsibility for decisions which have consequences in the 'real' world (Moliterno 1991: 117–8; Noone and Dickson 2001). Clinics also provide the opportunities for two important sources of character development. One is the influence of role models, who have been shown to have positive impact, even to the extent of inducing a warm or glowing feeling in the chest, which makes people want to morally better themselves and to help others (Algoe and Haidt 2009). Because of their perceived practical knowledge and skills, clinic supervisors may function as influential moral exemplars, modelling concern for others and an altruistic commitment to the community. Secondly, feelings of satisfaction or regret at their actions in representing actual clients and resolving real dilemmas may crucially affect the character development of law clinic students.

In addition, clinics reveal the extent of unmet legal need, and social and legal injustice, that legal practice can involve helping others, and that this can be rewarding as well as intellectually challenging. Finally, community work in general has been shown to encourage participants to identify as moral agents, which as we have seen is central to personal identity and character development, and to build the sort of self-confidence that contributes to the moral courage required of individuals to act on their convictions in challenging circumstances (Boss 1994: 192).

2: Clinics, Character and Calling: The Evidence

The potential for clinic work to inspire, or at least reinforce, altruistic aspirations in students has been asserted by many clinicians (Johnstone 1951: 537; Rees 1975: 136; Guggenheim 1995: 683; Kotkin 1997; Maresh 1997; Styles and Zariska 2001; Tranter 2002:13). Some support for a 'clinic effect' was found by Evans (2001) and Palermo and Evans (2008), but given that student views were not canvassed prior to entry, their conclusions were very tentative. However, further evidence emerges from the unpublished results of the survey of University of Strathclyde students discussed above and from a previously published analysis of the 23 reflective dairies of USLC students taking the optional Clinical Legal Practice (CLP) class (Nicolson 2010). Until recently, this class, which examines issues of ethics and justice, and is limited to experienced USLC members, was an exception to the otherwise extra-curricular nature of clinic involvement that can last for up to five years. The lengthy involvement of the 180 or so students who are USLC members at any one time means that some take on as many as 40 cases. The mean number of cases for those whose diaries were analysed was 4.75 cases and for 36 clinic members who took part in the unpublished survey it was 2.88, even though some of the latter had only recently joined the USLC and none had been members for more than 15 months. In fact, all students whose views were reported had between one and three years left in the clinic and hence even more exposure to come to the problems of those in need of legal services.

To the extent that the responses of the students surveyed and writing diary entries are reliable,[9] both groups indicate that clinic experience, and related teaching and reflection, influenced attitudes in numerous ways. One involved stimulating an awareness of the problems of justice and the need for lawyers to play a role in their redress. Thus when asked if and how their clinic experience had altered their opinion on access to justice one of the students surveyed stated that it 'illustrated [that] many people still struggle to get access to justice', and another that 'I have seen through clients that would otherwise have not had representation that access to justice is poorer than thought'. A similar question in relation to the 'importance of lawyers providing free legal representation to those in need' prompted the following:

- 'I understand the severity of the need more and the injustices of the system';
- 'I have seen that lawyers must provide more free representation as the numbers without access to justice are greater than I knew';
- '[T]he law clinic has made me realise how many people cannot afford a lawyer'.

As one CLP student responded when questioned in an oral examination about what she had most learnt from the USLC: 'Theoretically in Legal Process [a first year class] they tell you that there is an unmet legal need but that is one of those things that are intangible unless you really experience it'. Many also seemed to appreciate that they could use their knowledge and skills to make a difference to other people's lives. Thus the following responses were given to the question of whether USLC experience had altered their opinions on the value of law:

- '[It is] extremely valuable in making sure the underprivileged are served';
- 'I have gained a greater appreciation for the value of law through helping others';
- '[T]he legal system is invaluable to help peoples [sic] lives and feelings'.

---

9   Here it can be noted that the former had nothing to gain from their answers, whereas the fact that many of latter were prepared to challenge my views and USLC principles shows that not all were playing to the gallery.

The recognition of a possible 'clinic effect' was more explicit in the reflective diaries of CLP students. One opined that law clinics may enthuse 'the many students [who] enter the profession with a genuine desire to tackle society's access to justice problems'. Another stated that the 'possibility of making a positive difference to someone ... reminds you of why you wanted to become a lawyer in the first place ...' and a third that her satisfaction in successfully representing a client turned down by eight firms reinforced her desire to pursue a career which makes a difference to the community. Her admission that exposure 'to the wide variety of options other than commercial law' helped her to discover a 'social conscience' shows that law clinics can do more than reinforce existing values and actually change them. This emerges clearly from the diary entry of another student: '[b]efore my experience in the Clinic, I had imagined a career in a large law firm and hadn't really considered the larger ideal of social justice ... Now I find it impossible not to'. And lest it be said that the diaries only reveal thoughts and not actions, this student went on to donate to other law clinics a sophisticated case management system he had developed with his own money and now works for a law centre. The Clinic's ongoing effect can also be seen in the fact that those who retained their original plans to pursue careers in commercial firms but asserted an intention to engage in pro bono work once qualified are now volunteering for USLC evening advice sessions. In fact, such volunteers also come from ex-USLC members whose 'day job' involves serving those most in need such as through legal aid services.

The CLP diaries also confirm that clinics assist in character development by inducing feelings of satisfaction or regret at the conduct of cases. As one student stated:

> I didn't start my law degree to 'make a difference'. My goal was simply to earn enough money so I can afford some of life's luxuries and have no financial troubles. However, having seen the positive effect my time and effort has had on clients of the clinic has changed my perspective and now, my ultimate goal is to find a job that provides both financial security and a chance to help communities or less fortunate individuals.

We have also seen that guidance from others plays an important role in character development. Relevant here is the fact that all experienced USLC students mentor inexperienced members, with very experienced members taking responsibility for a 'firm' of around 30 others, thus increasing the number of cases to which they are exposed. Indeed, a few CLP students referred to learning from cases in which they acted as mentors and using their experience and learning to engage less experienced students in what some themselves described (no doubt influenced by their seminar reading) as moral apprenticeships. As regards role models, a number of CLP students cited the examples given by their teachers who combine voluntary legal work with work as lawyers or academics as inspiring them both in their career choices and to go the extra mile for their clients.

The other role that the teaching staff play is to guide student reflection – in 'surgeries' discussing cases and in responding to diary entries – and placing students' experiences in context by introducing them to academic literature on issues of ethics and access to justice. Here, the diaries revealed that the students were frequently stimulated by their classes to reflect on their personal values and ethical orientation, and how they might play out in practice, with many admitting to not having previously considered their motivating moral values, various issues of ethics and professionalism and even the justice of the legal system. Thus, a seminar made one student realise that: 'my ideals to altruism will be tested when I start practising as a lawyer … I suppose I have been naïve to think that I could uphold my ideals and still become a successful lawyer. The seminar set me thinking seriously about the kind of lawyer I wanted to be and what my values really are'.

The Clinical LLB: A Cradle-to-grave Approach to Character and Calling

However it was not only the students who were set thinking by their experiences. The diaries brought home to me the validity of much of the theoretical underpinning of clinical legal education. Thus the view that '[l]earning occurs not in the doing but in the reflection and conceptualisation that takes place during and after the event' (quoted by Brayne, Duncan and Grimes 1988: 47) echoed my impression that students were learning far more and far more deeply from the symbiotic relationship between experience, reflection and theory (for instance on professionalism, ethics and access to justice) than they would from experience or theory alone (see also the empirical findings of Boss 1994: 191). Indeed, Kolb's well-known learning circle (Kolb 1984) makes clear that one learns best by a process of reflection on experiences, leading to the adoption of new, or the adaptation of existing, theories about how to handle issues, which can then be put into practice when similar situations arise, providing the opportunity for further reflection, theory adaption, theory testing and so on.

At the same time, however, I realised that there were limitations to confining the process of reflective learning to a one-semester class in the third or fourth year. Opportunities for fine-tuning their approaches to issues of professionalism and ethics came late, were relatively short and, once the class ended, had to be continued without guidance from tutors, reading or class discussion. Certainly, if repetition of the learning cycle was going to help transform conscious theory into subconscious habit, it would have to be repeated more frequently than merely over the course of one semester.

Consequently, in order to integrate experience, theory and reflection throughout law students' academic training, I developed a Clinical LLB. This involves all the classes available on the standard LLB, but in addition:

- provides students with credit for the training and cases they would otherwise undertake on a voluntary basis;

- allows them to gain credit for reflection on the legal, practical and ethical aspects of their cases as part of the assessment in their courses;
- requires them to keep a regular diary to reflect on their clinical experiences; and,
- most importantly, tops and tails the degree with an introductory session and a whole final year class on ethics and justice.

While a few other universities go beyond standard one-semester or at best year-long clinical courses,[10] as far as I can gather the Clinical LLB is unique in its cradle-to-grave approach to clinical legal education (up to four years in total for Honours students, though only two for those taking the postgraduate accelerated LLB) and in the prominence given to exploring the ethical and altruistic aspects of legal professionalism. More specifically, it is hoped that, by comparison with the standard law degree, the Clinical LLB will:

- Enable a better understanding of how law operates in practice through opportunities to discuss clinic experiences and engage with relevant reading;
- Encourage students to develop life-long habits of reflection on their exercise of legal skills, but also on how these skills are employed, for whom and against whom;
- Start students on a journey towards altru-ethical professionalism in which they acquire and value not just competence, but also an awareness of the wider ethical and justice dimension to law and legal practice;
- Help students grapple with what it means to be a professional and what sort of professional they want to be – what area to practice, what sort of approach to adopt to clients (empathetic or more technocratic and so on), and how they might seek to meet their moral obligations to help ensure access to justice.

It is recognised, however, that these aims should not swamp the need to provide students with the basic building blocks of legal knowledge, and to learn how to think like a lawyer and critically evaluate law's values and social role: thus to gain

---

10 Most notably, Northumbria Law School students take a year-long one-clinical legal education course in their third year which involves some live-client work, and finally a double module in the fourth year involving much more live-client work. Similarly in Newcastle, Australia, after an initial two years of standard LLB courses, students can opt to take a more practical route in which they integrate professional training with the rest of their courses via clinical experience rather than continuing with the standard academic route. Before its demise Antioch Law School had a very extensive clinical legal education programme, which included a requirement that all students live with an under-privileged family and gain an idea of life from their perspective.

the Clinical LLB only one-third of courses must have a substantial or exclusive clinical content. Four of these are compulsory:

- Legal Methods (Clinical) adds training in basic legal skills (client interviewing, letter writing, case and data management) as well as an introduction to legal ethics to the standard legal methods class;
- Voluntary Obligations (Clinical) augments the standard contract class with training in advanced skills such as negotiation, advocacy and pleading in the second semester of the first year;
- Ethics and Justice, taken in the first semester of the final year, involves the renamed Clinical Legal Practice class;
- The new Clinical Legal Practice does not involve any teaching but gives students marks for their reflective diaries and case performance.

Lest it be thought that the USLC has been transformed from a largely extra-curricular clinic devoted primarily to serving the community into a vehicle for student learning in direct contradiction to my previously expressed preference for what I called social justice-oriented clinics (which are usually extra-curricular) over educationally oriented clinics (almost invariably credit bearing) (Nicolson 2006), it should be noted that safeguards exist to ensure what I regard as the three most important advantages of social justice-oriented clinics.

One disadvantage of educationally oriented clinics is that the focus on teaching students rather than simply ensuring quality legal services means that fewer cases can be taken on and hence less community service achieved. Compared to most clinics which have a staff-student ratio of as low as 1:6, but usually around 1:12 (Nicolson 2006), two part-time supervisors are responsible for around 180 USLC students. Maximising available resources is also significantly enhanced by the fact that USLC is largely run by a student committee enabling it to operate at a much lower cost than other law clinics undertaking similar levels of service. Secondly, there is the danger that students who see clinic participation largely in terms of learning and academic credit may tailor services according to their educational needs with subsequent harm to clients. Finally, and most importantly in terms of promoting altru-ethical professionalism, clinics which prioritise student needs over those of clients and community teach an important but negative ethical lesson to students, namely that it is their interests – now educational but later financial – that take precedence over those of clients and community. The impact of the contrasting orientation of the USLC was clearly illustrated when a CLP student, faced with the risk of jeopardising his career by suing a law firm decided to put his clients above his own, commented:

> The [USLC's] altruistic ethos helped to reinforce my beliefs and allowed me to feel comfortable making a selfless decision in a profession surrounded by greed and self-importance. Without the Clinic to strengthen and normalise my beliefs I do not know if I would have had the courage and conviction to act outside the

norm. In the future, I will try to use the Clinic as an example to justify acting altruistically rather than succumbing to peer pressure.

Indeed, as I have recently argued (Nicolson 2012), student responsibility for clinic management and direction through the committee leads to a sense of 'psychological ownership' of its ethos which translates into an even greater commitment to its altruistic values and the socialisation of non-committee members through mentoring and role-modelling by committee members.

Two safeguards are designed to secure these advantages. The first is that students must first be admitted to the USLC before they can register for the Clinical LLB and hence must undergo a rigorous application and interview process aimed at ascertaining whether their motivations for joining are more about helping others than themselves. Secondly, in order to ensure that those gaining credit for clinic work never exceed volunteers, only 25 students can be admitted to the Clinical LLB every year. In this way, it is hoped that the predominant ethos will remain volunteerist and oriented towards social justice, and that student 'ownership' of the USLC will continue to ensure that the existing ethos which places clients and community over students' needs is passed down from one generation to another though the mentoring system already mentioned and through committee decision-making.

Conclusion

It remains to be seen whether the strong altruistic ethos promoted in the USLC, reinforced through teaching and reflection on ethics and justice and now integrated into the learning experience of around an eighth of all full-time University of Strathclyde law students, will start a process in which students develop a professional moral character which sees law as a calling to promote justice rather than just a stimulating or materially rewarding career. The next step in researching the 'clinic effect' is to conduct follow-up interviews with students who have taken the CLP class and the CLLB to ascertain whether any commitment to altru-ethical professionalism they have developed is maintained in the face of the pressures of work and family life, although, as we have already seen, many ex-USLC members do in fact participate in evening advice sessions.

And even if those who obtain the intensive moral apprenticeship through USLC membership and cradle-to-grave ethics teaching through the CLLB are relatively limited in number, it is possible that starting even a small group on the road to altru-ethical professionalism will have a knock-on effect. Students who have already started the journey might encourage newer colleagues to join them, whereas those in practice may provide both encouragement and role models for similarly disposed neophytes. This, in turn, may water down the generally amoral environment of legal practice and perhaps also lead to areas of practice or isolated environments within practice which provide sustenance and support for altru-ethical professionalism. As research shows, those who display moral character tend to be involved in ongoing relationships with others who challenge, and thus sustain and expand, their sense of morality (Brandenberger, 2005: 316). In this way, a love of justice may flourish long after graduation from law school.

References

Abramson, E.M. (1993). 'Legal education, punching the myth of the moral intractability of law students: the suggestiveness of the work of psychologist Lawrence Kohlberg for ethical training', *Notre Dame Journal of Law, Ethics and Public Policy*, 7: 223–68.

Aiken, J.H. (1997). 'Striving to teach "justice, fairness, and morality"', *Clinical Law Review*, 4: 1–64.

Algoe, S.B. and Haidt, J. (2009). 'Witnessing excellence in action: the "other-praising" emotions of elevation', *The Journal of Positive Psychology*, 4: 105–27.

Aquino, K.F. and Reed, A. (2002). 'The self-importance of moral identity', *Journal of Personality and Social Psychology*, 83: 1423–40.

Aristotle (1987). *The Nicomachean Ethics* (translated by W.D. Ross). Amherst, NY: Prometheus Books.

Bebeau, M.J. (1994). 'Influencing the moral dimensions of dental practice', in *Moral Development in the Professions: Psychology and Applied Ethics*, edited by J. Rest and D. Narvaez. Hillsdale, NJ: Lawrence Erlbaum Associates.

Bebeau, M.J. (2006). 'Evidence-Based character development', in *Lost Virtue: Professional Character Development in Medical Education*, edited by N. Kenny and W. Shelton. Oxford: Elsevier Ltd, 47–86.

Blasi, A. (1980). 'Bridging moral cognition and moral action: a critical review of the literature', *Psychological Bulletin*, 88: 1–45.

Blasi, A. (1995). 'Moral understanding and the moral personality: the process of moral integration', in *Moral Development: An Introduction*, edited by W.M. Kurtines and J.L.Gewirtz. Needham Heights, MA: Allyn and Bacon.

Bloch, F. (1982). 'The andragogical basis of clinical legal education', *Vanderbilt Law Review*, 35: 321–54.

Boss, J.A. (1994). 'The effect of community service work on the moral development of college ethics students', *Journal of Moral Education*, 23, 183–98.

Boon, A. (2002). 'Ethics in legal education and training: four reports, three jurisdictions and a prospectus', *Legal Ethics*, 5: 34–67.

Brandenberger, J.W. (2005). 'College, character and social responsibility, moral learning through experience', in Lapsley, D. and Power, C. (2005). *Character Psychology and Character Education*. Notre Dame: University of Notre Dame Press.

Brayne, H., Duncan, N. and Grimes, R. (eds). (1998). *Clinical Legal Education: Active Learning in Your Law School*. London: Blackstone Press Ltd.

Carlo, G., PytlikZillig, L.M., Roesch, S.C. and Dienstbier, R.A. (2009). 'The Elusive altruist: the psychological study of the altruistic personality', in Narvaez, D. and Lapsley, D.K. (eds) (2009). *Personality, Identity and Character: Explorations in Moral Pyschology*. Cambridge: Cambridge University Press, 271–94.

Carr, D. (1991). *Educating the Virtues: An Essay on the Philosophical Psychology of Moral Development and Education*. London: Routledge.

Chapman, J. (2002). 'Why teach legal ethics to undergraduates?'. *Legal Ethics*, 5: 68–89.

Condlin, R. (1983). 'The moral failure of clinical legal education', in *The Good Lawyer: Lawyer's Roles and Lawyer's Ethics*, edited by D. Luban. Totowa, NJ: Rowman and Allanheld.

Cramton, C. (1978). 'The ordinary religion of the law school classroom', *Journal of Legal Education*, 29: 247–63.

Davidson, M.L. (2005). 'Harness the sun, channel the wind, the art and science of effective character education', in Lapsley, D. and Power, C. *Character Psychology and Character Education*. Notre Dame: University of Notre Dame Press.

Dreyfus, H.I. and Dreyfus, S.E. (1990). 'What is morality? a phenomenological account of the development of ethical expertise', in *Universalism and Communitarianism: Contemporary Debates in Ethics*, edited by D. Rasmussen. Cambridge, MA: MIT Press.

Duncan, N. (2002). 'Responsibility and ethics in professional legal education', in *Effective Learning and Teaching in Law*, edited by R. Burridge and K. Hinett. London: Kogan Page.

Economides, K. (1998). 'Legal ethics – three challenges for the next millennium', in *Ethical Challenges to Legal Education and Conduct*, edited by K. Economides. Oxford: Hart Publishing.

Emmons, R.A. (2009). 'Greatest of the virtues? Gratitude and the grateful personality', in Narvaez, D. and Lapsley, D.K. (eds) (2009). *Personality, Identity and Character: Explorations in Moral Pyschology*. Cambridge: Cambridge University Press.

Evans, A. (2001). 'Lawyers' perceptions of their values: an empirical assessment of monash university graduates in law, 1980–1998', *Legal Education Review*, 12: 209–66.

Eisele, T.D. (1987). 'Must virtue be taught?' *Journal of Legal Education*, 37: 495–508.

Francis, A. (2005). 'The business context: legal ethics, the marketplace and the fragmentation of legal professionalism', *International Journal of the Legal Profession*, 12: 173–200.

Glennon, T. (1992). 'Building an ethic of responsibility', *Hastings Law Journal*, 43: 1175–87.

Goldsmith, A. (1996). 'Heroes or technicians? The moral capacities of tomorrow's lawyers', *Journal of Professional Legal Education*, 14: 1–24.

Gordon, R.W. (1988). 'The independence of lawyers', *Boston University Law Review*, 68: 1–83.

Guggenheim, M. (1995). 'Fee-generating clinics: can we bear the costs?' *Clinical Law Review*, 1: 677–84.

Haan, N. (1985). 'Processes of moral development: cognitive or social disequilibrium?' *Developmental Psychology*, 21: 996–1006.

Jewell, M. (1984). Teaching law ethically: is it possible? *Dalhousie Law Journal*, 8: 474–519.

Johnston, I. and Treuthart, M.P. (1991). 'Doing the right thing: an overview of teaching professional responsibility', *Journal of Legal Education*, 41: 75–104.

Johnstone, Q. (1951). 'Law school legal aid clinics', *Journal of Legal Education*, 3: 535–54.

Kolb, D.A. (1984). *Experiential Learning: Experience as the Source of Learning and Development*. New Jersey: Prentice Hall.

Kotkin, M.J. (1997). 'The law school clinic: a training ground for public interest lawyers', in *Educating for Justice: Social Values and Legal Education*, edited by J. Cooper and L.G. Trubek. Aldershot: Ashgate.

Kronman, A.T. (1993). *The Lost Lawyer: Failing Ideals Of The Legal Profession*. Cambridge, MA: Harvard University Press.

Kupperman, J. (2005). 'How not to educate character', in Lapsley, D. and Power, C. *Character Psychology and Character Education*. Notre Dame: University of Notre Dame Press.

Lapsley, D. and Power, C. (eds) (2005). *Character Psychology and Character Education*. Notre Dame: University of Notre Dame Press.

LETR (Legal Education and Training Review) (2013). Setting Standards: Legal Services Education and Training regulation in England and Wales (accessed at http://letr.org.uk/wp-content/uploads/LETR-Report.pdf).

Lesnick, H. (1986). 'The integration of responsibility and values: legal education in an alternative consciousness of lawyering and law', *Nova Law Journal*, 10: 633–44.

Luban, D. (1988). 'The *noblesse oblige* tradition in the practice of law', *Vanderbilt Law Review*, 41: 717–40.

Luban, D. and Millemann, M. (1995). 'Good judgment: teaching ethics in dark times', *Georgetown Journal of Legal Ethics*, 9: 31–89.

Maresh, S. (1997). 'The Impact of clinical legal education on decisions of law students to practice public interest law', in *Educating for Justice: Social Values and Legal Education*, edited by J. Cooper and L.J Trubek. Aldershot: Ashgate.

Menkel-Meadow, C. (1999). 'The sense and sensibilities of lawyers: lawyering in literature, narratives, film and television, and ethical choices regarding career and craft', *McGeorge Law Review*, 31: 1–24.

Menkel-Meadow, C. (2000). 'Telling stories in school: using case studies and stories to teach legal ethics', *Fordham Law Review*, 69: 787–817.

Moliterno, J.E. (1991). 'An analysis of ethics teaching in law schools: replacing lost benefits of the apprentice system in the academic atmosphere', *University of Cincinnati Law Review*, 60: 83–134.

Narvaez, D. and Lapsley, D.K. (2005). 'Moral psychology at the crossroads', in Lapsley, D. and Power, C. (2005). *Character Psychology and Character Education.* Notre Dame: University of Notre Dame Press.

Narvaez, D. and Lapsley, D.K. (eds) (2009). *Personality, Identity and Character: Explorations in Moral Pyschology.* Cambridge: Cambridge University Press.

Nicolson, D. (2005). 'Making lawyers moral: ethical codes and moral character', *Legal Studies*, 25: 601–26.

Nicolson, D. (2006). 'Legal education or community service? The extra-curricular student law clinic', *Web Journal of Current Legal Issues* http://webjcli.ncl. ac.uk/2006/issue3/nicolson3.html.

Nicolson, D. (2008). 'Education, education, education: legal, moral and clinical', *The Law Teacher*, 42: 145–73.

Nicolson, D. (2010). 'Learning in justice: ethical education in an extra-curricular law clinic', in *The Ethics Project in Legal Education*, edited by M. Robertson et al. London: Routledge, 171–90.

Nicolson, D. (2011). 'Producing professionals: the impact of law shools and law clinics on the ethical attitudes of prospective lawyers', *Society of Legal Scholars Conference*, Cambridge September.

Nicolson, D. (2012). 'From South Africa to Scotland: the University of Cape Town legal aid legacy', paper to *Access to Justice Conference*, University of Kwazulu-Natal, Durban, South Africa, 10–12 December 2012.

Nicolson, D. and Webb, J. (1999). *Professional Legal Ethics: Critical Interrogations.* Oxford: OUP.

Noone, M.A. and Dickson, J. (2001). 'Teaching towards a new professionalism: challenging law students to become ethical lawyers', *Legal Ethics*, 4: 27–45.

Nucci, L.P. (ed.) (1989). *Moral Development and Character Development: A Dialogue.* Berkeley: McCutchan Publishing Corporation.

Palermo, J. and Evans, A. (2008). 'Almost there: empirical insights into clinical method and ethical courses in climbing the hill towards lawyers' professionalism', *Griffith Law Review*, 17: 252–84.

Paterson, A. (2011). *Lawyers and the Public Good: Democracy in Action.* Cambridge: CUP.

Pepper, S.L. (1986). 'The lawyer's amoral ethical role: a defense, a problem, and some possibilities', *American Bar Foundation Research Journal*, 613.

Peters, R.S. (1981). *Moral Development and Moral Education.* London: George and Unwin.

Pipkin, R.M. (1979). 'Law school instruction in professional responsibility: a curricular paradox', *American Bar Foundation Research Journal*, 4: 247–75.

Power, F.C. (1997). 'Understanding the character in character education. Paper to meeting of the American Educational Research Association', Chicago, March 1997, http://tigger.uic.edu/~lnucci/MoralEd/articles/powerunder.html.

Quigley, F. (1995). 'Seizing the disorienting moment: adult learning and the teaching of social justice in law school clinics', *Clinical Law Review*, 2: 37–73.

Rees, A., Thomas, P. and Todd, P. (2002). *Law Students: Investing in the Future*. Cardiff: Cardiff University.

Rees, M. (1975). 'Clinical legal education: an analysis of the University of Kent model', *Law Teacher*, 12: 125–32.

Rest, J. (1984). 'The major components of morality', in *Morality, Moral Behaviour and Moral Development*, edited by W.M. Kurtines and J.L. Gewirtz. New York: Wiley.

Rest, J. (1988). 'Can ethics be taught in professional schools? The psychological research', *Ethics Easier Said Than Done*, 1: 22–30.

Rest, J. (1994). 'The four components of acting morally', in Rest, J. and Narvaez, D. (eds), *Moral Development in the Professions: Psychology and Applied Ethics*. Hillsdale, NJ: Lawrence Erlbaum Associates.

Rest, J. and Narvaez, D. (eds) (1994). *Moral Development in the Professions: Psychology and Applied Ethics*. Hillsdale, NJ: Lawrence Erlbaum Associates.

Rest, J., Narvaez, D., Bebeau, M. and Thoma, S. (1999). *Post Conventional Moral Thinking: A Neo-Kohlbergian Approach*. Mahwah, NJ: Lawrence Erlbaum Associates.

Richards, D.A.J. (1981). 'Moral theory, the developmental psychology of ethical autonomy and professionalism', *Journal of Legal Education*, 31: 359–74.

Rhode, D.L. (1995). 'Into the valley of ethics: professional responsibility and educational reform', *Law and Contemporary Problems*, 58: 139–53.

Rhodes, R. and Smith, L.G. (2006). 'Molding professional character', in *Lost Virtue: Professional Character Development in Medical Education*, edited by N. Kenny and W. Shelton. Oxford: Elsevier Ltd, 99–114.

Sherr, A. (1995). 'Of super heroes and slaves: images and work of the legal profession', *Current Legal Problems*, 48: 327–43.

Sherr, A. and Webb, J. (1989). 'Law students, the market and socialisation: do we make them turn to the city?' *Journal of Law and Society*, 16: 225–49.

Sprinthall, N.A. (1994). 'Counselling and role taking: promoting moral and ego development', in Rest, J. and Narvaez, D. (eds). *Moral Development in the Professions: Psychology and Applied Ethics*. Hillsdale, NJ: Lawrence Erlbaum Associates.

Styles, I. and Zariska, A. (2001). 'Law clinics and the promotion of public interest lawyering', *Law in Context*, 19: 65–96.

Thoma, S. (1994). 'Moral judgments and moral action: establishing the link between judgement and action', in Rest, J. and Narvaez, D. *Moral Development in the Professions: Psychology and Applied Ethics*. Hillsdale, NJ: Lawrence Erlbaum Associates.

Tranter, K. (2002). 'Pro-bono ethos: teaching legal ethics', *Brief*, 29: 12–13.

Webb, J. (1996). 'Inventing the good: a prospectus for clinical education and the teaching of legal ethics in England', *Law Teacher*, 30: 270–294.

Webb, J. (1998a). 'Ethics of lawyers or ethics for citizens? New directions for legal education', *Journal of Law and Society*, 25: 134–50.
Webb, J. (1998b). 'Conduct, ethics and experience in vocational legal education: opportunities missed', in *Ethical Challenges to Legal Education and Conduct*, edited by K. Economides. Oxford: Hart Publishing.

Chapter 4

Public Interest Vocationalism: A Way Forward for Legal Education in Canada[1]

Richard Devlin and Jocelyn Downie

> Now is the winter of our discontent
> Made glorious summer by this sun of York;
> And all the clouds that lour'd upon our house
> In the deep bosom of the ocean buried.
>
> Shakespeare, *Richard III*

Introduction

Canadians often pride themselves on living in one of the best countries in the world. Global indices frequently confirm that this perception is not just patriotic hubris, but an objective reality (United Nations Development Programme 2011; Institute for Economics and Peace 2011). Key indicators of the success of Canada often include economic stability, responsible government, respect for human rights, commitment to the rule of law and access to justice (Legatum Institute 2011).

One key element of many of these indicators – the rule of law, respect for human rights and access to justice – is the legal profession. Lawyers play a vital role in many societies, and are often perceived to be foundational to the success of a liberal democratic society (Halliday and Karpik 1997). It is therefore somewhat disconcerting to recognize that, in the last five years in Canada there has been growing and widespread concern about the ability of the Canadian legal profession to fulfil its responsibilities. Increasingly, both the general public and leaders of many key institutions of Canadian society have been voicing significant criticisms of and sometimes even hostility towards lawyers.

In this chapter, we begin by identifying the nature of these criticisms to trace the root causes of this discontent. We then analyse the concept of vocationalism to determine if it can provide a useful vantage point from which to assess the perceived decline in the Canadian legal profession. Next, we turn our attention to how some of the insights of vocationalism can be converted into curriculum development that can anticipate and respond to the perceived decline in the

1 Thanks to Kate Fairbrother, Alex Hartwig and Molly Ross for their assistance in the preparation of this chapter. Research support was provided in part by the Schulich Academic Excellence Fund.

professionalism of Canadian lawyers. We conclude that, if the criticisms are to be more than rhetorical handwringing, then there must be a significant substantive reform of the educational processes for Canadian lawyers.

The Winter of our Discontent: External and Internal Critiques of the Legal Profession

At this moment in history there appears to be a contradiction, or at least a tension, in the status of the legal profession in Canada. On the one hand, the practice of law seems to be more popular than ever. There are now approximately 100,000 lawyers in Canada, the largest number in Canada's 145-year history. Law schools keep expanding their enrolments of law students, with, for example, approximately 3,500 graduating in 2012.[2] For the first time in 30 years, several new law schools have just opened their doors, or will do so in the near future.[3] A significant number of Canadians go abroad for a legal education, and several schools in the United Kingdom and Australia have a dedicated Canadian stream.[4] Furthermore, an increasing number of people who received legal training in other countries are seeking accreditation to practice in Canada.[5] Finally, the salaries of Canadian lawyers appear to be decidedly attractive, with one recent survey reporting the median net income of self-employed lawyers at $131,603 (Schmitz 2012) and, when broader than self-employed, $192,000 (Department of Justice Canada 2011). All of this suggests that these are the best of times.

However, in the course of the last ten years, there has been a chorus of voices claiming that these are the worst of times. The critics can be divided into two categories – the external and internal. The concerns of the first group may not come as much of a surprise, but those of the latter may be more startling for the legal profession. Let us explore both of these sets of criticisms separately.

There are a number of indicators of, and reasons for, public criticism of lawyers. First, public opinion polls indicate that, despite what the legal profession might think of itself, the majority of Canadians have a low regard for lawyers. In a 2011 Ipsos Reid Poll, 'Trust in the Professions', lawyers received a 25 per cent rating, which ranked them 19th out of 26 professions. The only ones below them were auto mechanics, new home builders, chief executive officers, local municipal

---

2   This figure is derived from third year (and for some schools, fourth year) class sizes in 2012.

3   New law schools include Thompson Rivers University in British Columbia and Lakehead University in Ontario. See Fodden, Simon, 2011.

4   Examples include Leicester University in the U.K. (http://www2.le.ac.uk/departments/law/undergraduate/canadian-applicants) and Bond University in Australia (http://oztrekk.com/programs/law/PG/bond.php).

5   The number of Certificates of Qualification issued by the National Committee on Accreditation in 2011 was 466, an increase from 260 in 2009 and 225 in 1999.

politicians, union leaders, national politicians and car sales people. Ahead of them are environmental activists, plumbers, chiropractors and daycare workers, as well as pharmacists, doctors, teachers and accountants. Second, there has been a massive increase in self-represented litigants in the last while. In part, this is because of the unaffordability of lawyers, but it is also due to the public's lack of faith in lawyers (Langan 2005). Third, in several provinces complaints to law societies about lawyers have been tracking upwards in recent years.[6] Fourth, some Canadians have been actively and publically mobilizing against lawyers, particularly in the area of family law where lawyers have been accused of overcharging and creating conflicts for financial gain (Sebesta 2012a; Tomlinson 2012).

The legal profession might be tempted to ignore all of this as the predictable, but hardly damning, frustrations of an ill-informed, mean-spirited and potentially envious general public. However, this is not a legitimate response because it is not fair or reasonable to characterize the critics in this way and there is a parallel set of criticisms coming from the leaders of the Canadian legal profession. There are four themes to the internal critiques: 1) the failure of the Canadian legal profession to ensure that there is access to justice; 2) the decline in the professionalism and civility of the legal profession; 3) the erosion of public trust in lawyers; and 4) the poor preparation of law students for the practice of law. While these themes often overlap, for discursive purposes we present them as discrete categories.

(a) The Failure to Ensure Access to Justice

In a series of speeches, the Chief Justice of Canada, Beverley McLachlin, has expressed serious concerns about access to justice in Canada and has explicitly identified the legal profession as part of the problem. At the Empire Club of Canada in March of 2007, she highlighted access to justice as one of four considerable challenges that needed tackling by Canada's justice system (along with long trials, delays in the justice system and endemic social problems). The concern is that middle-class Canadians are unable or unwilling to pursue litigation due to costs, and thus cannot afford justice. In her words, '(t)he most advanced justice system in the world is a failure if it does not provide justice to the people it is meant to serve' (McLachlin 2007).

More recently, at the 2011 Council of the Canadian Bar Association conference in Halifax, Chief Justice McLachlin reiterated that access to justice is the biggest challenge facing our justice system. She remarked that in the recent World Justice Project index, despite Canada's judicial system performing well on the whole, our lack of access to justice stands out as a blemish on an otherwise excellent record:

> We have a justice system that really is the envy of the world. The problem is that
> it is not accessible for far too many Canadians. In my view, access to justice is

---

6   British Columbia, Alberta and Saskatchewan have all seen increased complaints between 2006 and 2010 (Federation of Law Societies of Canada, 2006–10).

the greatest challenge facing the Canadian justice system. I am not alone in this regard ... On access to justice, the index ranks Canada 9th out of 12 wealthy Western European and North American countries. The most problematic areas, according to the index, are access to legal counsel and unreasonable delay in civil justice (McLachlin 2011).

The Chief Justice is not alone in her concerns. The Governor General of Canada, David Johnston, has also placed at least some of the responsibility for the lack of access to justice at the feet of the legal profession. Prior to becoming the Governor General, David Johnston was a corporate lawyer, a professor of law, a law dean and a university president. Like Chief Justice McLachlin, he is an ultimate insider. Also speaking at the 2011 Canadian Bar Association conference in Halifax, he singled out lawyers and judges as having a unique responsibility to ensure that justice is accessible:

> We in the legal community have a responsibility to take the lead in reforming the court system for the public good; remember our oath to 'improve the administration of justice'. Justice delayed is justice denied (Johnston 2011).

The core of the Governor General's remarks is that lawyers have a social contract with society, they have broken that social contract and that a remedy is required: we as legal practitioners need to craft a new conception of the legal professional.

Even more pointed are the remarks of the Chief Justice of Ontario in a question and answer session with the practicing bar in which he described a looming 'meltdown in the courts,' and called on lawyers to 'forgo their flashy suits and cars for their "moral duty" to represent the poor' (Sebesta 2012b). Even the CEO's of some of Canada's biggest law firms have joined the choir, characterizing access to justice as 'the legal profession's equivalent of global warming' (Melnitzer 2012).

(b) The Decline in Professionalism and Civility

Commentators have lamented the decline in professionalism and civility amongst legal practitioners (see for example Hunter 2012; but contra Woolley 2008, 2013). Michael Code (Code 2007) believes that civility in society is on a general decline, and that this holds true in law as well. He discusses several Ontario courts which have recently chastised lawyers for acting inappropriately and unprofessionally. Code noted that the decline may impact the fairness of trials as personal attacks distract both lawyers and triers of fact and delay court proceedings. A need for procedural fairness thus translates into a need for professionalism and civility amongst lawyers.

Former judges have also weighed in on this topic. In a report to the Attorney General of Ontario co-authored with Michael Code, Chief Justice Patrick LeSage examined causes of unduly long and complicated criminal law proceedings (2008).

Many faults were said to lie with Crown attorneys, from failing to make timely disclosures to calling witnesses irresponsibly. But most telling were comments on increased acrimony between Crown and defence counsels. The incivility of quarrelling counsel needlessly prolongs the proceedings, meaning that justice is not being done. Furthermore, as court cases take ever more time, the public is left with the impression that the judicial system cannot handle its own affairs competently (see also Goudge 2010).

(c) The Erosion of Public Trust in Lawyers

In a 2008 speech in Strasbourg, France, former Supreme Court Justice, Ian Binnie, bemoaned the fact that Canadian lawyers are among the least trusted of professionals, ranking with car dealers and politicians. His speech focused on conflicts of interest which a competent lawyer should be capable, but often seems incapable, of identifying and avoiding. These conflicts harm the parties whose interests the lawyers are trusted to uphold. This in turn harms the credibility of the entire profession. For Justice Binnie, this is a major concern which the profession does not take seriously enough. He concludes with a warning of what might follow should the public lose faith in the legal profession:

> It is in everyone's interest (especially that of the lawyers) to promote the trustworthiness of the legal profession in the eyes of the public. I don't see in the report of the CBA Task Force much recognition that the level of public trust in lawyers is seen as a serious risk, or that it is seen to be related in any significant way to the manner in which the profession deals with conflicts of interest. In contrast, the need to enhance public trust lies at the centre of the conflict of interest jurisprudence.
>
> It is difficult to believe that public trust is not shaken by lawyers who are prepared to work directly against the immediate interest of an existing client without telling the client what they are up to ... Maximizing business opportunities is a perfectly legitimate objective for those who are in the honourable trade of earning a living from a profession, yet, as the tale of Ulysses reminds us, there are some siren songs it is well to resist (Binnie 2008).

Governor General David Johnston also spoke of the need for trust in lawyers:

> Trust must also exist between the lawyer, the public and institutions such as the Canadian Bar Association and provincial and territorial law societies. Citizens must know there are effective and transparent measures in place to resolve their complaints, and they must trust in these institutions to govern the legal profession and be responsive to public need. That's the way it works (Johnston 2011).

(d) The Poor Preparation of Law Students

It has also been argued (directly or by implication) that law students are not being properly prepared for the practice of law. The Federation of Law Societies of Canada Task Force on the Approved Common Law Degree recently revisited the issue of the academic requirements for entry to bar admission programs, their final report being released in October of 2009. They obviously believed the current preparation of law students to be inadequate (at least at some schools) as they recommended the adoption of a 'national academic requirement for entry to the bar admission programs in Canadian common law jurisdictions' (FLSC 2009: 4). They proposed a national requirement with respect to 'basic skills, awareness of appropriate ethical values and core legal knowledge' (FLSC 2009: 4). The Task Force did not take a position with respect to how law schools are to ensure that their graduates meet the national requirement, with the notable exception of legal ethics and professionalism (for which they recommended a 'stand-alone course dedicated to the subject' FLSC 2009: 4).

Ian Holloway, a new Dean at the University of Calgary and the former Dean of the University of Western Ontario, believes that law students are not being adequately prepared for legal practice. According to Holloway, trends such as globalization and the outsourcing of legal work are threatening for individual Canadian lawyers, who need to become entrepreneurs and innovators in order to stay relevant. Law schools need to be aware of this reality, he writes, and they must bestow upon students the skills that are tailored to 21st century practice (Holloway 2011).

(e) Conclusion

The foregoing criticisms from both outside and inside the legal profession are strongly indicative of the fact that all is not well. The problems are complex, multi-faceted and structural. As a result there are no easy solutions, no silver bullets. In the remainder of this chapter we explore the potential of the discourse of 'vocationalism' to serve as one instrument to help address these problems.

Vocationalism

'Vocationalism' is derived from the Latin *vocation*, meaning 'a calling'. Historically, a vocation has been closely identified with religion – God calling someone into service. However, a review of the literature quickly reveals that 'vocationalism' has, over time, been disconnected from its religious connotations and become a much more diverse and protean discourse. As a result, it is often coupled with some modifier such as 'new' or 'old', 'liberal' or 'hedonistic', 'pseudo' or 'integrative', 'reductive' or 'moral' and 'critical', 'socially critical' and even 'anti-critical'.[7]

As a discourse, vocationalism has had a significant influence on a number of professions, particularly nursing and medicine as well as law.[8] From the multi-disciplinary literature on vocationalism, we have identified three main variations in what is seen to be the essence of a vocation – the religious, the aspirational and the technical. In the context of the Canadian legal profession we reject the religious but argue in favour of embracing both the aspirational and the technical in a state of creative tension.

In the context of law, the religious conception of vocationalism has had several defenders, particularly in the United States (see for example, Bahls 2003; Comartie 1996; Floyd 1998). Historically, this discourse has had a very low register in Canada. That, however, may be about to change. In 2012, one of Canada's few Christian universities, Trinity Western, has indicated its intention to create the first faith-based law school.[9] Trinity Western has not yet revealed the mission statement or objectives of this new law school, but the overall mission of the University is to be 'a place of rigorous academic scholarship and a people with a common vision – to transform lives through Christ-centered higher education' (Trinity Western 2010). In our opinion, it is an open question whether a law school can actually meet this mission and the accreditation requirements of the Federation of Law Societies of Canada (Federation of Law Societies of Canada 2011). However, we will not engage with that question here (see Craig 2013). Suffice to say that a religious conception of vocationalism is inadequate as the driver for a profession mandated to meet the legal needs of a diverse and pluralistic society, such as exists in Canada in the early 21st century (Kymlicka 1995).

---

7 This sampling was generated through a search on Google Scholar 30 May 2012. See also Schuurman 2004.

8 Nursing has long been conceptualized as a vocation with this being understood as acting for, and in, the best interests of the sick. While vocationalism's roots in nursing were religious (Florence Nightingale believed that God had literally called her to serve), it has more recently become more professionalized (in terms of training and regulation) and the links to religion have waned. However, it has retained the conceptualization as a vocation with this being grounded in a foundational commitment to the values of caring and compassion. Medicine too has long been conceptualized as a vocation with this being understood as acting for, and in, the best interests of the sick. While vocationalism's roots in medicine were also religious, here it has become more professionalized and the links to religion have waned. However, when compared to nursing, foundational commitments to a shared set of core values seem weak with a greater exclusivity of focus on scientific knowledge and technical skills and a lack of a foundational commitment to a set of shared values. See, for example: Osler 1919; Salvage 2004; White 2002; Yam 2004; Bradshaw 2010; Cox 2011; McKinlay and Marceau 2002; Koch and Jones 2010; Brody 1955; Siberski 1996; Kuczewski et al. 2003; Coleman 2006.

9 The idea was first communicated in a letter sent to the Council of Canadian Law Deans on 16 January 2012 [on file with the authors].

The second conception of vocationalism is what we have called the aspirational. Here 'vocation' is used in contradistinction to 'a job' or 'a career (see Osler 1919; Loxterkamp 2009; Ballantyne 1954' Velasco-Suarez 2000). Thus deployed, vocation is often aligned with the discourses of goals, values and norms. The third conception takes a different tack. Here 'vocation' is identified with practical and technical abilities. In this sense 'vocation' is used in contradistinction to 'academic', which is often characterized as abstract, conceptual and theoretical (see, for example, Klafter 1993; Veitch 1980; Boon 2001). Thus deployed, vocation is often aligned with the discourses of skills, competencies and proficiencies.

In the remainder of this chapter we want to suggest that the distinction between the second and third conceptions of vocation should not be overblown in the context of the Canadian legal profession. While each of the two conceptions is different, they can be conceived of as complementary rather than contradictory. One can be characterized as the ends (aspirational – the value of the public interest) and the other as the means (technical – the ability to practice law). We should not seek to prefer one over the other but rather we should embrace both and understand them as being not in opposition but rather in creative tension. In doing so, we may sow the seeds for a successful response to the problems with the legal profession outlined above.

The Sun of York: Public Interest Vocationalism

It is here that we want to introduce what we will call 'Public Interest Vocationalism' (PIV).[10] We ground this approach in the practice of law in Canada, which operates within a regime of delegated self-regulation (Devlin and Cheng 2010). Canada is a federal regime, in which legal authority is separated between federal jurisdiction and provincial/territorial jurisdiction. The ability to practice law falls under the jurisdiction of the 13 provincial and territorial governments. Each province and territory has passed legislation making it clear that the practice of law is a privilege not a right. Each province and territory has delegated to their law societies the authority to regulate the practice of law. In other words, the ability to practice law is a statutorily authorized monopoly to quasi-autonomous law societies. Of crucial importance, this delegating legislation outlines the core function of the law societies. In Nova Scotia, for example, s. 4(1) of the *Legal Profession Act* explicitly provides that the core obligation of the law society (the Nova Scotia Barristers Society) is to 'promote the public interest in the practice of law'.[11] It is this statement of 'the public interest in the practice of law', that lays the foundation

---

10   We were prompted to develop this concept of Public Interest Vocationalism by reading, in particular Peach (2010) *Socially Critical Vocationalism.*

11   *Nova Scotia Legal Profession Act* (s.4(1)), RSNS. Similarly, the recently amended British Columbia *Legal Profession Act* states the purpose as 'to uphold and protect the public interest in the administration of justice'. Legal Profession Amendment Act 2012

for our approach. If the obligation of the law societies is to promote 'the public interest in the practice of law' then, of necessity, those who practice law must be guided by the public interest. Their calling, their vocation, is not service to a god but rather service to the public interest through the practice of law. Hence our endorsement of what we have called 'Public Interest Vocationalism' and our suggestion that such vocationalism requires (technical) competencies as well as (aspirational) obligations to promote the public good.

The idea of 'the public interest in the practice of law' might strike some as being so amorphous and indeterminate as to provide little guidance for discerning substantive content for a revised conception of vocationalism. We resist such skepticism on two grounds. First, the statutory mandate to promote the public interest concretely rules out certain powerful (and perhaps disturbingly pervasive) approaches to the practice of law. For example, it makes it clear, at the level of principle, that entry into the legal profession is not just a private preference, personal career choice or exercise of an individual's liberty right. Rather, it is a publically conferred privilege, contingent on a larger social calling, which entails the fulfilment of certain obligations (Devlin 2002). Furthermore, PIV also suggests that, to the extent that the business model of the law firm has gained ascendency, those who endorse and promote such a model at the expense of the larger public interest have breached their obligations (for discussions see Gunz and Gunz 1994; Dodek 2008).

Second, in the Canadian context, we would argue that the public interest in the practice of law can be given substantive content by reference to Canada's constitutional principles and values. In the course of the last two decades, in a series of decisions the Supreme Court of Canada has outlined a number of written and unwritten constitutional values including:

- Federalism
- Democracy
- Constitutionalism and the Rule of Law
- Respect for Minorities
- Respect for the Inherent Dignity of the Human Person
- Commitment to Social Justice and Equality

---

s.3. It is the object and duty of the society to uphold and protect the public interest in the administration of justice by:

    (a) preserving and protecting the rights and freedoms of all persons;

    (b) ensuring the independence, integrity, honour and competence of lawyers;

    (c) establishing standards and programs for the education, professional responsibility and competence of lawyers and of applicants for call and admission;

    (d) regulating the practice of law; and

    (e) supporting and assisting lawyers, articled students and lawyers of other jurisdictions who are permitted to practice law in British Columbia in fulfilling their duties in the practice of law.

- Accommodation of a Wide Variety of Beliefs
- Respect for Cultural and Group Identity
- Faith in Social and Political Institutions which Enhance the Participation of Individuals and Groups in Society (*R. v Oakes* 1986, *Hunter v Southam* 1984, *Reference re Quebec Secession Reference* 1998).[12]

These constitutional values give content to the concept of the public interest. They provide the jurisgenerative foundation for public interest vocationalism tailored to the unique history and current context of Canada.

Furthermore, the effective pursuit of the public interest through the practice of law requires that lawyers focus not only on the aspirational but also on the technical aspects of the legal profession. Given space constraints as well as the fact that the technical aspects will be more familiar to the reader than the Canadian substantive content for the aspirational aspects, we do not detail these here. However, we have elsewhere spelled out the knowledge and critical understanding requirements as well as the requisite capabilities needed for the practice of law (Downie and Devlin 2012).

Burying the Clouds: How PIV Responds to the Internal and External Critiques

Earlier in this chapter, we identified four broad thematic concerns relating to the legal profession in Canada. Public Interest Vocationalism cannot guarantee a resolution of these concerns, but it can provide a foundation upon which we can attempt to build effective responses to them.

First, with regard to the access to justice issue, we note that PIV can serve as a strong reminder to lawyers that their primary obligation is to serve the public interest. PIV's focus on the public interest (understood in terms of the Canadian constitutional values such as 'respect for minorities', 'respect for the inherent dignity of the human person' and 'commitment to social justice and equality') can help to create a culture shift away from the overemphasis on the business model towards a more socially responsive legal profession. Furthermore, PIV's commitment to a complementary relationship between the aspirational and the technical seeks to empower lawyers with both the motivation and capabilities to facilitate greater access to justice.

Similarly, the concerns about the decline in civility and professionalism might also be addressed through PIV. There is good reason to believe that an excessive loyalty to one's client can lead to hyper-adversarialism and its consequential

---

12   They also indicate why a faith-based conception of vocationalism is antithetical to Canada's constitutional normativity in so far as religious exclusivity does not respect minorities, respect the inherent dignity of the human person, accommodate a wide variety of beliefs or respect cultural and group identity.

incivility and unprofessional behaviour. To the extent that PIV attempts to balance the duty of loyalty (which is an important legal good) with a larger set of constitutional values, especially the 'rule of law' and 'respect for the inherent dignity of the human person', it can potentially moderate the excesses of incivility and unprofessional behaviour. PIV can remind lawyers that the 'hired gun' model of lawyering is incompatible with fidelity to the larger public interest.

Third, the decline in public trust may also be alleviated through an explicit embrace of PIV. If lawyers are, and are seen to be, driven by the public interest, the public may begin to believe that, for example, lawyers are not all motivated solely by their own interests or the interests of the clients with the deepest pockets.

Finally, PIV also provides a response to the concerns about the poor preparation of law students. While we do not endorse the approach imposed by the Federation of Law Societies of Canada or that suggested by Dean Holloway, we do suggest that PIV generates somewhat of a revision of the dominant model of legal education in Canada. Because it explicitly embraces both the aspirational and the technical in a creative tension, PIV seeks to encourage law students to have a broader conception of their roles and responsibilities. We will illustrate this potential in the remainder of this chapter by exploring how PIV can be implemented within Canadian legal education.

So if we are right that a promising response to the criticisms lodged against the legal profession is an embrace of PIV, then the next question becomes, 'how do we implement PIV?' One path, we believe, is through legal education. In this section, we will attempt to illustrate how PIV can be infused into legal education by discussing how we have attempted to put some elements of PIV into our own teaching of legal ethics at the Schulich School of Law at Dalhousie University, and through a continuing professional development module on cultural competency.

(a) Through the Lens of Undergraduate Legal Ethics Education – the Schulich School of Law

As of 2012, there are three opportunities for the teaching of legal ethics at our law school: (a) as part of the compulsory first year introductory Orientation to Law course; (b) pervasively through any other courses in the curriculum; and (c) as a compulsory one-term third year course.[13]

(i) Introductory Lecture
Orientation to Law is a course for the incoming class of 165 first year students. It is composed of a series of sessions designed to provide a general introduction to law and the legal profession. A broad range of topics is covered including the historical origins of common law, cultural competence, natural law and legal realist theories,

---

13 In our opinion these are insufficient. However, as of 2012, the Schulich School of Law is commencing a curriculum reform project which, we hope, will include a consideration of public interest vocationalism as a solid foundational concept for a curriculum.

aboriginal law and international law. Three of these sessions implicitly or explicitly address legal ethics. The first is a panel discussion delivered by several judges which exposes first year law students to judicial reasoning through the judges' testimonials. The panel share their experiences, field questions and provide general ethical and professional guidance. The judges also address the role of a lawyer in Canadian society. The second is a lecture given by the Executive Director of the Nova Scotia Barristers Society. It provides an overview of the legal profession and its responsibilities. The third was a new addition in 2011. It expressly engages with legal ethics. This lecture does two things. First, it introduces students to two idealized types of lawyers – 'the zealous advocate' and 'the minister of justice' – and explores the implications of each of these for the legal practice and the pursuit of justice. Second, the lecture introduces a fictional character, Al, and follows her career trajectory from pre-law school, through law school, legal practice and then to the bench.[14] At each stage, Al encounters a variety of ethical challenges in both her professional and private life (all of which are based in reality). The class discusses and votes upon various courses of ethical conduct. The main messages that emerge from the discussion of Al's life are that ethical challenges are pervasive and often unexpected, and that the ethically responsible lawyer needs to develop both an ethical skill set and a larger conception of herself as an ethical agent committed to the promotion of the public interest.

These sessions, by addressing the practice of law in light of broad themes, alert students to the fact that the practice of law is more than a series of private pursuits and is rather a pursuit of the public interest: the hope is that students embrace and internalize the aspirational aspects of Public Interest Vocationalism (teaching and learning of the technical skills that will allow them to realize these goals come later in the program).

(ii) Pervasive

The Schulich School of Law has not formally adopted the pervasive method for teaching legal ethics.[15] However, one of the authors regularly teaches a first year compulsory Contracts course and explicitly engages with issues of ethics on at least three occasions in the course. The first emerges from the classic privity of contract case, *Beswick v Beswick* (1966). The case commences with Lord Denning's description of old Peter Beswick and his nephew visiting the office of a lawyer, Mr Ashburn, to draft up a contract transferring the coal company from the uncle to the nephew. This enables the class to have a discussion about two things: first, how potential ethics problems can arise unannounced in the most mundane situations; and second, the basic principle of a duty of loyalty and potential conflicts of interest.

---

14   Al's persona is enhanced through a series of cartoons drawn by a member of the staff at the Sir James Dunn Law Library, Andre Richard.

15   The pervasive method is described, for example, in Rhode and Luban 1995; Cranston 1995.

The second opportunity arises out of a Canadian case, *D.C.B. v Zellers Inc.* (1996), where a lawyer working for a major retail chain sent demand letters threatening civil action against the parents of children who shoplift, even though there was no legal foundation for such a suit. The contract question relates to the issue of whether a promise to forbear on an alleged right to sue is legally sufficient consideration. The ethical issues are:

- What do you do as a lawyer if a deep-pocketed client instructs you to draft and send such letters?
- What is the relationship between the duty of loyalty and duties to respect the administration of justice? and
- Should the Law Society investigate and potentially discipline a lawyer who engages in such behaviour?

The in-class conversation is enriched by a recent discipline decision out of British Columbia.[16] A lawyer from Ontario wrote a similar demand letter to some parents in British Columbia. The lawyer for the parents, Mr Laaraakker, wrote back a letter which berated the Ontario lawyer for his actions. He also went onto a website and referred to the Ontario lawyer as a 'sleazy operator' and 'the kind of lawyer that gives lawyers a bad name' (*Law Society of British Columbia v Laarakker* 2011). The lawyer from Ontario complained to the Law Society of British Columbia, which then found that Mr Laarakker's remarks were unprofessional and fined him $1,500 plus $3,000 in costs. Consideration of these cases leads to a fruitful conversation about the potential limits of resolute advocacy, the nature of professionalism and civility, as well as a discussion of whether the Law Society was really targeting the proper person.

A third opportunity for teaching legal ethics in contract law emerges from a Canadian case on unconscionability (*Morrison v Coast Finance Ltd* 1965). Here an elderly woman was being taken advantage of by two rogues and a finance company. The facts indicate that the lawyer for the finance company and his student-at-law had some interaction with the elderly woman, but the judge, while finding unconscionability on the part of the company, went out of his way to indicate that the lawyer should not be blamed as the elderly woman was not his client. This fact situation generates two questions. The first is whether the judge is correct that the duty of loyalty trumps. The second is what options the student-at-laws have when their senior acts this way. In relation to this second question, the students usually react in several different ways ranging from silence/ acquiescence to protest. Each option is put on the chalkboard. Then the students are asked to vote. At least two things become obvious in this exercise – many students are conflicted between what they believe is the right thing to do (protest) and what they believe is their only option if they want to keep their job (silence). Furthermore, the students enthusiastically and passionately engage in a debate as

---

16 See also Alice Woolley's blog: *Lawyers Regulating Lawyers?* (2011).

to the ethical obligations of the contract lawyer – hardly the most exciting of the cast of ethical characters in the practice of law (compared, for example, to criminal lawyers or tax lawyers).

The three examples from the contracts course are illustrative of the dual ambitions of PIV. On the one hand, they introduce students to some of the core technical competencies of an ethical lawyer (for example, knowledge of some of the basic principles of legal ethics such as resolute advocacy and the duty of loyalty) and they allow them to practice some preliminary skills of ethical analysis and reasoning. On the other hand, they also engage students in reflection on larger aspirational issues such as what sort of lawyers they might want to be, the structural frameworks within which they might find themselves, and the core values that should underlie their ethical decision-making while practicing law in Canada.

(iii) Compulsory Third year Course

Legal Ethics and Professional Responsibility is a compulsory two-credit third year course. The two authors both teach this course, sometimes separately, sometimes together. Over the years we have developed a number of strategies for teaching in this area, heavily affected by our commitment to PIV.

First, we provide the students with a clear list of course objectives and outcomes.

This course is intended to develop students':

- awareness of and ability to identify and resolve ethical problems in a legal context;
- awareness of the need for cultural and emotional competence in the practice of law;
- understanding of the legal and ethical duties and responsibilities of lawyers and the legal profession;
- understanding of the different possible roles for lawyers, the legal profession and the legal system;
- knowledge of the relevant legislation, regulations, rules of professional conduct and common or case law;
- knowledge of legal and quasi-legal responses to unethical conduct and professional incompetence; and
- ability to make informed and reasoned contributions to the development of the legal profession and legal system.

Upon successful completion of the course, it is hoped that students will be able to:

- make informed and reasoned decisions when they are confronted with ethical dilemmas during law school;
- make informed and reasoned decisions about what kinds of lawyers they want to be (if any) and how they want to use their law degrees (if at all);

- meet Law Society legal ethics and professional responsibility requirements;
- make informed and reasoned decisions when they are confronted with ethical issues after graduation;
- act in a professionally and ethically appropriate manner;
- make informed and reasoned contributions to the development of the legal profession and legal system;
- clearly express and defend positions on a range of issues in legal ethics and professional responsibility; and
- conduct a respectful discussion of controversial legal ethics and professional responsibility issues with individuals holding contrary views.

Second, we provide students with substantive knowledge through the use of the textbook *Lawyers' Ethics and Professional Regulation* which contains a comprehensive discussion of codes of conduct, court decisions and discipline decisions that constitute the 'law of lawyering' (see Woolley et al. 2012).

Third, we seek to help students to develop their capacity for ethical reasoning, again through the use of *Lawyers' Ethics and Professional Regulation* which is peppered with more than 100 scenarios – some fictional, most based on real cases – which students have an opportunity to work through. We have also constructed a number of heuristics that we believe help to develop their capacity for ethical reasoning. One such device is a pair of drawings that make manifest the fact that lawyers inevitably exist in a complex web of relationships and that these relationships generate a complex set of obligations. We begin with a simple graphic (Figure 4.1) that will seem familiar to the students inasmuch as they have thought about their obligations as lawyers already.

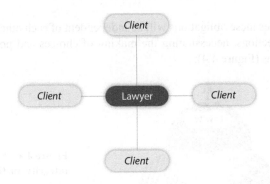

Figure 4.1   A lawyer's web of relationships

We then move to a more complicated graphic (Figure 4.2) that we argue is more representative of the complex reality within which lawyers exist and which should form the backdrop for their analysis of ethical issues.

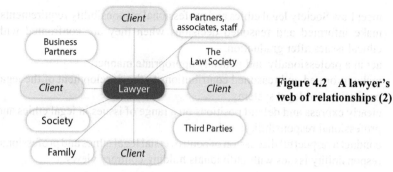

Figure 4.2   A lawyer's web of relationships (2)

Another heuristic we have developed is a Venn diagram (Figure 4.3) which shows that, broadly speaking, there are three categories of responsibilities for lawyers: a duty of loyalty to one's client; a duty to uphold the administration of justice; and a duty of integrity. At times, all three will overlap, generating an ethical sweet spot.

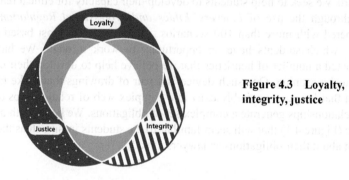

Figure 4.3   Loyalty, integrity, justice

But at other times these obligations will be independent of each other and will pull in opposite directions, necessitating the making of choices and posing potential ethical dilemmas (Figure 4.4).

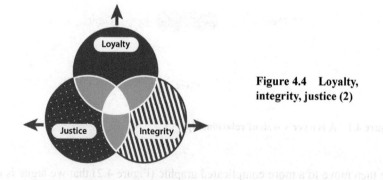

Figure 4.4   Loyalty, integrity, justice (2)

Having highlighted the relationships and values implicated in legal practice, we then provide the students with our third heuristic, A Framework of Ethical Analysis, that can serve as a template for working through ethical challenges:

1. Get the facts
2. Investigate the governing 'rules'
   - Act
   - Regulations
   - case law
   - Codes of Ethics
   - disciplinary decisions of Bar Societies
3. Reflect on the underlying spirit and philosophy of the 'rules'
   - theories, principles, norms, values, virtues
4. Ascertain the client's interests, wishes, rights and obligations (where there is a client involved)
5. Reflect on the interests of other affected parties
6. Reflect on one's duties (to the public, the court, the profession, colleagues, one's family)
7. Identify one's own personal theories, principles, norms, values, and virtues that are implicated in
   - the situation
   - family, culture, community, religion
   - philosophy;
8. Identify the choices available
9. Assess the possible consequences of each of the choices
   - probability and nature (severity) or possible harms and benefits
10. Identify the constraints on particular choices
   - for example, illegal, contrary to Code of Ethics, contrary to personal ethics
11. Discuss with others
   - more senior colleagues
   - Bar Society
   - external ethics experts
12. Engage in self-reflection
13. Identify priorities
14. Choose and implement a course of action/inaction
15. Review choice
   - the result
   - the processes
   - the need for change (personal, professional, institutional).

On one occasion when we co-taught the course, while one of us gave a lecture on some of the basic rules and principles governing the formation and termination of the lawyer-client relationship, the other was simultaneously locating on a chalkboard behind the lecturer these rules and principles under headings and subheadings reflecting the principles captured by the Venn diagram (loyalty, justice and integrity), the web of relationships, the competing models of the practice of law (business vs. profession) and competing interests (public vs. lawyers'). The point of this teaching method was to convey the core content of the rules but also, and at the same time, to visually represent the theoretical (and value-laden) framework playing out in concrete rules.

The foregoing four heuristics were designed to serve the goal of developing the cognitive capacities with respect to legal ethics but they are of limited utility in developing the affective and emotional intelligence of law students.[17] Consequently we have also experimented with several other exercises to enrich students' learning experience in the context of legal ethics education.

For example, in the very first class, before we turn to our course objectives or substantive rules we use a modest exercise in creative thinking. Each student is given a page which is blank, except for a heading which states 'My Picture of a Lawyer'. We give the students three minutes to draw a picture. Then we ask the students to turn the page over and draw a second picture under a new heading 'The Lawyer as seen by the General Public'. After a few moments of nervous laughter, the students begin drawing their second picture. After a few more minutes we call on volunteers to come to the front of the room and share their work (via an overhead projector). Strong patterns quickly emerge – the majority of the first pictures are relatively benign illustrations – lawyers are portrayed holding scales of justice, a sword, a shield, the *Canadian Charter of Rights and Freedoms* and advocating passionately in front of a judge on behalf of a disadvantaged client. The second set of pictures is much more negative – there are many pictures of lawyers as rats and sharks, and lawyers are portrayed as fancy-suited, well-dressed drivers of expensive cars (convertibles, Hummers), laden with bags or pockets full of money. But they also portray lawyers as stressed and overworked substance abusers (Jack Daniels is a favourite!). We discuss the pictures as they are presented by the volunteers and we also collect these pictures and weave them into later classes in the course.

We have also tried to promote more experiential learning. Occasionally we have used some of the exercises in the textbook as an opportunity to role-play. For example, in one scenario involving confidentiality, a husband who has tested HIV positive indicates to his lawyer that he does not plan to tell his wife of his diagnosis. After asking the students about the lawyer's options and responsibilities, the instructor takes on the role of the recalcitrant husband and calls on one or two volunteer students to conduct the interview. The tension in the room is palpable and the exercise is frustrating for the students. In part the tension arises because of the indications of the potentially explosive anger of the client, a common phenomenon in family law matters. The frustration stems from the fact

---

17   For further discussion of the importance of, and the recent literature on emotional intelligence see Devlin and Downie 2010.

that the students struggle with the choice between maintaining client confidence, a concern about the welfare of the spouse, and the risk of being fired by a client. For example, if the students indicate that it is appropriate to breach the confidence, we ask, 'to whom'? If the students say 'the spouse', we proceed to role-play that conversation ... one group of students begins to protest. If the students say 'the police' ... another group of students begin to protest. On the other hand, if the students claim they can say nothing, some of them feel guilty, even demoralized.

We have also created an assignment for which students are required to contact a lawyer and to ask them to identify and discuss one or two moments in their career where they had an ethical dilemma or a challenge to their ethical identity. We provided the students with the following template as a rough guide (inviting them to follow their own interests and the conversation wherever it takes them):

- Can you identify one or two instances in your career that challenged your professionalism or generated an ethical dilemma?
- How did you respond to these challenges or dilemmas?
- Did you seek any assistance as you attempted to resolve these challenges or dilemmas?
- In retrospect, would you do anything differently?

Each student was asked to submit a two-page synopsis of the interview. The exercise generated several insights. First, it reinforced for many of the students the reality that ethical challenges are pervasive for lawyers and that they are often unanticipated. Second, when we received all of the assignments, we were able to identify particular issues that came up most frequently as well as a number of core themes. We were able to feed these back to the students. Some of the most common issues included conflicts, loyalty and confidentiality. The interviews also highlighted the issues of discretion exercised by prosecutors, the duty to report other lawyers and even clients, competency, sharp practice, adversarialism and hostility, protection of vulnerable clients and unrepresented litigants. Some of the themes that surfaced included the tension between personal and professional values, the temptations of adversarialism, professional reputation, the pervasiveness of ethical issues, the contextual nature of ethical decision-making, the significance of the size of the community in which one practices, the importance of keeping notes about ethical challenges, the influence of instinct and gut reaction, the value of consulting with other lawyers, the reality of physical danger to oneself and others and self-respect. As a result of this exercise, students were able to engage in some, admittedly modest, experiential learning not only with an individual lawyer but also vicariously through their classmates with a very broad range of lawyers (criminal lawyers, prosecutors, family lawyers, corporate lawyers, poverty lawyers and so on) and their diverse ethical dilemmas.

Finally, again in the pursuit of experiential learning we ran one of our classes as a two hour 'Ethics Fair'. In order to achieve this we invited five lawyers – legal aid, in-house, criminal defence, prosecution and government – to facilitate one-hour workshops on legal ethics matters arising in their area of practice. Each workshop was offered twice. Students were given the opportunity to enrol in two different workshops and were required to read the relevant chapters from the textbook as preparation. Once again the goal of the exercise was to build upon the students' cognitive knowledge and to gain some insights into the affective and emotional aspects of the ethical challenges in the practice of law.

In sharing these reflections on ethics pedagogy at the Schulich School of Law, we are not claiming total success in the pursuit of public interest vocationalism. As with most experiments, there are moments of achievement and moments of failure. Rather what we are attempting to illustrate is what can be done when trying to blend the aspirational with the technical. But law school is only the beginning and continuing professional development is also a critical locus for legal education. It is to this that we now turn.

(b)Through the Lens of Cultural Competency Education in Programs of Continuing Professional Development

In the last few years, after much debate and significant resistance, the majority of the law societies in Canada have adopted some form of mandatory continuing legal education. The remaining law societies are expected to do the same in the near future. The preferred nomenclature for these initiatives is 'continuing professional development (CPD)'. As we have argued elsewhere, this is a welcome development for at least two reasons (Devlin and Downie 2009). First, it is an acknowledgement by regulators that they have an institutional obligation to ensure the ongoing competencies of members of the legal profession. Secondly, it is a salutary reminder to practicing lawyers that education is not just an inoculation … you don't just get it once in law school and then assume it's over.

However, while CPD has its benefits, as is currently unfolding, its promise is not being maximized. The approach adopted by most law societies is relatively minimalist, merely requiring 12 hours per year, two of which must be focused on 'professionalism/ethics/practice management'. Furthermore, most law societies seem to be favouring a free market approach whereby a variety of providers (including for-profit providers) can seek accreditation. Most of the current offerings focus on reviews of substantive law and some practical skills. To the extent that these initiatives enhance technical competencies they fulfill one aspect of PIV, but few fully engage the aspirational aspects of PIV. Let us suggest one example of how this gap might at least be partially filled, that is, through the development of a cultural competency module.

In June 2012 one of the authors co-designed, organized and participated in just such a module for CPD. The module focused on the case of *R. v Fraser* (2011). In this case, the Nova Scotia Court of Appeal struck down the jury's conviction of a black high school teacher on the charge of sexual interference with a minor, a white female student. The primary basis for allowing the appeal was that the accused did not receive a fair trial because he did not have effective counsel.

The court catalogued the failures of defence counsel as including the following: the ineptitude of his declared defence strategy; his refusal to consider the importance of the accused's wife as a material witness; his failures to effectively challenge the Crown's case on material issues; his failures to interview and call potentially effective defence witnesses; his failure to seek an adjournment when facing last-minute information; his failure to advise his client of his right to challenge prospective jurors for cause on the basis of potential racial bias; and his dismissal of his client's concern about facing an all-white jury by stating, 'don't worry about it, I got lots of black guys off with all-white juries before'.

Although the Court of Appeal never used the phrase, this case might be seen by some as a classic example of 'cultural incompetence' – a situation in which the lawyer's knowledge, skills and attitude demonstrates an incapacity to understand and respond to the social context of his/her client (Woolley et al. 2012). One reason why this case is such an important foundation for a module on the challenges of being culturally competent is that the lawyer involved is one of the most senior defence counsel in the province of Nova Scotia. If lawyers at this level of seniority and stature can run into difficulty with cultural competency, then clearly there is much work to be done.

This module on cultural competency clearly dovetails with both the aspirational and technical dimensions of public interest vocationalism. On the aspirational level, it demonstrated a failure to respond to several of Canada's core constitutional values, especially 'respect for minorities', 'respect for the inherent dignity of the human person', 'a commitment to social justice and equality' and 'respect for cultural and group identity'. On the technical level, it illustrated a failure of the concrete knowledge and skills of a proficient defence lawyer. It did not require the lawyers to don hair shirts, but it did require them to think carefully about the goals of the Canadian justice system, their responsibilities within that system and their own individual knowledge, skills and attitudes.

Conclusion

In the same way that practicing law is a socially conferred privilege, so too is the teaching of law. In this chapter we have reflected upon and described the way in which we have attempted to respond to the obligations engendered by our socially conferred privilege. The first step in any project of reconstruction or rehabilitation is to acknowledge that there is a problem. In Part I, we have done just that by identifying the trenchant criticisms of the Canadian legal profession by both outsiders and insiders. The second, reconstructive, stage is to explore and imagine an alternative path, which we have done through an articulation of Public Interest Vocationalism, with its double focus on the aspirational and the technical. The third step is to put the reconstruction into practice.

There are multiple ways to do this, depending upon one's personal situation and institutional location. As law teachers, our focus has been on how legal education can be reconfigured and redesigned to promote PIV. We have suggested how this can, and should, be done not only in the law schools but also in continuous professional development. Such efforts, however, require a willingness to experiment, to innovate and to take risks ... but surely a vocation demands at least this much.

References

Bahls, S. (2003). 'Leading students to distinguish between career and vocation: reflections from a Lutheran law school', *University of Toledo Law Review*, 35(1): 11–18.

Ballantyne, D.A. (1954). 'Medicine: a job or vocation', *New Zealand Medical Journal*, 53(293): 47.

Beswick v Beswick [1966] 1 Ch. 538, [1966] 3 All E.R. 1(C.A.)

Binnie, Ian (2008). *Sondage Après Sondage ... Quelques Réflexions sur les conflits d'intérets ('Poll After Poll: A Few Thoughts about Conflicts of Interest')*, speech 4 July, Strasbourg France.

Boon, Andy (2001). 'Making good lawyers: challenges to vocational legal education', *UK Centre for Legal Education*. [Online]. Available at: http://www. ukcle.ac.uk/resources/employer-engagement/boon [accessed: 4 June 2012].

Bradshaw, A. (2010). 'An Historical Perspective on the Treatment of Vocation in the Briggs Report (1972)', *Journal of Clinical Nursing*, 19: 3459–67.

Brody, I. (1955). 'The decision to study medicine', *The New England Journal of Medicine*, 252(4): 130–134.

BusinessGrad.ca. (2010). *Top ten highest paying careers*. 30 Dec. [Online]. Available at http://www.businessgrad.ca/uncategorized/salary/top-ten-highest-paying-careers-2010-edition [accessed 4 June 2012].

Code, M. (2007). 'Counsel's duty of civility: an essential component of fair trials and an effective justice system', *Canadian Criminal Law Review*, 11(2): 97–139.

Code, M. and LeSage, P. (2008). *Report on the Review of Large and Complex Criminal Case Procedures*. Toronto: Ontario Minister of the Attorney General.

Coleman, A. (2006). 'Vocation lost? Hospitals must bring physicians back into the mission of medicine', *Health Progress*, 54–8.

Comartie, J. (1996). 'Reflections on vocation, calling, spirituality and justice', *Texas Tech Law Review*, 27(3): 1061–8.

Cox, J. (2011). 'Doctors, clergy and the troubled soul: two professions, one vocation?' *Royal College of Psychiatrists*. [Online]. Available at http://www. rcpsych.ac.uk/pdf/Report%20on%20SPSIG%20meeting%202.11.11.%20 Cox.pdf [accessed: 26 November 2011].

Craig, E. (2013). 'Is it reasonable to for a regulator acting in the public interest to endorse a program of legal education founded on principles of discrimination against queers?: The Case of Trinity Western' (forthcoming *Canadian Journal of Women and the Law*).

Cranston, R. (1995). *Legal Ethics and Professional Responsibility*. Oxford: Clarendon Press.

D.C.B. v Zellers Inc. [1996] MJ No. 362, 138 DLR (4th) 309.

Devlin, R. (2002). 'The new economy: access to justice and the ethical responsibilities of the legal profession', *Dalhousie Law Journal*, 25(2): 335.

Devlin, R. and Cheng, A. (2010). 'Re-calibrating, re-visioning and re-thinking self-regulation in Canada', *International Journal of the Legal Profession*, 17(3): 233–81.

Devlin, R. and Downie, J. (2010). 'And the learners shall inherit the earth': continuing professional development, life long learning and legal ethics education', *CLEAR* 151–68.

Downie, J. and Devlin, R. (2012). 'The great Canadian lawyer: A Manifesto, Eh', in D. Blaikie et al. (eds), *Why Good Lawyers Matter* (Toronto: Irwin Law).

Dodek, A. (2008). 'Canadian legal ethics: ready for the twenty-first century at last', *Osgoode Hall Law Journal*, 46: 1–49.

Federation of Law Societies of Canada (2006–10). *Statistical Report*. Ottawa: Federation of Law Societies of Canada.

Federation of Law Societies of Canada (2011). *Common Law Degree Implementation Committee: Final Report*. Ottawa; Federation of Law Societies of Canada. [Online]. Available at http://www.flsc.ca/_documents/Implementation-Report-ECC-Aug-2011-R.pdf [accessed 21 June 2012].

FLSC (2009). *Task Force on the Canadian Common Law Degree: final report*. Ottawa: FLSC.

Floyd, T. (1998). 'The practice of law as a vocation or calling', *Fordham Law Review*, 66(4): 1405–24.

Fodden, S. (2011). 'Federation of law societies approves programs of two new law school hopefuls', *Slaw*. Available at http://www.slaw.ca/2011/02/14/federation-of-law-societies-approves-programs-of-two-new-law-school-hopefuls/ [accessed: 4 June 2012].

Google Scholar (2012). [Online]. Available at http://scholar.google.ca [accessed: 24 November 2011].

Goudge, S. (2010). 'Looking back and looking forward on learning in professionalism', *Canadian Legal Education Annual Review*, 4: 109–17.

Gunz, H.P. and Gunz, S.P. (1994). 'Ethical implications of the employment relationship for professional lawyers', *University of British Columbia Law Review*, 28: 123–39.

Halliday, T.C. and Karpik, L. (1997). *Lawyers and the Rise of Western Political Liberalism: Europe and America from the Eighteenth to Twentieth Centuries*. New York. Oxford University Press.

Holloway, I. (2011). 'The Canadian lawyer in the twenty-first century', *The Advocate*, 69(5): 691–9.

Hunter v Southam Inc. [1984] 2 SCR 145, 1984 CanLII 33.

Hunter, J. (2012). Keynote address, International Legal Ethics Conference, Banff, Alberta, July 2012.

Institute for Economics and Peace (2011). *Global Peace Index: 2011 Methodology, Results and Findings*. [Online]. Available at http://www.visionofhumanity.org/ GPI_Indicators. [accessed: 5 June 2012].

Ipsos Reid (2011). *A Matter of Trust*. Toronto: Ipsos Reid.

Johnson, D. (2011). *The legal profession in a smart and caring nation: a vision for 2017*, speech 16 August, Halifax NS. Available at www.gg.ca/document. aspx?id=14195. [accessed: 26 August 2011].

Department of Justice Canada (2011). *Net Income of Canadian Lawyers as Reported by CRATax Year 2000, Excluding Income Below $60,000*. [Online]. Available at http://www.justice.gc.ca/eng/dept-min/pub/jcbc-cerj/annex2.html [accessed 15 June 2012].

Kendyl, S. (2012). 'Family practitioners targeted by protests', *Law Times*, 19 March.

Klafter, C. (1993). 'The influence of vocational law schools on the origins of American legal thought', *American Journal of Legal History*, 37(3): 307–31.

Koch, T. and Jones, S. (2010). 'The ethical professional as endangered person: blog notes on doctor-patient relationships', *Journal of Medical Ethics*, 36: 371–4.

Kuczewski, M., Bading, E., Langbein, M. and Henry, B. (2003). 'Fostering professionalism: the Loyola model', *Cambridge Quarterly of Healthcare Ethics*, 12: 161–6.

Kymlicka, W. (1995). *Multicultural Citizenship: A Liberal Theory of Minority Rights*. Oxford: Claredon Press.

Langan, A. (2005). 'Threatening the balance of the scales of justice: unrepresented litigants in the family courts of Ontario', *Queen's Law Journal*, 30: 825–62.

Law Society of British Columbia v Laarakker 2011 LSBC 29.

Legatum Institute (2011). *The 2011 Legatum Prosperity Index: Canada*. [Online]. Available at http://www.prosperity.com/country.aspx?id=CA.

Loxterkamp, D. (2009). 'Doctors' work: eulogy for my vocation', *Annals of Family Medicine*, 7(3): 268.

McLachlin, B. (2007). *The challenges we face*, speech 8 March, Toronto ON. Available at http://www.scc-csc.gc.ca/court-cour/ju/spe-dis/bm07-03-08-eng.asp [accessed 6 June 2012].

McLachlin, B. (2011). *A busy court, access to justice, and public confidence*, speech 16 August, Halifax NS. Available at http://www.ipolitics.ca/2011/08/16/ beverley-mclachlin-address-to-the-council-of-the-canadian-bar-association [accessed 6 June 2012].

McKinlay, J. and Marceau, L. (2002). 'The end of the golden age of doctoring', *International Journal of Health Services*, 32(2): 379.

Melnitzer, J. (2012). 'David Scott warns of profession's global warming equal', *Law Times*, 13 February.

Morrison v Coast Finance Ltd (1965), 54 WWR 257, 55 DLR (2d) 710 (BCCA).

Nova Scotia Legal Profession Act 2004 (s.4(1)), RSNS.

Osler, W. (1919). 'The vocation of medicine and nursing', in *Essays on Vocation*, edited by B. Mathews. London: Oxford University Press, 119.

Peach, S. (2010). *Socially Critical Vocationalism*. Philadelphia: Routledge.

R. v Fraser 2011 NSCA 70 [2011] NSJ No. 400

R. v Oakes [1986] 1 SCR 103 [1986] SCJ No. 7.

Reference re Secession of Quebec [1998] SCJ No. 61, 161 DLR (4th) 385.

Rhode, D. and Luban, D. (1995). *Legal Ethics*. 2nd ed. Westbury, NY: Foundation Press.

Salvage, J. (2004). 'The call to nurture', *Nursing Standard*, 19(10): 16.

Sebesta, K. (2012a). 'Family practitioners targeted by parents', *Law Times*, 19 March.

Sebesta, K. (2012b). 'Winker lectures bar about access to justice', *Law Times*, 2 April.

Schmitz, C. (2012). *Lawyers Weekly*, 30 March, 3.

Schuurman, D.J. (2004). *Vocation: Discerning our callings in life*. Grand Rapids: W.B. Eerdmans Pub Co.

Siberski, J. (1996). 'Medicine: vocation or job?', *America*, 174(18): 22–4.

Tomlinson, K. (2012). 'BC Women May Lose Home Over Huge Lawyer Bill', 3 December 2012 www.cbc.ca/news/canada/british-columbia/story/2012/11/30bc-legalbills.html.

Trinity Western University (2010). *About TWU: Our Vision*. [Online]. Available at http://twu.ca/about/our-vision.html [accessed: 4 June 2012].

United Nations Development Programme (2011). *2011 Human Development Index*. [Online]. Available at http://hdr.undp.org/en/media/HDR_2011_EN_Complete.pdf. [accessed: 5 June 2012].

Velasco-Suarez, M. (2000). 'Evaded bioethics and the vocation of medicine – the future at stake', *Surgical Neurology*, 53: 193.

Veitch, E. (1980). 'The vocation of our era for legal education', *Saskatchewan Law Review*, 44(19): 19–37.

White, K. (2002). 'Nursing as vocation', *Nursing Ethics*, 9(3): 279.

Woolley, A. (2008). 'Does civility matter', *Osgoode Hall L.J.*, 46:175.

Woolley, A. (3 November 2011). *Lawyers Regulating Lawyers?* [Online]. Available at http://ablawg.ca/wp-content/uploads/2011/11/blog_aw_laarakker_nov2011.pdf [accessed 6 June 2012].

Woolley, A., Devlin, R., Cotter, B. and Law, J. (eds) (2012). *Lawyers Ethics and Professional Regulation* (2nd ed) Toronto: LexisNexis.

Woolley, A. (2013). '"Uncivil by too much civility"?: Critiquing five more years of civility regulation in Canada', *Dalhousie L.J.* (forthcoming).

Yam, B. (2004). 'From vocations to profession: the quest for professionalization of nursing', *British Journal of Nursing*, 13(16): 978.

PART IV
Contract

Chapter 5

Professions and their Social Contracts: A Basis for Teaching Lessons of Professionalism from Medicine

Sylvia R. Cruess and Richard L. Cruess

> Professional schools are not only where expert knowledge and judgment are communicated from advanced practitioner to beginner; they are also the place where the profession puts its defining values and exemplars on display, where future practitioners can begin to both assume and critically examine their future identities (Sullivan et al. 2007: 4).

Introduction

While this quote is from a recent analysis of legal education in the United States, it emphasizes a generic truth which has been understood for many generations. Professional education involves the acquisition of the knowledge and skills essential for professional practice. Students in professional schools must move from being amateurs in their domain to acquiring a detailed knowledge of professional practice. Few would argue with this statement, and, in fact, most would further indicate that this represents the easy part. More difficult is the transition in status from being a member of the lay public to an individual who consistently demonstrates professional behaviour (Merton 1957). Students must acquire the identity of a professional.

Historically in medicine, and we believe in law, professionalism was not taught explicitly (Cruess and Cruess 1997b). Students were expected to develop their professional identities by patterning their behaviour on that of respected role models. While data is difficult to obtain, it seems likely that this system worked reasonably well. Those entering professional practice were aware of what it meant to be a professional and had a real, if somewhat disorganized, idea of their professional responsibilities. However, the system depended heavily upon the fact that the professions were male-dominated and homogeneous in racial and cultural terms, as were the societies that they served (Starr 1984; MacDonald 1995; Krause 1996). There was a strong sense of shared values. In addition, the structure and organization of society was relatively simple and stable with an inherent sense of tradition. None of these conditions are now true. In virtually every country, both society and the professions show a wonderful diversity in terms of gender, culture and national origin (Krause 1996). Based on this and other considerations, in the field of medical education it is now believed that professionalism must be taught explicitly.

There are other reasons for the current emphasis on teaching professionalism which spring directly from the above. For almost half a century there has been a genuine concern that the professions are under threat with, for example, common themes for conferences structured around the question 'Can the professions survive?' The concerns arise from two main sources (Cruess and Cruess 1997a). The first is based on the perceived behaviour of individual professionals and their organizations. They are believed to put their own interest above that of those they serve and of the general public (Freidson 1970; Starr 1984; Krause 1996). The second source springs from the nature of the system within which professionals must function. This is particularly true of medicine, where the incentives and disincentives inherent in current health care systems can actively subvert professional values and encourage unprofessional behaviour (Cohen et al. 2007; Relman 2008; Cruess and Cruess 2008).

The modern professions arose in the guilds and universities of medieval Europe and England. Although the term profession had been in use in medicine since at least Roman times (Pellegrino and Pellegrino 1988), their impact on society was limited to the aristocracy and the wealthy until the Industrial Revolution provided sufficient wealth that the average citizen could afford the services of a professional (Krause 1996). At that time, society was becoming more complex and individuals began to require more of the services provided by professionals. In medicine, science provided a greater understanding of the nature of disease and treatment, thus making health care essential to the well-being of each individual citizen. Society, faced with the need for some organizing principle around which to deliver the complex services it required, turned to the pre-existing concept of the professions. Without study groups or Royal Commissions, and without question encouraged by the members of the professions and the organizations representing them, society granted the major professions a monopoly over the use of their knowledge base by establishing licensure (Krause 1996). In medicine this occurred around the middle of the 19th century throughout the developed world. Although the term was not used at the time, it is clear that a social contract was established as society delegated authority to the professions on the understanding that there would be tangible benefits in return (Starr 1984; MacDonald 1995; Krause 1996). The professions were granted autonomy in practice, the privilege of self-regulation, prestige and substantial financial rewards. In return, individual professionals and their organizations were expected to place the interests of those served and of society above their own (altruism), assure the competence of those practicing the profession, demonstrate morality and integrity in all of their activities and address issues of societal concern. This was, and remains, the essence of the social contract between society and professionals and professions.

The 'bargain' appeared to function well until the middle of the 20th century. In spite of Shaw's comment that 'professions are a conspiracy against the laity' (Shaw 1915), social scientists studying the professions believed that professions constituted an effective method of organizing work, and in particular the delivery of complex knowledge-based services. While the tension between altruism and self-interest was recognized, it was actually believed that the commitment to service of individual professionals would lead to altruistic behaviour (Parsons 1939). This changed dramatically in the middle of the 20th century (Freidson 1970; Johnson 1972; Larsen 1977; McKinley and Arches 1985). The reasons are many and complex. Society itself became skeptical of all forms of authority and the professions represented authority. The nature of professional practice became more complex and more costly. This change was dramatic in medicine as science revolutionized practice, making medicine much more effective and therefore necessary. Medicine changed from a cottage industry to one which consumes a significant portion of the wealth of every developed country. As this occurred, the financial risk of illness to an individual citizen became intolerable and third-party payers emerged in order to diminish the risk. The original social contract had almost always been expressed in the relationship between a patient and a physician. As the state and/or the commercial sector became actively involved in the business of medicine, the incentives and disincentives inherent in the system altered dramatically (Starr 1984). In countries with national health systems, as expenses rose there were resulting pressures to be more efficient and effective. Where the commercial sector was predominant, these pressures were even stronger. The autonomy of individual physicians was threatened by government interventions and by guidelines. As the opportunity for financial gain became greater, financial and non-financial conflicts of interest emerged as major issues. Medicine's fiduciary duty to patients came into conflict with the needs of wider society and with the wishes of both commercial organizations and ministries of health (Relman 2007). Medicine's professional values and its professionalism were threatened by these changes. A recent editorial in the *New York Times* indicates that similar pressures are found in the law. It suggested that in the legal profession professionalism and professional ideals have become 'camouflage' to hide the pursuit of narrow economic self-interest (New York Times 2012).

While it was conscious of the threat to its professional status, the medical profession initially did not respond well. It appeared defensive and unresponsive to the need for change (Freidson 2001). Social scientists became extremely critical, proposing that medicine was pursuing a project which used its privileged position to advance its own interests (Larsen 1977), that it self-regulated poorly, protecting physicians rather than the general public (Freidson 1970), and that its claims to altruism were not supported by its actions (Freidson 2001). Krause (1996) has recorded similar pressures in the legal profession, with the source of the pressures varying depending upon the country and culture. While trust in individual physicians was reasonably well maintained, trust in the profession as a whole dropped from its previous high levels (Schlesinger 2002; Mechanic 2004). Gradually the medical profession came to realize that action was necessary and many initiatives were undertaken. These included attempting to address conflicts of interest and to improve self-regulation, including re-licensure, recertification and revalidation (Irvine 2003). A major effort was initiated to ensure that students, residents and registrars and practitioners understood the nature of professionalism and professional identity, their relationship to the social contract and the obligations necessary to maintain professional status (Cruess and Cruess 1997a and b). It thus became necessary to develop a curriculum for the teaching and evaluation of professionalism at all levels as previously none had existed (Cohen 2006).

Teaching Professionalism

Because the professions occupied such an important place in modern society, social scientists began studying them early in the 20th century and a large body of literature existed as the century drew to a close (Cruess and Cruess 1997a). While all major professions were included in these studies, medicine and the law received the most attention. Unfortunately, none of this work appeared in sources readily available to members of the medical profession and it is probable that a similar situation existed in the law. Without question, physicians and those representing them remained largely unaware of the literature in spite of the fact that much of it referred to them. Essentially, there was no medical literature on the nature of professionalism, nor was there literature on how best to teach it.

As a first step in developing a curriculum, it became important to define professionalism. There are now several satisfactory definitions available to serve as the basis for educational programs. The International Charter on Medical Professionalism is a joint effort by the American Board of Internal Medicine and the European Federation of Internal Medicine (ABIM 2002). The Royal College of Physicians of London (2005) and the Royal College of Physicians and Surgeons of Canada (2007) each have their definitions and Swick (2000) has published an excellent normative definition. We have developed and published the following generic definition of the word 'profession' based on that of the *Oxford English Dictionary* and the social sciences literature which is specifically designed to serve as a basis for the teaching of professionalism.

Profession: An occupation whose core element is work based upon the mastery of a complex body of knowledge and skills. It is a vocation in which knowledge of some department of science or learning or the practice of an art founded upon it is used in the service of others. Its members are governed by codes of ethics and profess a commitment to competence, integrity and morality, altruism and the promotion of the public good within their domain. These commitments form the basis of a social contract between a profession and society, which in return grants the profession a monopoly over the use of its knowledge base, the right to considerable autonomy in practice and the privilege of self-regulation. Professions and their members are accountable to those served, to the profession and to society (Cruess et al. 2004).

The Challenges

There are two distinct educational challenges which must be overcome as students and trainees undergo the transformative process of acquiring the identity characteristic of the skilled professional (Merton 1957; Cruess et al. 2008). The first is the relatively straightforward need to ensure that the cognitive base of professionalism is both taught and learned. This base includes the nature of professionalism including a working definition, the attributes of the professional and an understanding of the meaning of professionalism and professional identity. The obligations necessary to maintain professional status must be learned and the reasons for their existence understood. There appear to be distinct educational advantages to presenting professionalism as the basis of a profession's social contract with society as part of the cognitive base. In our postmodern and largely secular society it no longer appears appropriate to appeal to tradition or the presence of long-held values in an attempting to influence the behaviour of the current generation of learners. 'Most young people no longer respond to appeals to duty; instead, they want to know exactly why they are doing something' (Twenge 2009: 404). Thus educators who wish to assist students entering a profession in the internalization of professional values as a means of promoting professional behaviours must provide a rational basis for both the values and behaviours. Teaching professionalism as the basis of medicine's social contract with society is one means of accomplishing this objective (Cruess and Cruess 2008).

General agreement has recently emerged on the fact that professionalism serves as the basis of a series of social contracts between professions and society (Cruess and Cruess 2008). The organization of occupations devoted to the delivery of knowledge-based expertise essential to society is built around the social contract and the public expectation is that practitioners will at all times demonstrate professional behaviours. The reason for the presence of these contracts is a 'set of common goals shared by the public and for which different professions take responsibility' (Sullivan et al. 2007). Professional privileges are granted based on the willingness of the professions to commit to these goals.

The concept of the social contract is three centuries old, having been developed by early philosophers in a time of hereditary monarchies. Originally intended to propose organizing principles for society as a whole, it has always emphasized the idea of reciprocity between citizens and the state, with rights and privileges being balanced by obligations on both sides. In modern times, this approach has been modified to explain the relationship between various sectors and the society that they serve (Cruess and Cruess 2008; Sullivan et al. 2007) It has been suggested that medicine (Sullivan 2005; Wynia 2008), law (Rosenblatt et al. 1997; Sullivan et al. 2007), science (Lubchenko 1998; Gibbons 1999) and universities (Kennedy 1997) all are unique sectors with individual social contracts with society.

A useful definition of social contract is: 'the rights and duties of the state and its citizens are reciprocal and the recognition of this reciprocity constitutes a relationship which by analogy can be called a social contract' (Gough 1957).

Obviously there is no formal structured written contract. Rather, the social contract between a profession and society is a mixture of the written and the unwritten (Cruess and Cruess 2008). The written portions include laws establishing licensure and regulation and codes of ethics. These impose legal and ethical obligations on professionals and their organizations. Of at least equal importance, however, are the unwritten portions. It is not possible to legislate altruism or commitment which represent such fundamental public expectations. These must come from within the person and spring from the presence of a strong professional identity.

Inherent in the idea of a social contract is the presence of expectations on the part of the parties to the contract (Sullivan 2005; Cruess and Cruess 2008). Society, which is made up of patients, the general public and those chosen to govern them, expects professionals to place their own interests below those they serve, understand and uphold the moral nature of their relationship, demonstrate honesty and integrity, self-regulate well and to address issues of societal concern. Professionals for their part wish sufficient autonomy to make independent decisions in the best interest of those they serve, to be trusted, to be able to self-regulate and be rewarded financially and to occupy a position of prestige in society.

The teaching of professionalism is further aided by highlighting the fact that there will be obvious consequences if either party feels that their legitimate expectations are not met. As an example, the untoward incidents in Bristol England involving cardiac surgery in newborns demonstrated that the medical profession had failed to self-regulate with sufficient rigor (Irvine 2003). Society, which grants professional status to the medical profession, altered the regulatory framework by withdrawing some of these privileges. Medicine's social contract and its professionalism were changed significantly by these actions. The medical profession also has expectations of society which, if unmet, will lead to consequences. In the United States, reliance on the commercial sector for many aspects of both cost and quality control has forced physicians to alter their behaviour to become entrepreneurs in a competitive marketplace, a situation which threatens their professional values (Relman 2007).

Teaching professionalism around the concept of the social contract thus provides a justification for the presence of professional obligations and can explain in a rational fashion the consequences resulting from a failure to meet these obligations. Furthermore, it illuminates the necessity to actually negotiate a social contract that supports professional values (Wynia et al. 1999; Cruess and Cruess 2008).

The second educational challenge is less concrete, more difficult to communicate and of paramount importance. It is to ensure that every individual entering practice has acquired the identity of a skilled professional. *The Oxford English Dictionary* (1985) defines identity as 'a set of characteristics or a description that distinguishes a person or thing from others' but professional identity is somewhat more complex. Hafferty (2009) puts it succinctly: professional identity is characterized by 'what one is rather than what one does'. Essential to the development of a professional identity is socialization: 'the process by which a person learns to function within a particular society or group by internalizing its values and norms' (Oxford English Dictionary 1985) There is general agreement that fundamental to the process of socialization is experiential learning, 'a combination of experience and reflection upon experience' (Hilton and Slotnik 2005).

Thus any educational program designed to 'teach professionalism' must address both of these challenges. The cognitive base must be taught and learned and an educational environment must be created in which the process of socialization can ensure the acquisition of the identity of a professional.

Some lessons have been learned as experience has been gained in teaching professionalism in the field of medicine. The concept of the social contract has proved to be useful in providing a rationale for the presence of both the professions themselves and professional obligations. In addition, some general principles have emerged which can assist in the establishment of programs on teaching professionalism.

General Principles

The general principles that can assist in the establishment of a teaching program are (Cruess and Cruess 2006, 2009b):

1. Institutional Support

Experience has shown that it is difficult to initiate a program in which professionalism is actively taught and the development of a professional identity addressed without strong institutional support (Brater 2007; Smith et al. 2007; Wasserstein et al. 2007). Professionalism crosses departmental boundaries, its teaching requires financial and administrative support and time in the curriculum must be found for the program. The support of the Dean and major department chairs is required, as what is frequently needed is a culture change in which professionalism becomes an institutional priority (Inui et al. 2009). Ensuring that each graduate demonstrates the behaviour of the professional cannot be accomplished without strong leadership.

2. Allocation of Responsibility

An individual must be responsible for the program and be accountable for its performance. In medicine, most institutions have chosen to establish a committee on the teaching of professionalism with members drawn from major departments. The chair is generally expected to fill the necessary role of 'champion' of the program. It is advisable for the chair to be an individual respected as a professional throughout faculty with strong links to major departments.

3. Continuity

The definition of professionalism, its attributes and the behaviours characteristic of a professional serve as the basis of instruction at all levels-undergraduate, postgraduate and professional practice (Brater 2007; Smith et al. 2007; Wasserstein et al. 2007). Ideally they should inform the admission policies of the professional school, be used for teaching and evaluating students, postgraduate trainees and faculty and for continuing professional development. The unifying theme is a common understanding of the nature of professionalism (Cohen 2006; Cruess and Cruess 2006). How it is taught and evaluated will vary depending upon the educational level. There is general agreement that stage-appropriate educational activities, including assessment, should be devised and that they should represent an integrated entity throughout the continuum of professional education.

4. An Incremental Approach

A comprehensive program for teaching professionalism is difficult to implement at all levels simultaneously. One should start with those activities devoted to the teaching of professionalism that are usually already in place such as ethics, communication skills and so on. New programs often represent a combination of these activities and new learning experiences developed specifically to complement what was previously taught. Once the objectives for the program on teaching professionalism have been developed the program can be designed and implemented in an incremental fashion.

5. The Cognitive Base

The cognitive base of professionalism constitutes a body of knowledge which must be understood by those aspiring to become professional. It is important that a common vocabulary, understood by the entire academic community, be developed. As stated earlier, the teaching program, which relies only on students and trainees becoming professional by patterning their behaviour after respected role models alone is no longer effective, if indeed it ever was. Each institution must either select a definition from those available in the literature or develop one which is acceptable to its faculty. A caveat must be mentioned. Developing a definition with faculty input has the potential to promote buy-in to the definition and the program itself. However, because professions operate using authority delegated by society, it is society that ultimately defines professionalism. The current interpretation of societal desires is contained in the laws on licensure and regulation that actually delegate authority as well as in the current literature on professionalism, most of which is in the social sciences. Therefore any definition, developed by a faculty must be consistent with the literature on the subject and must not 'cherry pick'. It must include all items deemed important in the literature. Thus if a professional faculty wishes to develop its own definition, this definition must be consistent with the literature on the subject. The definition used by the Faculty of Medicine at McGill University has already been presented (Cruess et al. 2004).

In addition to the definition, it is desirable to develop a list of the attributes of the professional. In medicine, professionalism is used to organize the services of the healer (Cruess and Cruess 1997a; Sullivan 2005). The attributes of the healer and professional in use at McGill University are shown in Figure 5.1 (Cruess et al. 2009a). If one wishes to create a similar diagram for a lawyer it should be relatively easy to substitute the attributes specific to the 'adjudicator of disputes' in the left-hand portion of the left circle of the Venn diagram.

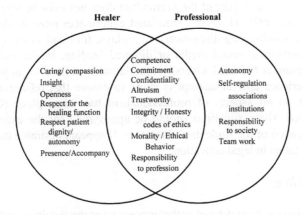

Figure 5.1   Attributes of the physician/medical professional
Source: Cruess and Cruess 2009a.

The attributes traditionally associated with the healer are shown in the left-hand circle and those with the professional on the right. As can be seen, there are attributes unique to each role. Those shared by both are found in the large area of overlap of the circles. This list of attributes is drawn from the literature on healing and professionalism.

The definition and list of attributes, along with the relationship of professionalism to the social contract, which will be discussed below, constitute the cognitive base which should serve as the basis for the teaching of professionalism and the development of a professional identity from the process of admission of students and throughout training and practice. Ideally this should permeate the entire educational exercise of the teaching and evaluation of the professionalism of all members of the academic community.

6. Experiential Learning and Self-reflection

The introduction of the cognitive base provides learners with both knowledge of the nature of professionalism and its value system. The professional values must then be internalized so that they serve as the foundation of a professional identity (Hafferty 2009). There is wide consensus that students must experience situations in which these values become relevant and are challenged as a necessary first step in the process of internalization. Learners must also have opportunities and time to reflect upon these experiences in a safe environment (Schon 1983, 1987; Epstein 1999). In medicine the basis of experiential learning is found in clinical exposure on the wards where students begin to accept responsibility for patient care under close supervision. A major difference found between the teaching of medicine and of the law is that the equivalent of formal and structured clinical experience as a routine part of the curriculum does not exist in legal education (Sullivan et al. 2007). Therefore, simulated experiences must be developed in Moot Courts, small-group discussions, role-plays, film and videotape reviews, narratives, portfolios, social media or directed reading. In the undergraduate medical program at McGill University, simulation is utilized to supplement real clinical experience and an attempt is made to ensure that reflection in a safe environment on all aspects of professionalism has taken place (Cruess and Cruess 2009b). These situations should be appropriate for the experience and level of education of the students and trainees. It appears desirable that a similar approach be taken in legal education.

7. Role-modelling

Role-modelling has been defined as that process whereby faculty members exhibit knowledge, attitudes and skills; demonstrate and articulate expert thought processes; and manifest positive professional behaviours and characteristics (Irby 1986). All studies have indicated that they are fundamental to the process of transmitting those intangibles which make up the value system of the profession. They are central to the development of the sense of collegiality without which a profession has a greatly diminished ability to self-regulate (Ihara 1988). Unfortunately in medicine it is clear that the modelling of unprofessional behaviour on the part of clinical teachers is common. The impact of teaching programs designed to promote professionalism is often undermined by this behaviour. Students frequently state that they are being judged by higher standards than are their teachers (Brainard and Bilson 2007). Observed unprofessional behaviour is tolerated and its presence in the 'hidden curriculum' has a negative impact on the learning environment (Hafferty 1998).

Role models in professional education model broad categories of characteristics. Professional competence is of course essential, but teaching skills and personal qualities also have a profound impact (Wright et al. 1998). Within these categories, there are characteristics that can either have a positive or negative impact on learning depending on how they are modelled (Cruess et al. 2008). Knowledge and skills, the ability to communicate, being explicit about what is modelled, taking time to teach, demonstrating respect for students and their needs, providing feedback in a timely fashion and encouraging reflection are all essential characteristics of good role models. Showing compassion, demonstrating honesty and integrity, demonstrating enthusiasm for teaching and professional practice are equally important. Finally, the presence of good humor is always an added benefit.

Because role-modelling is of such importance, it has received increasing amounts of attention within faculties of medicine. Faculty development programs have been established to increase the awareness of role-modelling by teachers and to improve their performance (Steinert et al. 2005, 2007). Structured feedback is being included in performance assessments and programs to evaluate the professionalism of role models are being established and included in this feedback (Arah et al. 2011; Young et al. 2012). Finally, efforts are being made to identify outstanding role models and reward them and identify those role models who require remediation. If remediation fails, negative role models must be removed from teaching.

9. Faculty Development

Within medicine, recognition that a professional degree does not automatically include training to teach was long in coming. The past few decades has seen the establishment of faculty development programs in virtually all faculties of medicine. When it was deemed desirable to actively teach professionalism, it became apparent that most faculty members did not fully understand professionalism and hence found it difficult to communicate and model it in a structured way. It has been concluded that in order to establish a formal program on the teaching and learning of professionalism, faculty development is essential (Steinert et al. 2005, 2007) While the stated objective of such programs is to assist faculty members in the teaching and evaluation of professionalism, there are secondary objectives which are equally important. They are to familiarize the faculty with the cognitive base and the vocabulary chosen to underpin the program, to obtain buy-in for the program and to influence the learning environment by increasing the awareness of the importance of professionalism and professional behaviour in faculty members. In fact, a well-planned program of faculty development can assist in curricular change design to promote the teaching of professionalism (Steinert et al. 2007).

10. Continuity

Because the acquisition of a professional identity, which must include knowledge of the nature of professionalism, is a process which takes place throughout the educational continuum, there must be educational activities throughout professional education (Brater 2007; Smith et al. 2007; Wasserstein et al. 2007;

Cruess and Cruess 2009b). A single lecture or series of lectures will have a minimal effect. The cognitive base should be presented to incoming students early in their experience and be reinforced throughout the curriculum. Reflection upon both real and simulated experiences must also take place throughout the educational process. These experiences should be appropriate to the educational level of the students and opportunities for reflection must be provided on a regular basis. The capacity of students to acquire and reinforce their professional identities expands as their exposure to experiences takes place. A schematic representation of this process is shown in Figure 5.2.

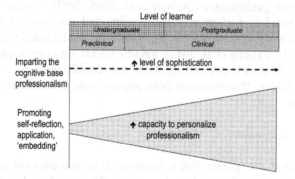

Figure 5.2   Capacity of students to acquire and reinforce professional identities
Source: Cruess and Cruess 2009b.

The cognitive base of professionalism should be presented to students on a regular basis throughout the curriculum. Students, residents and practitioners have an increasing capacity for reflection on professionalism as they gain in experiential learning. This is an important aspect of professional identity formation. Stage-appropriate opportunities for reflection should therefore be provided.

In medicine, most faculties have found it expedient to establish integrated programs on teaching and learning of professionalism throughout undergraduate and postgraduate training, with the early emphasis being on the cognitive base. Professional identity and professional attitudes and behaviours are emphasized as students' professional experience is acquired.

11. Evaluation

There are powerful reasons why the evaluation of professionalism is of paramount importance (Arnold 2002; Stern 2005; Sullivan and Arnold 2009). In the first place, the acquisition of a professional identity is so fundamental to professional practice that the evaluation of the professionalism of students and graduates is a societal responsibility. In medicine it has been demonstrated that unprofessional behaviour identified in students and postgraduate trainees is associated with unprofessional behaviour in practice (Papadakis et al. 2005a and b, 2008). For this reason, faculties of medicine are required to carry out summative assessment of the professionalism of their undergraduate and postgraduate students. However, of at least equal importance is the fact that formative evaluation of the professionalism of students and trainees coupled with feedback has a profound impact on the development of a professional identity (Sullivan and Arnold 2009).

There are two aspects to the evaluation of professionalism. The first is relatively simple. Knowledge of the cognitive base of professionalism can be evaluated using techniques developed to evaluate all forms of knowledge. Thus multiple choice questions, short answer questions, essays and so on can be used to determine whether students and trainees have mastered the subject.

Much more difficult is the task of determining whether individuals destined for professional practice have acquired and internalized the attitudes and values characteristic of the professional. Attitudes and values cannot be reliably and reproducibly evaluated because of their inherently subjective nature. However, the behaviours indicative of these attitudes and values can be observed and assessed (Stern 2005). Once more, the importance of definitions and lists of attributes becomes apparent. A major thrust in medicine during the past decade has been to develop lists of observable behaviours which are reflective of the characteristics of the good professional. While there still is deemed to be a lack of reliable tools (Wilkinson 2009), progress is being made and psychometrically valid methods of assessment are emerging. In addition, structured programs designed to utilize these evaluations in both a formative and summative fashion are in use (Arah et al. 2011; Young et al. 2012).

A final point on the assessment of professionalism must be made. Because of the corrosive nature of unprofessional behaviour of faculty members on the learning environment (Brainard and Bilson 2007), it has been realized that faculty professionalism must also be evaluated and tools are being developed to accomplish this (Todhunter et al. 2010). Obviously, methods of using this information to improve faculty performance are also emerging in parallel with the development of the methods (Hickson 2007).

Conclusion

It has been proposed that the objective of a legal education is to provide society with lawyers who exhibit 'the capacity for judgment, guided by a sense of professional responsibility' (Sullivan et al. 2007). In order to achieve this objective, we offer that it is necessary to explicitly teach the nature of professional responsibility and the reasons for its existence.

References

ABIM. (2002). (American Board of Internal Medicine) Foundation. ACP (American College of Physicians) Foundation. European Federation of Internal Medicine. Medical professionalism in the new millennium: a physician charter, *Ann Intern Med.*, 136: 243–6. *Lancet*, 359: 520–523

Arnold, L. (2002). 'Assessing professional behaviors: yesterday, today, and tomorrow', *Academic Medicine*, 77: 502–15.

Arah, O.A., Hoekstra, J.B.L., Bos, A.P. and Lombarts, K.M. (2011). 'New tools for systemic evaluation of teaching qualities of medical faculty: results of an ongoing multi-center survey', *PLos ONE*, 6(100): e25983.

Brainard, A.H. and Bilsen, H.C. (2007). 'Learning professionalism: a view from the trenches', *Academic Medicine*, 82: 1010–14.

Brater, D.C. (2007). 'Infusing professionalism into a school of medicine: perspectives from the Dean', *Academic Medicine*, 82: 1094–7.

Cohen, J.J. (2006). 'Professionalism in medical education, an American perspective: from evidence to accountability', *Med Educ.*, 40: 607–17.

Cohen, J.J., Cruess, S.R. and Davidson, C. (2007). 'Alliance between society and medicine: the public's stake in medical professionalism', *JAMA*, 298: 670–673.

Cruess, R.L. and Cruess, S.R. (1997a). 'Teaching professionalism in the service of healing', *Academic Medicine*, 72: 941–52.

Cruess, S.R. and Cruess, R.L. (1997b). 'Professionalism must be taught', *BMJ*, 7123: 1674–7.

Cruess, S.R., Johnston, S. and Cruess, R.L. (2004). 'Profession, a working definition for medical educators', *Teaching and Learning in Medicine*, 16: 74–6.

Cruess, R. and Cruess, S. (2006). 'Teaching professionalism: general principles', *Medical Teacher*, 28: 205–8.

Cruess, S.R., Cruess, R.L. and Steinert, Y. (2008). 'Role modeling: making the most of a powerful teaching strategy', *BMJ*, 336: 718–21.

Cruess, R.L. and Cruess, S.R. (2008). 'Expectations and obligations: professionalism and medicine's social contract with society', *Perspectives in Med and Biol.*, 51: 579–98.

Cruess, S.R. and Cruess, R.L. (2009a). 'The cognitive base of professionalism', in *Teaching Medical Professionalism*, edited by Cruess R.L., Cruess S.R. and Steinert Y. New York, NY: Cambridge Univ. Press, 7–31.

Cruess, R.L. and Cruess, S.R. (2009b). 'Principles for designing a program for the teaching and learning of professionalism at the undergraduate level', in *Teaching Medical Professionalism*, edited by Cruess, R.L., Cruess, S.R. and Steinert, Y. New York, NY: Cambridge Univ. Press, 73–92.

Epstein, R.M. (2007). 'Assessment in medical education', *NEJM*, 356: 387–96.

Freidson, E. (1970). *Professional Dominance: The Social Structure of Medical Care*. Chicago, Aldine.

Freidson, E. (2001). *Professionalism: The Third Logic*. Chicago: University of Chicago Press.

Gibbons, M. (1999). 'Science's new social contract with society', *Nature*, 402: C81–C84.

Gough, J.W. (1957). *The Social Contract: A Critical Study of its Development*. Oxford, The Clarendon Press.

Hafferty, F.W., McKinley, J.B. (1993). *The Changing Medical Profession: an International Perspective*. Oxford: Oxford Univ. Press.

Hafferty, F.W. (1998). 'Beyond curriculum reform: confronting medicine's hidden curriculum', *Academic Medicine*, 73: 403–7.

Hafferty, F.W. (2009). 'Professionalism and the socialization of medical students', in *Teaching Medical Professionalism*, edited by Cruess R.L., Cruess S.R. and Steinert Y. New York: Cambridge Univ. Press, 53–73.

Hickson, G.B., Pichert, J.W., Webb, L.E. and Gabbe, S.G. (2007). 'A complimentary approach to promoting professionalism: identifying, measuring, and addressing unprofessional behaviors', *Academic Medicine*, 82: 1040–1048.

Hilton, S.R. and Slotnick, H.B. (2005). 'Proto-professionalism: how professionalization occurs across the continuum of medical education', *Med Ed.*, 39: 58–65.

Ihara, C.K. (1988). 'Collegiality as a professional virtue', in *Professional Ideals*, edited by Flores, A. Belmont, CA: Wadsworth, 56–65.

Inui, T.S., Cottingham, A.H., Frankel, R.M., Litzelman, D.K., Suchman, A.L. and Williamson, P.R. (2009). 'Supporting teaching and learning of professionalism-changing the educational environment, and students' navigational skills', in *Teaching Medical Professionalism*, edited by Cruess, R.L., Cruess, S.R. and Steinert, Y. New York, NY: Cambridge Univ. Press, 108–24.

Irvine, D. (2003). *The Doctor's Tale: Professionalism and Public Trust*. Abington UK. Radcliffe Medical Press.

Irby, D.M. (1986). 'Clinical teaching and the clinical teacher', *J Med Ed.*, 61: 35–45.

Johnson, T. (1972). *Professions and Power*. London: Macmillan Press.

Kennedy, D. (1997). *Academic Duty*. Cambridge, MA: Harvard Univ. Press.

Krause, E. (1996). *Death of the Guilds: Professions, States and the Advance of Capitalism, 1930 to the Present*. New Haven: Yale University Press.

Larson, M. (1977). *The Rise of Professionalism: A Sociological Analysis*. Berkeley, CA: University of California Press.

Lubchenko, J. (1998). 'Entering the century of the environment: a new social contract for science', *Science*, 279: 491–7.

Macdonald, K.M. (1995). *The Sociology of the Professions*. London: Sage.

McKinley, J.B. and Arches, J. (1985). 'Toward the proletarianization of physicians', *Int. J. Health Serv*, 15: 161–15.

Mechanic, D. (2004). 'In my chosen doctor I trust', *BMJ*, 329: 1418–9.

Oxford English Dictionary, 2nd ed. 1989. Oxford: Clarendon Press.

Merton, R.K., Reader, L.G. and Kendall, P.L. (eds) (1957). *The Student Physician: Introductory Studies in the Sociology of Medical Education.* Cambridge, MA: Harvard University Press.

New York Times. 2012. Editorial: The cautionary tale of Dewey and LeBoeuf: 6 May, Page A 22.

Papadakis, M. and Loeser, H. (2005a). 'Using critical incident reports and longitudinal observations to assess professionalism', in *Measuring Medical Professionalism*, edited by Stern, D.T. New York, NY: Oxford Univ. Press, 159–75.

Papadakis, M.A., Teharani, A., Banach, M.A., Knettler, T.R., Rattner, S.L., Stern, D.T., Veloski, J.J. and Hodson, C.S. (2005b). 'Disciplanary action by medical boards and prior behavior in medical school', *NEJM*, 353: 2673–82.

Papadakis, M.A., Arnold, G.K., Blank, L.L., Holmboe, E.S. and Lipner, R.S. (2008). Performance during internal medicine residency training and subsequent disciplinary action by state licensing, *Ann Intern Med*,148(11): 869–76.

Parsons, T. (1939). 'The professions and social structure', *Social Forces*, 17: 457–67.

Pellegrino, E.D. and Pellegrino, A.A. (1988). 'Humanism and ethics in Roman medicine: translation and commentary on a text of Scribonius Largus', *Literature and medicine*, 7: 22–38.

Relman, A.S. (2007). 'Medical professionalism in a commercialized health care market', *JAMA*, 298: 2668–70.

Rosenblatt, R.E., Shaw, S. and Rosenbaum, S. (1997). *Law and the American Health Care System.* New York, NY: Foundation Press.

Royal College of Physicians of London. (2005). *Doctors in Society: Medical Professionalism in a Changing World.* London UK: Royal college of Physicians of London.

Royal College of Physicians and Surgeons of Canada. (2007). The CanMeds roles framework. 2005. http://rcpsc.medil.org.canmeds/index.php. Accessed 5 February 2007.

Schlesinger, M. (2002). 'A loss of faith: the sources of reduced political legitimacy for the American medical profession', *Milbank Quarterly*, 80: 185–235.

Schon, D.A. (1983). *The Reflective Practitioner: How Professionals Think in Action.* London: Basic Books.

Schon, D.A. (1987). *Educating the Reflective Practitioner: Toward a New Design for Teaching and Learning in the Professions.* San Francisco: Jossey-Bass.

Shaw, B. (1946). *Introduction to 'The Doctor's Dilemma'.* London: Penguin Books, 75.

Smith, K.L., Saavedra, R., Raeke, J.L. and O'Donell, A.A. (2007). 'The journey to creating a campus-wide culture of professionalism', *Academic Medicine*, 82: 1015–21.

Starr, P. (1984). *The Social Transformation of American Medicine.* New York: Basic Books.

Steinert, Y., Cruess, S.R., Cruess, R.L. and Snell, L. (2005). 'Faculty development for teaching and evaluating professionalism: from program design to curricular change', *Med Ed.*, 39: 127–36.

Steinert, Y., Cruess, R.L., Cruess, S.R., Boudreau, J.D. and Abraham, F. (2007). 'Faculty development as an instrument of change: a case study on teaching professionalism', *Academic Medicine*, 82: 1065–7.

Stern, D.T. (ed). (2005). *Measuring Medical Professionalism*. New York: Oxford University Press.

Sullivan, W. (2005). *Work and Integrity: The Crisis and Promise of Professionalism in North America*. 2nd ed. San Francisco, CA: Jossey-Bass.

Sullivan, W.M., Colby, A., Wegner, J.W., Bond, L. and Shulman, L.S. (2007). *Educating Lawyers: Preparation for the Profession of Law*. San Francisco, CA: John Wiley and Sons.

Sullivan, C. and Arnold, C. (2009). 'Assessment and remediation in programs of teaching professionalism', in *Teaching Medical Professionalism*, edited by Cruess, R.L., Cruess, S.R. and Steinert, Y. New York, NY: Cambridge Univ. Press. 124–50.

Swick, H.M. (2000). 'Towards a normative definition of professionalism', *Academic Medicine*, 75: 612–6.

Todhunter, S., Cruess, S.R., Cruess, R.L., Young, M. and Steinert, Y. (2011). 'Developing and piloting a form for student assessment of faculty professionalism', *Advances in Health Sci Edu.*, 16: 223–38.

Twenge, J.M. (2009). 'Generational changes and their impact in the classroom: teaching Generation Me', *Med Ed.*, 43: 398–405.

Wasserstein, A.G., Brennan, P.J. and Rubenstein, A.H. (2007). 'Institutional leadership and faculty response: fostering professionalism at the University of Pennsylvania School of Medicine', *Academic Medicine*, 82: 1049–56.

Wilkinson, T.J., Wade, W.B., and Knock, L.D. (2009). 'A blueprint to assess professionalism: results of a systematic review', *Academic Medicine*, 84: 551–8.

Wright, S.M., Kern, D.E., Kolodner, K. Howard, D.M. and Brancati, F.L. (1998). 'Attributes of excellent attending-physician role models', *NEJM*, 339: 1986–93.

Wynia, M.K., Latham, S.R., Kao, A.C., Berg, J.W. and Emanuel, L.L (1999). 'Medical professionalism in society', *New. Engl. J. Med.*, 341: 1612–6.

Wynia, M.K. (2008). 'The short and tenuous future of medical professionalism: the erosion of medicine's social contract', *Perspectives in Biology and Medicine*, 51: 565–78.

Young, M.E., Cruess, S.R., Cruess, R.L. and Steinert, Y. (2012). 'The professionalism assessment of clinical teachers: the reliability and validity of a novel tool to evaluate professional and clinical teaching behaviors', *Under revision for Advances in Health Sciences Education*.

Chapter 6

Enabling Fitness to Practice in Medical Education

Sam Leinster

Introduction

The concept of medicine as a profession has a long and honourable history. It is obvious from the Code of Hammurabi that there was a distinct group of individuals who were recognised as authorised to deliver health care (King 2012). The sanctions against those who were found to be negligent in the administration of health care were somewhat more draconian than those currently in force in most legal jurisdictions. While it is possible to appeal against erasure from the Medical Register, the amputation of a hand if the patient suffered serious complications is rather more final.

Self-regulation is one of the features that define a profession and this is first evident in the *Oath of the Hindu Physicians* which dates from the 16th century BC (Rampe 2009). The *Hippocratic Oath* is better known, dating from the 5th century BC and originating from the guild of practitioners founded by Hippocrates on the island of Kos. How much of it is the work of Hippocrates himself is not clear. Although it is now regarded as the root of our modern concepts of medical professionalism, the Hippocratic School was only one of a number of competing schools of medicine, not all of which adhered to the same ethical code.

Similar oaths were developed in Japan and among the Jewish physicians practicing in the Arab world in the Middle Ages (Ogunbanjo and van Bogart 2009). All of the oaths contain concepts which are now accepted as defining at least some aspects of medical professionalism such as:

- the physician's responsibility for care of the patient;
- the central importance of confidentiality in the doctor-patient relationship;
- the need for probity in one's personal life; and
- the physician's duties towards present and future colleagues.

In 1948, following revelations in the Nuremberg War Crimes Tribunal of serious misconduct by doctors under the orders of the Nazi regime, the World Medical Association drew up a new code, The Declaration of Geneva, which reaffirmed the principles of the older codes while removing their religious overtones and making them more relevant to modern medical practice. The Declaration has been revised on a number of occasions, most recently in 2006 and is accepted as the foundation statement of current medical ethics (World Medical Association 1948). It is supported by more specific codes such as the Declaration of Helsinki (World Medical Association 1964) which deals with the ethical conduct of medical research, and the Declaration of Tokyo (World Medical Association 1975) which explicitly prohibits the participation by doctors in torture.

The terms of the codes are very general and are therefore open to interpretation. Because of this the General Medical Council, which is responsible for regulating the medical profession in the UK, has produced a guide *Good Medical Practice* (General Medical Council 1995). An important part of producing this guide was the involvement of representatives of the public in determining what constitutes good practice. This guide and its summary, 'The Duties of a Doctor', form the explicit working definition of what is regarded as appropriate professional attitudes and behaviour in the UK today.

Medical education was for many years focused on the knowledge that was needed to practice safely and successfully as a doctor. Concern over standard of medical education in the USA in the early part of the 20th century led the Carnegie Foundation to commission a lawyer, Abraham Flexner, to carry out an investigation of standards in medical schools throughout the USA. His report, published in 1910, was influential in determining the shape of medical education in Europe and in the then British Empire as well as the USA (reproduced in Flexner 2002). He recognised the importance of science in the practice and ongoing development of medicine and recommended that medical education should start with two years of scientific study before clinical studies were undertaken. The clinical studies were to be experiential as well as theoretical. This pattern of a period of so-called pre-clinical studies followed by clinical studies remained universal until the end of the 20th century when there was a move towards greater integration of the basic sciences with clinical studies. The length of time spent in each phase varied from country to country, partly determined by the different traditions of medical education in each country.

Although a discussion of the content of the ideal medical curriculum as early as 1827 had emphasised the need for medical jurisprudence and ethics to be taught (Medicus 1827), most curricula during the 20th century focused almost exclusively on scientific knowledge. Clinical skills were acquired at the bedside, largely by observing one's teachers. It was expected that professional attitudes and behaviours would be learnt in the same way. Interestingly, this process of education by osmosis appears to have been effective. Despite the lack of formal teaching sessions on professional behaviour, the mores of the profession were transmitted from generation to generation. This was probably due in large part to the relatively small size of medical classes with consequent close relationships between the teachers and the students. Up to the 1970s the average medical school class in London had fewer than 100 students while in the Scottish and provincial schools the number was never greater than 150. Students were taught at the bedside in groups of no more than six and in many instances in one-to-one situations. Skills and attitudes were taught by example and, on the whole, the students were treated as junior colleagues although ritual humiliation as depicted in *Doctor in the House* did occur (Gordon 2008).

By the late 1990s, class sizes had grown in all schools with some classes exceeding 400 students. Personal interaction with a small number of motivated teachers became unfeasible. While it is possible to deliver lectures in basic science and medical theory to very large numbers in a lecture theatre, clinical experience became more difficult to facilitate. Many medical schools had to disperse their students to distant hospitals with attendant difficulties in maintaining a sense of belonging among the students and assuring the quality of the teaching that was delivered. In fairness to the district general hospitals that were involved in this dispersed teaching it should be said that student evaluations tended to rate the experience in these smaller units as more enjoyable and more useful than time in the teaching centres.

The Challenge to Complacency

The medical profession is very conservative and operates on the assumption that the way things are done is the best way for them to be done. Few within the profession doubted that we were training doctors who would uphold the best traditions of professional behaviour while ensuring that medicine would continue to advance scientifically.

This view was not necessarily shared by those outside the profession. As people's expectations of what could be achieved by modern medicine grew in response to media reports of the wonders of modern science, so their tolerance of medical failure or medical error diminished. Indeed, they began to perceive all medical failure as necessarily being the result of medical error or incompetence. Legal challenge of alleged medical negligence became commonplace in the USA and is now firmly established in the UK. Formal complaints processes developed within health services alongside the legal process. One factor that emerges in examining both routes of redress is the part played by poor communication by health professionals in the patient's dissatisfaction. An important study of Canadian medical graduates showed that individuals' scores in the communication skills component of the Licensing Examination (which all doctors in Canada are required to sit) were highly correlated with complaints against those individuals in the first 12 years of practice (Tamblyn et al. 2007). Their findings are concordant with a substantial international body of literature that they cite in their paper. The increasing awareness of the central role that communication plays in the doctor-patient relationship led to increasing debate among medical educators about the need to improve the teaching of communication skills, which are now seen as an important component of professionalism.

The robustness of the medical professionalism in the UK was challenged by a number of high-profile scandals in the mid-1990s. The two best known are the Bristol paediatric cardiac surgery case (Kennedy 2001) and the case of the doctor-cum-serial killer, Harold Shipman. Perhaps the more influential of these was the Shipman case. Certainly, it was the one that provoked the government into setting up an official enquiry chaired by an eminent judge Dame Janet Smith (Smith 2002–05). She was tasked with examining the role and effectiveness of the GMC in regulating the medical profession and made a series of recommendations that have resulted in major restructuring of the regulatory system and contributed to a fresh awareness of the role of education in forming professional attitudes. It is ironic that public anxiety was triggered by the behaviour of an aberrant individual while the more systemic problems raised by the behaviour of the medical team in Bristol received less attention.

The Meaning of Professionalism

Other parts of the world had their own incidents. Such external factors added fuel to an international debate that was already taking place within the medical education literature on the meaning of professionalism in the context of medical education (Hodges et al. 2011). The concept proved to be elusive, probably because of its complexity. Professionalism is necessarily based in part on knowledge. It is interpreted by many people as relating to attitudes but it manifests itself through overt behaviours. In the absence of any universally agreed definition, medical schools began devising their own courses on professionalism. These sometimes were stand-alone modules occurring at a fixed point in the course. In other schools, professionalism formed a theme running across different modules and years of the course. The courses were often a mixture of communication skills, ethics and law.

Within the UK the debate became part of a more general review of the nature and content of medical education. Since its inception in 1858, the GMC had issued reports and recommendations on medical education at regular intervals. These reports appeared to have little effect and the overall approach to preparing doctors for practice changed very little with time. The second half of the 20th century was marked by an explosion in medical knowledge. More and more content was poured into the curriculum and very little was removed. By the late 1980s there was considerable unease about the medical undergraduate curriculum. A variety of sources highlighted the disillusionment experienced by medical students who felt overwhelmed by the mass of information with which they were faced. A worryingly large percentage of students in the later years of medical courses said that they regretted the decision to study medicine.

The GMC review which occurred at this time resulted in the publication in 1993 of a new set of recommendations called *Tomorrow's Doctors* (General Medical Council 1993). Among its other recommendations it mandated a reduction in the factual content of undergraduate medical courses. This was to be achieved by defining a minimum core of factual knowledge that should be learnt by all students. Wider educational outcomes such as cognitive skills would be developed by additional optional material in the form of 'Student Selected Modules'. Professional values and ethics were specified as core requirements.

Unlike its predecessors this report led to major changes within medical education. A number of factors contributed to this effect, not least the decision by the GMC that, during their routine visits to medical schools, the extent to which the school was compliant with the recommendations would be evaluated. The provision by the Chief Medical Officer of financial support for a curriculum coordinator in each medical school was a further driver (Leinster 1995).

Since 1993 there have been two revisions of *Tomorrow's Doctors*. The latest, published in 2009 (General Medical Council 2009a) has been restructured to facilitate its use in accreditation and quality assurance visits by the regulator. It is divided into two parts. The first is a list of learning outcomes which define the expected content of the course. The second part describes in some detail the structures and procedures that should be in place for its delivery and defines the evidence that is expected to prove that the specified criteria have been met. The outcomes are classified under three headings: *The doctor as scholar and scientist*; *The doctor as practitioner*; and *The doctor as professional*. The latter is closely aligned to *Good Medical Practice*.

Although medical schools are expected to be able to demonstrate that their graduates have achieved the learning outcomes listed in *Tomorrows Doctors* (including those under *The doctor as professional*), the recommendations do not specify how these outcomes should be taught or assessed.

Assessing Professionalism

There are widely accepted robust methods for assessing knowledge but assessing professionalism presents challenges (Wilkinson et al. 2009). Part of the difficulty arises from the existence of two components – attitudes and behaviour. Various attempts to assess attitudes have been made. Most of these take the form of questionnaires which attempt to elicit respondents' reaction to a variety of scenarios thought to highlight professional attitudes (Campbell et al. 2007; Roland et al. 2011). Other approaches involve *situational judgement tests* which are now routinely used in the assessment of trainee general practitioners and are shortly to be introduced as an element in the selection of graduates for their first post in the NHS (Lievens and Coetsier 2002). In the situational judgement test the subject is given a series of dilemmas and asked to rank a number of possible responses. The response profile is compared with that given by an expert panel. The method has been shown to be robust and reproducible (Patterson et al. 2012). The major shortcoming of such efforts is that candidates are well aware of the accepted answers to the questions posed and may give what they perceive to be the acceptable response rather than the one that represents their true attitude.

A similar problem faces efforts to measure behaviour at a discrete point in time. Most people are aware of the range of behaviours that are regarded as acceptable.

Candidates will make the effort to behave in an acceptable way during a short period of observation when they are under scrutiny. For this reason, it is now recognised that assessing professionalism needs observation over a long period in a real-life setting.

Methods of Real-life Observation

In educational settings, real-life observation usually entails some form of tutor report. At Norwich Medical School, each student is a member of a tutorial group comprising 10 students who remain together for a whole academic year. The group has a tutor for problem-based learning and a different tutor for primary care clinical placement who see the group weekly throughout the year. Each tutor reports on the professional behaviour of each student within the tutor group at the end of every module. The tutors use proformas which specify the domains that are to be assessed. For each domain they give a global judgement ranging from *unsatisfactory* through *needs attention* to *good* and *excellent*.

The students are seen individually by the tutors and the report is discussed with them. They sign the report to confirm that they have received feedback on it and also indicate whether or not they agree with the assessment. The form is returned to the Chair of the Professional Behaviour Committee. Students who receive successive *unsatisfactory* reports are discussed in detail as are students who receive persistent *needs attention* grades. A range of actions is open to the committee. The lowest level of intervention is an informal letter from the Chair of the Professional Behaviour Committee reinforcing the areas that are a cause for concern and requiring the student to improve in these areas. If the matter is more serious, or if the unacceptable behaviour persists, the student will be interviewed by a senior member of faculty and a formal written warning will be issued. The formal warning is entered in the student's record and must be reported to the GMC at the time of application for provisional registration. A second formal warning will result in the student being reported to the University Professional Misconduct and Unsuitability Committee for fitness-to-practice proceedings to be initiated. These proceedings can also be initiated if a student's behaviour gives rise for sufficient concern. There is a formal process by which members of staff or students can report attitudes or behaviours which they regard as unacceptable. The report form requires the reporter to identify themselves. Anonymous reports are not accepted.

Fitness-to-practice proceedings are governed by university statutes and have a formal structure. When the head of school is made aware that there may be an issue with a particular student, he or she is required to appoint an Investigating Officer who must be an experienced member of faculty who has no previous personal contact with the student. The student will be sent a letter advising that an allegation has been made and explaining the process that will take place. Attention will be drawn to the relevant university regulations governing the process. The investigating officer is responsible for collecting evidence with regard to the alleged offence. This will normally mean interviewing the complainant, the student against whom the allegations are made and any witnesses. In some cases there will be documentary evidence such as inappropriate entries on social networking sites, written complaints from members of the public or police reports. The investigating officer prepares a report for the head of school. If there appears to be a case to answer, the head of school forwards the report to the University Academic Registrar who is the senior administrator responsible for student discipline who then convenes a Fitness-to-Practice Panel of three members. The panel is chaired by a senior academic from another school with a senior NHS clinician and a senior academic from the medical school who have no previous personal contact with the student and is supported by a University Senior Assistant Registrar with experience in this area.

This panel holds a formal hearing at which the student is entitled to be accompanied by a 'friend' who may be a legal representative or a representative of the Student Union. The School's case is put by the Head of School who may present written evidence and call relevant witnesses. The student may also call witnesses. All of the witnesses may be questioned by the panel and either party. After due deliberation the panel announces its decision. If it finds that inappropriate attitudes or behaviours have been displayed, it has a range of sanctions which it may apply.

It may issue a formal warning which has the same significance as a formal warning from the Head of School. If the matter is more serious, it may suspend the student's studies. His or her return may be made contingent on fulfilling certain conditions, for example successful completion of an anger management course or a course on equality and diversity. The ultimate sanction is termination of studies when the offence is judged to be of a nature that casts serious doubt on the student's ability to behave in a professional manner throughout his or her future career. The student has the right of appeal in which case a new panel would be convened. An appeal panel would be expected to include a senior clinical academic from another medical school who has experience in fitness-to-practice matters. A list of such individuals who are willing to participate is held by the Medical Schools Council.

All medical schools in the UK are now required by the GMC to have similar procedures. These procedures are specifically addressed in *Tomorrow's Doctors* and may be subject to review at a GMC quality assurance visit. When the GMC began to emphasise the role of the medical schools in ensuring that graduates were fit to practice some universities were initially resistant. University statutes made clear provision for failing a student for academic underperformance but there was no defined mechanism for removing a student whose academic performance was good but whose behaviour was deemed to be unprofessional. University authorities were anxious that a student whose studies might be terminated on non-academic grounds might sue the university for loss of potential earnings. Student support services were concerned that the system was open to abuse with students being dismissed as the result of personality clashes with members of faculty. It is fair to say that this anxiety was shared by the students who thought that any expression of dissent or dissatisfaction would result in fitness-to-practice procedures being initiated.

The system has been in operation for ten years and these concerns have, in the main, been allayed. The university recognised that the risk of successful litigation was small if proper procedures were in place and were followed. The reputational risk of being sued by a patient who was harmed by a graduate who had been identified as unsafe but nevertheless allowed to graduate was seen to be greater.

Discussions took place with the senior members of the student support service to reassure them that a robust evidence base indicating persistent poor behaviour would be required before action would be taken against a student. The primary purpose of the process is remediation with disciplinary action being invoked when attempts at remediation fail. Once the system was operational it became clear to the support staff and students that the system was fair and transparent. There is now a general acceptance that the procedures are an essential part of medical education and reports of unprofessional behaviour are as likely to be made by students as by staff.

Curiously, monitoring professional behaviour was never an issue with nursing students who, for many years, in addition to passing their final examinations, were required to have a Certificate of Fitness-to-Practice signed by the Head of School before they were allowed to enter the Register of Nurses.

Among fitness-to-practice concerns, plagiarism has a special place in that it is also recognised as a significant issue among students who are not on professional courses. The problem ranges from unascribed quotation from original sources (often on the Internet) to wholesale passing off of downloaded material as original work. All universities now have systems for detecting and dealing with plagiarism with specific members of academic staff being given the responsibility for handling cases. Medical students who are caught plagiarising will be dealt with through the university-wide system rather than being subject to fitness-to-practice procedures. The matter will appear on their record and they are required to inform the GMC at the point of provisional registration.

The criteria on which fitness-to-practice should be judged have gradually become crystallised. In 2009, the GMC and the Medical Schools Council jointly published a guide to medical student behaviour (General Medical Council 2009b). This includes a clear list of behaviours that the GMC will regard as serious bars to registering as a medical practitioner on qualification.

Role of the Regulator

There have been calls for the GMC to assume direct responsibility for medical student conduct. Students in the Allied Health Professions are registered with the appropriate professional body such as the Chartered Society of Physiotherapists. In New South Wales, students are registered with the Medical Council and disciplinary hearings are conducted by the Council. The argument is made that registration with the GMC and a consequent centralisation of disciplinary procedures would result in greater consistency in application of the criteria. Although no formal studies have been done, the mythology of the profession suggests that there are differences in the way apparently similar offences are dealt with between medical schools with some schools being thought of as more lenient than others. Currently, most opinion among medical educators and in the GMC itself is opposed to the idea of student registration. There is a pragmatic argument that a centralised system would be unwieldy and would result in delays in decision-making. More importantly, local processes provide greater opportunities for remedial action to be taken.

Following graduation, medical students are provisionally registered by the GMC. Full registration is obtained after a year of supervised practice as a Foundation Doctor in recognised posts within the NHS. In addition to passing the Finals Examinations, students are required to self-certify that they have no fitness-to-practice issues, including issues relating to their health. They are asked specifically if they have faced disciplinary proceedings while at Medical School and whether they have any form of criminal record. The GMC does not itself ask for Criminal Records Bureau checks although the medical schools and NHS employers do. Although the process is one of self-certification, it is common practice for the medical school to check the form before it is submitted and remind the student of any relevant matters that they may have 'forgotten' to declare. Non-declaration is in itself *serious professional misconduct* that would, if it came to light, result in a hearing before the GMC. It is therefore a high risk strategy. When a student reports an issue, the GMC registration department investigates in more detail, essentially seeking reassurances that the medical school has dealt with the problem appropriately and is happy to confirm that the student is fit to practice medicine. The system has only recently been introduced and to date only a handful of students have been refused provisional registration.

Ongoing Matters

Cases of professional misconduct will always occur. Our duty as medical educators is to minimise the risk of misconduct by providing effective learning methods that will develop professional attitudes and behaviours. At the same time, we must have robust systems that identify those students who are unable or unwilling to conform to professional mores and remove them from the course at as early a stage as possible. The challenge is to distinguish this recalcitrant group from the much larger group who commit a misdemeanour but respond to appropriate guidance and remediation and become exemplary medical practitioners. Finding the balance between the rights of the professional and the good of the public is a difficulty that we share with the other professions that interact directly with the public.

References

Campbell, E.G., Regan, S., Gruen, R.L. et al. (2007), 'Professionalism in medicine: results of a national survey of physicians', *Annals of Internal Medicine*, 147: 795–802.

Flexner, A. (2002), 'Medical education in the United States and Canada: a report to the Carnegie Foundation for the advancement of teaching'. Reproduced in *Bulletin of the World Health Organization*, 80 (7): 594–602.

General Medical Council (1993), *Tomorrow's Doctors*. GMC: London.

General Medical Council (1995), *Good Medical Practice*. Available at: http://www.gmc-uk.org/static/documents/content/GMP_0910.pdf [accessed 19 September 2012].

General Medical Council (2009a), *Tomorrow's Doctors*. Available at: http://www.gmc-uk.org/static/documents/content/GMC_TD_09__1.11.11.pdf [accessed 19 September 2012].

General Medical Council (2009b), *Medical Students: Professionalism and Fitness to Practice*. Available at: http://www.gmc-uk.org/static/documents/content/GMC_Medical_Students.pdf [accessed 19 September 2012].

Gordon, R. (2008), *Doctor in the House*. House of Stratus: London.

Hodges, B D., Ginsberg, S., Cruess, R. et al. (2011), 'Assessment of professionalism: recommendations from Ottowa 2010 Conference', *Medical Teacher*, 33: 354–63.

King, L.W. (2012), (translator) *Hammurabi's Code of Laws*. Available at: http://www.fordham.edu/halsall/ancient/hamcode.asp [accessed 19 September 2012].

Kennedy, I. (2001), *The Report of the Public Inquiry into children's heart surgery at Bristol Royal Infirmary 1984–1995*. Available at: www.bristol-inquiry.org.uk/final_report/index.htm [accessed 19 September 2012].

Leinster. S.J. (1995), Resourcing changes in the medical curriculum. A report on an ASME workshop – 28 February 1995, *Medical Education*, 29: 382–4.

Lievens, F. and Coetsier, P. (2002), 'Situational tests in student selection: an examination of predictive validity, adverse impact and construct validity', *International Journal of Selection and Assessment*, 10: 245–7.

Medicus (1827), *Thoughts on Medical Education and a Plan for its Improvement*. London: Longman, Rees, Orme, Brown and Greene, 16–18.

Ogunbanjo, G.A. and van Bogaert, K. (2009), 'The hippocratic oath: revisited', *SA Family Practice*, 51: 30–31.

Patterson, F., Ashworth, V., Zibarras, L. et al. (2012), 'Evaluation of situational judgement tests to assess non-academic attributes in selection', *Medical Education*, 46: 850–868.

Rampe, K. (2009), 'Do we need the hippocratic oath?' *Student BMJ*, 17: b1032.

Roland, M., Rao, S.R., Sibbald, D. et al. (2011), 'Professional values and reported behaviour of doctors in the USA and UK: quantitative survey', *BMJ Quality and Safety*, 20: 515–21.

Smith, Dame Janet (2002–05), *The Shipman Inquiry – Reports*. Available at: http://www.shipman-inquiry.org/reports.asp [accessed 19 September 2012].

Tamblyn, R., Abrahamowicz, M., Dauphinee, D. et al. (2007), 'Physician scores on a national clinical skills examination as predictors of complaints to medical regulatory authorities', *JAMA*, 298: 993–1001.

Wilkinson, T.J., Wade, W.B. and Knock, L.D. (2009), 'A blueprint to assess professionalism: a systematic review', *Academic Medicine*, 84: 531–58.

World Medical Association (1948), *The Physician's Oath*. Available at: http://www.mma.org.my/Portals/0/Declaration%20of%20Geneva.pdf [accessed 19 September 2012].

World Medical Association (1964), *Declaration of Helsinki – Ethical Principles for Medical Research involving Human Subjects*. Available at: http://www.wma.net/en/30publications/10policies/b3/ [accessed 19 September 2012].

World Medical Association (1975), *Declaration of Tokyo Guidelines for Physicians Concerning Torture and Other Cruel, Inhuman or Degrading Treatment or Punishment in Relation to Detention or Imprisonment*. Available at: http://www.wma.net/en/20activities/10ethics/20tokyo/ [accessed 19 September 2012].

PART V
Culture

Chapter 7

Collaboration:
A Crucible for Cultivating Common
Understanding in Professional Legal Education

Craig Collins and Suzanne Webbey

The original meaning of 'to have a vocation' is 'to be addressed by a voice'

C.G. Jung (1954)

Introduction

'Vocation' is an Old French word derived from the Latin *vocare*, 'to call', and in early English this referred to a spiritual calling (Ayton 1990: 561). The root *voca* refers to the voice and from the same root is derived 'vocabulary'. Central to the 'calling of law' is speech – and this is especially so within the common law tradition, with its reliance upon 'unwritten' laws and custom. Alan Atkinson captures the effect (or affect) arising from the distinction between the spoken and written word:

> Speech creates an island of understanding, high and dry, and the habits of speech lead to a sense of place and of particularity. There is power in utterance, in filling a silence, and listeners are easily made into subjects, at least for the moment. None of this is true when talk is crystallised by writing ... Words on a page as distinct from words in the air, lose some of the sharper resonance of locality, gender and race...Words pass from warm breath into cold storage (Atkinson 1997: 17–19).

Law, then, is not only created, contested, shaped and transmitted by speech in or about courts of law, but so too is the *persona* of lawyers. One's *persona* is 'the mask assumed in order to play a social role' or the 'face' presented to the outside world in one context or another (Wickes 1988: 65). Accordingly, the professional *persona* necessary to perform the role of lawyer is shaped by 'the persons by whom it is surrounded, noting what is considered respectable, worthy and desirable in the chosen circle in which it moves' (Wickes 1988: 65).

For Professional Legal Education (PLE), our central argument is that a 'collaboration of voices' or 'group-work' is not only an effective, but also necessary, crucible for inculcating a basic, entry-level competency with the language, processes, customs, ethics and social behaviour (or culture) of Australian lawyers.

We say 'necessary' because it seems to us that group dynamics have been the engine driving the development of legal culture over time. This is also the mechanism by which individual lawyers develop expertise, and even wisdom, today.

Taking a large view of learning within the discipline, we seek to lift our gaze beyond the specific learning objects (for example the 'what' – the content, skills, values and so on) and towards the different *kinds* (or cultures) of learning that occur within our discipline. In making our argument, and drawing out the implications for PLE, we suggest that two distinct cultures of learning law operate today: 'learning as a student' (with a heavily individualist orientation) and 'learning as a lawyer' (with group dynamics emphasised).

One implication of this is that, rather than conceiving PLE as some kind of 'bolted on' appendage to undergraduate law, PLE occupies a vital pivotal space directed towards re-orientating and transforming one's very approach to engaging with law. Indeed, we argue, it is only when so equipped that one can begin developing as a lawyer.

Finally, by reference to recent innovations with the Graduate Diploma of Legal Practice program at the Australian National University, we show how the Maharg model of simulated learning in 'virtual law firms' has been adapted to an entirely distance-education cohort. We seek to show how collaboration through group-work – predominantly as peer-to-peer online interactions between students performing as lawyers within their virtual firms – has been central to the effectiveness of the program.

Law and Culture

The word 'culture', according to Raymond Williams, is 'one of the two or three most complicated words in the English language' (Teo and White 2003: 3). Indeed, the Australian historian, Greg Dening, has counted 366 extant definitions of the word (Teo and White 2003: 3). This chapter adopts an anthropological definition of 'culture' as 'the customs, ideas, and social behaviour of a particular people or group' (Stevenson 2007; Teo and White 2003)[1] – for our purposes, Australian lawyers. Accordingly, we focus upon the relationship between *legal* culture and legal education.

We also adopt James Boyd White's expansive definition of a discipline 'as a community of discourse organized around its disagreements, its way of disagreeing, as well as its agreements' (White 1994: 16).[2] It follows that, within

---

1   Fogel, A. 1993. *Development Through Relationships: Origins of communication, self and culture*. Chicago: University of Chicago Press, 6, suggests to similar effect that '[c]ulture is the set of tools, media, communication conventions and beliefs that mediate all of our relational experiences'.

2   See also: Collins, C. 2007 'The Discipline of Law: A Developmental and Historical Perspective', *Australian Law Postgraduate Network Paper Series*, 1. Available at:

the common law tradition, the discipline of law can be painted as a broad image of mind and talk rather than just as a package of rules and enforcement. To similar effect, Michael Lobban attributes to Sir Edward Coke (in the 17th century) the idea 'that the common law was a system of reasoning, that the source of law lay in the way that judges thought about legal problems' (Lobban 1991: 7). This practitioner view of law also helps to explain the renowned adaptability of the common law. Indeed, '[t]he law could change simply because it was not a fixed set of rules, but a reasoning process, working with a system of remedies'(Lobban 1991: 54).

And so, as Fogel observes, while 'culture reflects the history of a community' (Fogel 1993: 6), including the 'tools of communication and the rules that regulate its occurrence' (Fogel 1993: 13), at the same time 'cultural systems are not static' (Fogel 1993: 13):

> Like the mind and like personal relationships they develop, they shrink and expand, they are varied in relation to the context and purpose of action. Cultures are relational and embodied, expressed as the actions and products of the participants (Fogel 1993: 13).

If law is to be understood as patterns of thinking variably recomposed over time and place, but vulnerable to regression – and if practising law in society today at a level of developed expertise requires an advanced cognitive capacity for reasoning about justice and morality – then it is vital to explore and understand in more detail the relationship between the culture of lawyers and legal education.

Two Cultures of Learning Law

Using broad brush-strokes, we suggest that there are two distinct cultures of learning law in Australia (and elsewhere). The distinction we draw is between 'learning as a student' and 'learning as a lawyer'.

Learning as a Student

Learning law as a student in a university-based law school is still a relatively recent phenomenon in the common law tradition. David Lemmings argues that 'it was social elitism, rather than educational utility, which lay behind the principal shift in the structure of legal education: from clerical apprenticeship to university and pupilage' (Lemmings 2003: 57).

In Australia, and in the absence of an established culture of legal learning centred around Inns of Court or similar institutions, the Sydney (1855) and Melbourne (1857) University Law Schools trace back to the mid-19th century.

http://www.alpn.edu.au/publications/2007-alpn-paper-series [Online].

But it is only since the mid-1940s that Australian law schools began to take their modern shape, with the wide adoption of William Langdell's 'case method' from the United States, the publication of Australian textbooks and, from a small base, a growing body of full-time legal academics (Campbell 1977). Indeed, in the English context, William Twining recognises that 'the standard accounts provide strong support for the proposition that the modern English law school is in most important respects a post Second World War creation' (Twining 1994: 26).

Twining also observes that 'for most practical purposes, law in universities ... has been treated as just one, relatively small and insignificant part of the humanities and social sciences' and, further, that 'changes in undergraduate legal education ... have much more closely reflected changes in higher education than changes in legal practice and the legal system' (Twinning 1994: 28). One implication of this development, amplified below, is a widening schism between the two cultures of learning law.

The university approach to learning law builds upon the attempts by Sir William Blackstone and Jeremy Bentham to impose system and coherence upon the common law by delineating positivist rules and narrow sources of law. But Michael Lobban argues persuasively that this 'law as rules' approach remained 'outside the mainstream of what lawyers thought the law was about' (Lobban 1991: 13) and actually failed to take hold in practice. Yet, for all of its limitations as recognised by practitioners, Blackstone's *Commentaries* became the standard, base reference for legal education in the common law world – especially in the Australian colonies where legal reference books were for a long time in short supply.

The scholastic approach to law, consistently with university approaches to learning canon and civil (continental) law, elevated the text – far beyond the oral and inter-personal bent of the common law tradition. Indeed, in developing the case-book method of university legal education – and in removing students from the 'crucible' of courts and into the silence of libraries – Langdell espoused that:

> [L]aw is a science, and ... all the available materials of that science are contained in printed books. If law be not a science, a university will consult its own dignity in declining to teach it. We have ... inculcated the idea that the library is the proper workshop of professors and students alike; that it is to us all that the laboratories of the university are to the chemists and physicists, the museum of natural history to the zoologists, the botanical garden to the botanists (Twining 1994: 91).[3]

Roger Burridge and Julian Webb argue that this 'dominant pedagogical form of legal rule, factual proposition and problem resolution only pretends a social relevance. Facts are presented as unproblematic; alternative non-legal solutions

---

3 Citing Christopher Columbus Langdell, 1887 'Speech at Harvard University', 3, *Law Quarterly Review*: 123, 124.

are ignored; wider issues of justice, environment and culture become irrelevant' (Burridge and Webb 2008: 263, 267).

And, as a counterpoint to the culture of learning as a lawyer described below, Burridge and Webb note that at law school, '[t]he pursuit of independent and original thought is a product of individual achievement. Collaborative approaches to learning are felt to be suspect' (Burridge and Webb 2006: 263, 267). Indeed, they go further with the observation that 'scholarship is essentially a selfish pursuit' (Burridge and Webb 2006: 267). This theme is reinforced by the American legal psychologist, Benjamin Sells, when he refers to the 'cloistered mentality' and 'self-confident isolation' spawned in students by law schools (Sells 1994: 50). He adds that, '[m]any of the mental habits taught in law school promote a distorted and burdensome sense of individuality' (Sells 1994: 50–51).

The implications of this approach to learning were highlighted recently by the Business Council of Australia, which advocated 'a broadening of the curricula to produce people who can work on a range of issues, solve problems and work in teams' (Hare 2011: 29). The spokesman added that 'universities were [still] failing to heed the call' (Hare 2011: 29).

While the case-method makes sense as an approach for those entirely new to the study of law as a means of focusing attention upon pure legal reasoning, unhindered by complicating context, undergraduate legal education hardly ventures beyond this method over the course of an entire five-year combined degree. Accordingly, graduates emerge from their undergraduate legal education with a distorted and often inflated sense of their mastery of the discipline. Of course, such inflation is readily generated within a learning space largely devoid of contact with outstanding lawyers – or, indeed, any community of lawyers of varying experience, maturity and wisdom. And this distortion ought to be no surprise when, as Burridge and Webb observe of an undergraduate legal education, '[i]ts primary purpose is not the development of 'good lawyers', welcome or tolerated though this secondary objective may be' (Burridge and Webb 2008: 263–4).

The question arises as to whether the culture of learning law as a student has now become so qualitatively different and disconnected from the culture of learning law as a lawyer, as to retard any true sense of progression from the former towards the latter.

Learning as a Lawyer

By contrast with the 'learning as a student' approach discussed above, we say that, for lawyers, development and expertise occurs through group dynamics. As an eminent American lawyer, Fred Bartlitt once said: '[w]e work in small groups of highly motivated, interesting people, addressing ever-changing, complex problems where there is a lot at stake' (quoted in Maister 1997: 25). Within this dynamic, 'cognitive conflict' operates as a significant source of developmental propulsion. Such conflict sits at the core of our adversarial system of law and seems to correspond with 'the mechanism of progress' identified by Jean Piaget

(Ginsberg and Opper 1979: 230), as children progress through the stages of moral reasoning:

> Social interaction inevitably leads to arguments and discussion: The child's views are questioned, and he must defend and justify his opinions. This action forces the child to clarify his thoughts, for if he wants to convince others of the validity of his own views, the child must present them clearly and logically. In addition, other people may not be as tolerant of his inconsistencies as is the child himself and they do not hesitate to point them out. Thus social interaction helps the child recognise the shortcomings in his thinking and forces him to see other points of view which may conflict with his own (Ginsberg and Opper 1979: 230).

Indeed, drawing upon Piaget, the significance of group dynamics and cognitive conflict is central to Charles Radding's argument that the initial spark which ignited the discipline of law (in the West, and as we know it today) was a monumental cognitive shift on a cultural scale brought about by the collapse of traditional authority within the law courts of the eleventh century. This collapse created the conditions in which lawyers,

> ... had to learn ways of persuading their peers by showing their interpretation of the text was correct, by answering the arguments of their opponents, and in general by appealing to the good sense of their audience. The effort to adapt to this necessity stimulated the development of cognitive skills that had rarely been required since the time of Cicero (Radding 1985: 155).

We represent this group dynamic as a 'crucible', adopting Fogel's observation that 'relationship processes are the conflagrations out of which information is forged. Morality, aesthetics and affiliation do not exist in the Platonic sense before or after the dialogue: they emerge from its heat' (Fogel 1993: 182). Within the forum of the court, old patterns of thinking combust as lawyers' strain to recompose and explain a legal problem and advocated solution under the intense heat generated by the combination of peer challenge; public transparency; novelty; and necessity. A similar dynamic is at play in the context of transactional negotiations performed by lawyers.

Within this milieu and under these conditions, legal expertise is propelled by 'continually tackling challenges that lie just beyond one's competence' (Ross 2006: 66) or, differently expressed, 'purposeful engagement involving direct instruction, active participation, role modeling, and reward' (Sternberg 2003: 71). Interaction with others is crucial, as higher psychological functions (including legal culture) are first experienced on the social level before they can begin a process of internalisation. As Lev Vygotsky said, '[a]ll the higher functions originate as actual relations between human individuals' (1978: 57) and this external orientation can take 'a long time before definitively turning inward' (1978: 57). He also postulated a 'zone of proximal development' (1978: 86) which represents the reaching forward to the next stage of cognition or the 'processes that are currently in a state of formation, that are just beginning to mature and develop' (1978: 86). Significantly, this potential stage can actually be achieved 'under adult guidance or in collaboration with more capable peers' (1978: 87). In other words, learning and development can be accelerated with an injection of the right kind of collaboration. Historically, and for the reasons amplified below, the legal profession evolved through guild structures which supported opportunities for progressive development.

We also suggest that, as a rule of thumb, developing legal expertise takes time, perhaps no less than 10,000 hours or 10 years of challenging engagement within the discipline (Gladwell 2008). One implication of our distinction between different cultures of learning law, and something which law students are often surprised to hear suggested, is that this time frame really only begins upon admission to practise rather than at the point of entry into law school (some six years earlier in the Australian context). And to reinforce the point about developing recognised expertise over time, there is an account – which does not seem atypical – of a new Reader at Grays Inn who, in 1622, and following 'sanctioned advancement through the fixed hierarchy of ranks' and degrees of law, took 26 years to attain 'full maturity as a member of the inn' (Lemmings 2003: 58).

Further, in the legal practice setting, developed expertise goes beyond expert domain knowledge to include performance and application. In turn, according to Robert Sternberg, these are necessary but not sufficient conditions for the cultivation of wisdom, which he describes as a particular kind of practical thinking, applied towards the common good. The wise individual, says Sternberg:

- has 'much the same analytical reasoning ability as the intelligent individual … [but] has a certain sagacity not necessarily found in the intelligent person';
- 'listens to others, knows how to weigh advice, and knows how to deal with a variety of different kinds of people';
- 'reads between the lines as well as making use of the obviously available information';
- 'is especially able to make clear, sensible and fair judgments, and in doing so, takes a long-term as well as a short-term view of the consequences of the judgments made';
- profits 'from the experience of others' and learns from their own and others' mistakes';
- 'is not afraid to change his or her mind as experience dictates';
- offers solutions to complex problems which tend to be the right ones; and
- is 'a conserver of worldly experience' (Sternberg 2003: 158).

The culture of lawyers, then, is conducive not only to developing expertise but also to the cultivation of wisdom. The key aspect here is law in action. As Sternberg says, '[w]isdom is not just a way of thinking about things; it is a way of doing things. If people wish to be wise, they have to act wisely, not just think wisely' (Sternberg 2003: 158). Accordingly, one should not be surprised to find wisdom prevalent amongst those with 10 years or more experience.

It follows that, to the extent that legal education is directed towards achieving acculturation and adaptation to the patterns of thinking, language and argument of lawyers, then the importance of interaction and discussion is highlighted. In other words, the object of legal education is not so much learning 'the rules' or 'the skills' (in any narrow, deconstructed sense) as developing a certain capacity for social and professional interaction – and of discipline-specific mind and talk.

Kohlberg's Stages: Reasoning About Justice and Morality

If it is accepted that learning within the discipline of law may be painted as a broad image of mind and talk rather than just as Langdell's 'case-book method' – and if, as suggested above, expertise is propelled forward by the challenging experiences of 'cognitive conflict' inherent within the discipline – then Lawrence Kohlberg's framework for reasoning about justice and morality might usefully be applied. This framework offers a backdrop for comparing the two cultures of learning law and for situating PLE within (or, more accurately, across) those cultures.

Kohlberg's (1981, 1984) theory is built upon the earlier work of Piaget, which found that qualitatively different forms of reasoning emerge, although not inevitably so, with age. He identified four major stages of development to describe 'the organized cognitive possibilities and limits that characterize a child's thinking and feeling processes at a given point in the child's development' (Reimer et al. 1990: 25). Piaget's central ideas have withstood thousands of empirical studies and remain resilient and breathing. Kohlberg extends Piaget's work beyond childhood and argues for six distinct stages of reasoning about justice and morality. This developmental sequence is fixed in the sense that one cannot achieve a higher stage without first passing through the preceding stages. The later stages involve 'mastering cognitive operations that are logically more complex than the operations characterising the earlier stage' (Reimer et al 1990: 53). Further, one's reasoning can comprise a mixture of adjacent stages and can regress under stress (Reimer et al. 1990: 53).

Learning law as a student in Australia usually begins with entrance into a university law school at or about age 18. Moving beyond the developmental stages of childhood and early adolescence, longitudinal studies – albeit not confined to a law specific population – suggest that typically:

- from ages 16–18, 'stage 3 is predominant, with stages 1/2 and 2 continuing to fall off, stage 2/3 falling rapidly and stage 3/4 emerging strongly';
- from ages 20–22, 'stage 3/4 is predominant, with stages 1/2 and 2 dropping out, stage 2/3 continuing to fall off, stage 3 falling off slightly, and stage 4 emerging';

- from ages 24–30, 'stage 3/4 remains predominant, with stage 2/3 dropping out, stage 3 falling rapidly, and stage 4 holding at a minority position. Stage 4/5 first emerges'; and
- from ages 32–6, 'stage 4 rises to share the predominant position with stage 3/4. Stage 3 drops off, and stage 4/5 holds constant at a minority position' (Reimer et al. 1990: 100).

One conclusion drawn from Kohlberg's research is that stage 3, along with stage 4, represents 'the major stage for most adults in our society' (Reimer et al. 1990: 74). And while stage 3 'proves an adequate mode for dealing with most conflicts arising from people who know one another … [i]ts inadequacy surfaces when one must deal with problems at a societal level' (1990: 74). Stanley Greenspan reinforces this conclusion by noting that conflict resolution 'is not a purely cognitive enterprise or a rational weighing of options. It involves other capacities as well: the ability to empathize and a moral sensibility, both of which stem from mastery of the different levels of emotional development' (Greenspan 1997: 234).

It seems to follow that a stage 4 capacity for moral reasoning is a necessary condition for practising law in our society today. Indeed, it is said that '[l]aw emerges for stage 4 reasoners as a central value' (Reimer et al. 1990: 75).

The key transition required of legal education – through to the point of entry into the profession – is to facilitate the shift from a stage 3 to a stage 4 capacity for moral reasoning. In short, the required shift recognises that,

> … [w]hereas stage 3 role taking is primarily characterized by the ability to take the third-person perspective of *significant* others, stage 4 role taking is primarily characterized by the ability to take the shared point of view of the *generalized* other. That is, a person takes the perspective of the social system in which he participates: his institution, society, belief system, and so on (Reimer et al. 1990: 74).

In effect, this shift requires the remnants of a polarised – 'us versus them' and 'all or nothing' – mindset to be broken down. Within the specific context of conflict resolution, Greenspan amplifies the distinction underlying this necessary shift:

> Lasting resolution of conflicts demands a high level of moral development. It involves equitable, empathetic negotiation of the true needs of both parties. A resolution by which both parties give up a little and gain a little requires maturity on both sides. Immature but streetwise individuals, for their part, may negotiate merely to gain further advantages, not necessarily to resolve conflicts. Such 'resolutions' are rarely stable. The conflict is temporarily smoothed over until one party discovers that the box is empty (Greenspan 1997: 235).

Towards the start of this chapter we adopted an anthropological definition of 'culture' as the customs, ideas and social behaviour of Australian lawyers. It follows that, rather than just inculcating a capacity for 'thinking like a lawyer' or a cognitive-rational approach to dispute resolution within the narrow boundaries of Langdell's case-method, this shift demands a wider cultivation of a lawyerly perspective. And towards achieving this shift, while still recalling Vygotsky's 'zone of proximal development' mentioned above, the vital developmental impetus performed by 'collaboration with more capable peers' is reinforced (Vygotsky 1978: 87).

Situating Professional Legal Education

If we accept that there are two cultures of learning law, then where does PLE fit into such a scheme? Our own experience is drawn from the Australian National University (ANU), where the Graduate Diploma of Legal Practice (GDLP) program takes graduate law students and seeks to bring them up to the prescribed 'entry-level' standards of the Australian legal profession. In other words, students seeking to be admitted to practice in a ceremony held in one of the Australian State Supreme Courts must go beyond having a recognised law degree and passing various prescribed undergraduate law subjects (known as the 'Priestley 11'). Following graduation, students must also take a further course of studies (PLE) or articles of clerkship. For the PLE component, a set of competency standards developed by the Australasian Professional Legal Education Council (APLEC) have been adopted by the State admitting authorities (APLEC and LACC 2000).

Accordingly, we suggest that, rather than a 'bolted on' appendage to undergraduate law, PLE sits at a pivotal point in the transformation from 'learning as a student' to 'learning as a lawyer'. Our assumption is that PLE students – who generally come to us more or less adept at 'learning as a student' – need to be reorientated towards beginning to 'learn as a lawyer'. And part of this reorientation is to ensure that the shift from Kohlberg's stage 3 to stage 4 moral reasoning – and a capacity to 'get' law and grasp 'the societal point of view' – is firmly established.

We seek to represent life-long learning within the profession at large, and the pivotal position occupied by PLE, in the figure below. In this model we are integrating the learning journey of a person from first year undergraduate law through to status as a legal professional with recognised expertise. This combines academic and professional learning and experience in law over time.

- PAE = post-admission experience (years)
- UG = undergraduate (years)
- Kohlberg stages of reasoning about justice and morality (see Figure 7.1 opposite)

As described below, a new approach to PLE was adopted by ANU towards more effectively orientating students away from the culture of 'learning as a student' and towards the culture of 'learning as a lawyer'. Central to this approach has been student-mentor collaboration and group-work.

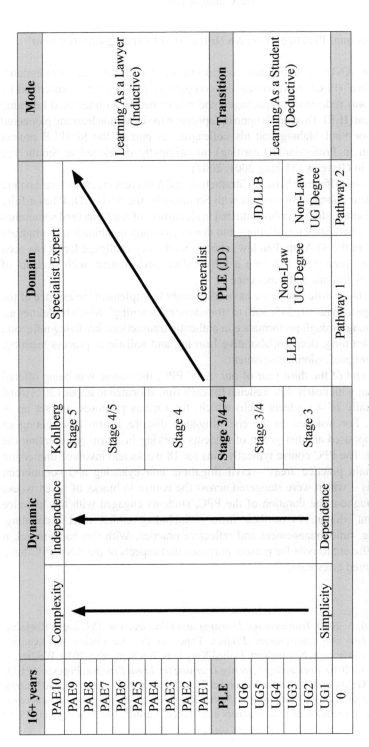

Figure 7.1 Life-long learning in law (developing expertise)

16+ years	Dynamic		Domain	Mode
	Complexity	Independence	Kohlberg	
PAE10			Stage 5	Learning As a Lawyer (Inductive)
PAE9				
PAE8			Stage 4/5	
PAE7				Specialist Expert
PAE6				
PAE5			Stage 4	
PAE4				
PAE3				Generalist
PAE2				
PAE1				
PLE			Stage 3/4–4	PLE (JD)	Transition
UG6			Stage 3/4		JD/LLB
UG5				Non-Law UG Degree	Non-Law UG Degree
UG4			Stage 3		Learning As a Student (Deductive)
UG3				LLB	
UG2					
UG1	Simplicity	Dependence		Pathway 1	Pathway 2
0					

The Professional Practice Core: An 'Integrated Learning Environment'

In 2010 at ANU, a significant component of the GDLP, the 'Professional Practice Core' (PPC), representing the compulsory practice areas prescribed by APLEC – was redesigned, repackaged and relaunched as an Integrated Learning Environment (ILE). This builds upon the approach to simulation learning pioneered by Professor Paul Maharg and his colleagues as part of the SIMPLE project (SIMulation in Professional Learning), as originally developed at Strathclyde University in Glasgow (Maharg 2001, 2007).

The central difference between Strathclyde and ANU reflects the different nature of the student cohorts. By contrast with Strathclyde, the ANU GDLP has a fully external, distance student cohort situated in all corners of Australia (and sometimes overseas), across State jurisdictions and drawn from any combination of graduate students from the 32 Australian law schools. So the key challenge for us has been to adapt our version of ILE into a fully online environment, with students of variable backgrounds and experience.

Despite these differences, we have still sought to implement the essence of the Maharg approach (2001: 345, 360) to 'transactional learning', which he defines as: active learning through performance in authentic transactions involving reflection in and on learning, deep collaborative learning and holistic or process learning, with relevant professional assessment.

By the end of the third year of our 'new' PPC, the course was being offered twice a year, with nearly 450 students for each run, allocated to about 120 'virtual firms' (usually of 4 students each) which, for various purposes, are set up in opposition. For instance, in the civil litigation dispute, a firm representing an applicant opposed another group of students working in a firm representing the respondent. The PPC course typically runs for 18 weeks and involved immersion in three main practice areas – civil litigation, conveyancing and commercial transactions – which were staggered across the course in blocks of seven weeks each. Throughout the duration of the PPC, students engaged with the 'practice management' dimension of their firms – including ethics, trust accounting, file-keeping, time-management and reflective practice. With this background, it may be sufficient to note for present purposes that aspects of the ANU PPC have been presented elsewhere.[4]

---

4   Steed, A. 2010. *Transactional Learning at a Distance: The ANU Legal Workshop Integrated Learning Environment Project.* Paper to the Association for Learning Technology conference, Nottingham, United Kingdom, 7–9 September 2010; Webbey, S. and Collins, C. 2010. *Facilitating Effective Learning for Legal Practice.* Paper to APLEC conference, Gold Coast, Australia, November 2010; Westwood, F., Rowe, M. and Murray, M. 2011. *From Kilts to Kangaroos – Embedding professionalism in legal education.* Paper to the Association of Law Teachers conference, Cardiff, United Kingdom, 15–17 April 2011.

Making the Transition: From Learning as a Student to Learning as a Lawyer

The educational psychologist, David Ausubel, famously said:

> If I had to reduce all of educational psychology to just one principle, I would say
> this: The most important single factor influencing learning is what the learner
> already knows. Ascertain this and teach him accordingly (Ausubel 1968: 63).

> We would adopt, but also extend this (if necessary, for the avoidance of any doubt)
> to include, 'how the learner already learns'. And, further, 'effective teaching must
> tune in to the [person's] own developmental level' (Greenspan 1997: 221).

One striking feature of the new PPC for us has been the extent to which we find students habituated, and unable quickly to adapt, from the culture of learning as a student. For some students, this translates to considerable discomfort, if not active resistance, towards learning in any other way. Common student pleas towards the start of the PPC – reflecting the curriculum structure of undergraduate learning – include 'just give me the content' or 'just tell me what to do'. By simulating legal practice and engaging practically with transactional learning, students must necessarily grapple with fewer 'givens' as a starting point.

Accordingly, we suggest that it is important not to underestimate the extent to which we are inducing 'cognitive conflict' in students, at the level of metacognition, causing them at least to become conscious of, if not question, their own unstated assumptions about the nature and scope of learning law. Indeed, this is one of our objectives, particularly with the aid of periodic reflection tasks.

One thing has become clear to us through the early iterations of the PPC: it is neither effective nor desirable just to lift students out of their 'learning as a student' culture and then drop them straight into a 'learning as a lawyer' simulation, and expect them to apply their pre-existing knowledge and skills in this new environment without much more. The 'culture shock' of doing so might be just as dramatic as that experienced by a law student entering a law-firm and being expected to perform without any PLE, prior experience of the practice of law or exposure to the culture of lawyers.

It follows, we suggest, that the PPC necessarily includes a combination of both approaches to learning law – the deductive mode (the way students already know how to learn law, as brought into the PPC from their LLB or JD studies) and also the inductive mode (with which they are more or less unfamiliar, depending upon exposure to working in law firms – perhaps as paralegals, secretaries or summer clerks).

In structural and design terms, this has led to the solidification of, and sharper demarcation between, these two cultures of learning within the overall online learning space of the PPC. In effect, the PPC website (Wattle) presents as a space with many components that will be familiar to students from past learning experience and which still facilitates individual learning and assessment.

Taking the Civil Litigation Practice Area of the PPC as an example, the website included: a course outline; educational task guidelines; references and materials in a searchable library database (cross-referenced from the guidelines); and a discussion forum for engaging directly with the Civil Litigation convenor. Perhaps the main difference for students was the inversion of the usual hierarchy of deductive student learning – with 'the task' now foregrounded and the discursive materials and text extracts concerning relevant fields of law buried within the library, to be drawn upon only as necessary and relevant to the task.

As the PPC course progresses, students were increasingly expected to immerse themselves in the Virtual Office Space (VOS) – and to engage with their peers, 'characters' and opponents through there and only have recourse to the Wattle website as necessary (for supporting materials) or as a last resort (for resolving task queries).

Group Learning within the PPC

Of course, activity within the VOS does not in fact replicate the professional practice environment, nor does it attempt to do so – the constraints of time, technology and curriculum make this impossible. As Maharg (2007: 184) says, 'simulation, though, is not reality'. We only take aspects of the professional practice environment (or, for the VOS, fragments of a legal practitioner's psyche – as per the characters) for the teaching and reorientation purposes identified above.

In seeking to construct a crucible for learning, and by reference to Figure 6.2, within the VOS Civil Litigation practice area we sought to generate five key conditions or features of relative emphasis, namely:

- widening context;
- elevated dynamic;
- practical, not academic, mode of learning;
- learning as a lawyer, not as a student; and
- developing self-efficacy as the primary motivation.

Widening Context

The undergraduate focus upon primary sources of law was opened up within the VOS to expose students to more of the surrounding context. Whereas at undergraduate level facts are a 'given' in the task of applying law, students within the VOS were exposed to the uncertainty and ambiguity of 'messy' and incomplete facts. Further, performing within the VOS recognises that the task of taking instructions from a client is not something which occurs within a laboratory but, rather, as something frequently overlaid with the emotion and angst of a real person. The widening of context also introduces other elements of realism, such as the constraints of time and resources. Students of a 'perfectionist' disposition had to adapt and make the shift from 'being right' towards 'exercising judgment' within client- and court-imposed constraints of time and cost.

Elevated Dynamic

The widening context mentioned above serves to generate an elevated dynamic of learning, with shifting expectations of students moving from dependence towards independence, and from simplicity towards complexity (see Figure 6.2). Student pleas about what to read or what to do were met by in-character senior lawyers within the VOS pointing to the client problem as the starting point before asking students to propose their own answers to those questions. In this way, students are guided towards independent self-sufficiency and a level of exposure to working within a 'shades of grey' environment. These progressions are captured in Robert Sternberg's 'developing-expertise' model (Sternberg 2003: 72), which recognizes that:

> ... [t]he novice works towards expertise through deliberate practice ... Eventually, one reaches a kind of expertise, at which one becomes a reflective practitioner of a certain set of skills. But expertise occurs at many levels. The expert first-year graduate or law student, for example, is still a far cry from the expert professional. People thus proceed through many cycles on the way to successively higher levels of expertise (Sternberg 2003: 74–5).

Importantly, students are challenged for their usual tendency to take a one-sided or partisan perspective of their client's problem – perhaps when overstating the chances of success or turning a blind eye to glaring deficiencies with their own case. This dialogical testing helps students to acquire and demonstrate Kohlberg's stage 4 capacity for reasoning about justice and morality – and to adopt 'the societal point of view' necessary for professionalism.

Practical, Not Academic, Mode of Learning

Sternberg observes that analytical abilities 'are engaged when information-processing components are applied to relatively familiar problems that are largely academic because they are abstracted from the substance of everyday life' (Sternberg 2003: xiv). He distinguishes analytical intelligence from practical intelligence which, he finds, 'derives largely from the acquisition and utilization of *tacit knowledge* – the procedural knowledge not explicitly taught and often not even verbalized that one needs to know to succeed in an environment' (Sternberg 2003: xv).

Accordingly, the Civil Litigation component of the VOS was constructed to allow for the kind of incidental interaction by which tacit knowledge is gained – in this case, by creating a virtual tea-room within each firm. This space was utilised by an experienced lawyer performing the character of 'Shelly Yu' popping into the tea-room for informal interludes. The Shelly character was an Associate of the law firm just 2–3 years more experienced than the student practitioners (refer above to Vygotsky's 'zone of proximal development'). By contrast with formal instruction in law, Shelly offered a friendly source of support – offering incidental tips, asides, insights, hints and revelations, help with framing the right question, directing attention by asking 'have you considered ...', and suggestions for thinking laterally about the client problem.

In addition, Sternberg notes that 'teaching for practical thinking is teaching students to adopt certain attitudes in their intellectual work', including:

  a. combating the tendency to procrastinate;
  b. organizing oneself to get one's work done;
  c. figuring out how one learns best;
  d. avoiding the tendency to use self-pity as an excuse for working hard; and
  e. avoiding blaming others for one's own failings (Sternberg 2003: 81).

Towards achieving this end, each virtual firm was allocated a 'Practice Mentor' to support the substantive work on the Civil Litigation client tasks. The importance of teaching a practical mode of learning at PLE level is reinforced when it is recognized that practical intelligence is the bridge linking analytical intelligence (emphasised at undergraduate level) with our ideal of the wise legal expert.

Learning as a Lawyer, Not as a Student

The shift from learning as a student towards learning as a lawyer is discussed at length above. Within the VOS, we moved from deductive to inductive learning – where the process begins with a real problem, not with the law. The VOS was populated by a community of lawyers, including: the task-master (an experienced practitioner performing the character of Senior Partner) – also modelling effective supervision and leadership; the Practice Mentor (as mentioned above); a helpful (one step above peer) guide and source of encouragement and support (Shelly Yu); and peer-to-peer support (for example where, in a real firm, the article clerk intake for a given year tends to bind together). This collaboration and support structure fosters opportunities for breaking through to, or cementing, Kohlberg's stage 4.

Developing Self-efficacy as the Primary Motivation

Self-efficacy motivation refers to 'persons' beliefs in their own ability to solve the problem at hand' (Sternberg 2003: 74). Indeed, such motivation sits at the centre of, and propels, Sternberg's developing-expertise model (Sternberg 2003: 74–5). Within the VOS, and consistently with Radding's above characterisation of the crucible of the courts, students must face up to the (virtual) reality of what a client, opposing lawyer, court official (or even judge) might say about their work and/or professionalism.

Collaboration Within the Crucible

Accordingly, within our constructed crucible and towards students forging a professional *persona* of their own, we surround them with virtual characters tasked with shaping and influencing their sense of 'what is considered respectable, worthy and desirable' with the chosen circle of the profession. The various supporting roles – real and fictional – both within the Wattle site and the VOS may be summarised as follows:

Wattle: Learning as a Student		VOS: Learning as a Lawyer	
Project Convenors	Teacher-student	Senior Partner#	Task-master/standards
Practice Mentors	Teacher-student	Associate#	Helpful guide/ motivator
GDLP Help	Help-desk	Client#	Standards/satisfaction
		Opposing lawyer*	Probing for weakness/ opportunistic
		Peer colleague*	Mutual support

= *expe*rienced lawyers in-character; * = student roles

Figure 7.2   List of PPC supporting roles

Importantly, the simulation nature of the VOS means that this is still a safe and supported environment where students can afford to make mistakes and learn from them without causing 'real' harm to their clients or their own professional reputations.

Conclusion

We have sought to demonstrate our central argument that, at the vital pivot-point represented by PLE, a 'collaboration of voices' – or 'group-work' – is not only an effective, but also necessary, crucible for inculcating a basic, entry-level competency with the language, processes, customs, ethics and social behaviour (or culture) of Australian lawyers.

At the same time, learning law by collaboration and verbal intercourse reconnects with modes of cultural transmission represented by the common law tradition. In many ways, lawyers have always – and still do – learn in this particular kind of way. And, to the extent that undergraduate law students may be shielded by universities from this fundamental precept of our vocation, their development within the discipline is not only stunted, but diminished. The 'calling of law', then, remains something muffled, remote and elusive through the university learning phase – even as entry-level law students (by their thousands) purport to respond to 'the call'.

And yet, the object of practising law at a level of developed expertise both requires – and reflects – an advanced cognitive capacity for reasoning about justice and morality (not just 'law' in its narrowest sense). Through these qualities of mind and talk, the culture of lawyers has a powerful and shaping influence upon our wider culture – upon society, or our nation, at large. The culture of lawyers contributes to the critical mass of reflective thinkers, social conscience and institutionalised structures necessary 'to maintain a society that is both stable and creative, both cohesive and flexible' (Greenspan 1997: 300) – and as a bulwark against polarization, resort to violence and tyranny, especially when society falls under pressure.

By connecting with this larger purpose, surely the culture of learning as a lawyer, the cultivation of a 'lawyerly perspective', the development of professional *persona*, the acquisition of a high-order moral sensibility, the collegiality of our vocation and the attainment of recognised expertise (even practical wisdom) within our discipline ought to be sufficient goals for heeding the 'warm breath' of 'the calling of law'.

References

APLEC and LACC (2000), *Competency Standards for Entry Level Lawyers*. Available at: http://www.aplec.asn.au/Pdf/Competency_Standards_for_Entry_Level_Lawyers.pdf, [accessed at 13 March 2009].
Atkinson, A. (1997), *The Europeans in Australia: A History*. Volume 1 of 3. Melbourne: Oxford University Press.
Ausubel, D. (1968), *Educational Psychology: A Cognitive View*. Austin: Holt, Rinehart and Winston.
Ayto, J. (1990), *Bloomsbury Dictionary of Word Origins*. London: Bloomsbury.
Burridge, R. and Webb, J. (2008), 'The Values of Common Law Education Reprised', *The Law Teacher*, 42(3).
Campbell, R. (1977), *A History of the Melbourne Law School, 1857–1973*. Parkville Vic.: Faculty of Law, University of Melbourne.
Collins, C. (2007), 'The Discipline of Law: A Developmental and Historical Perspective', *Australian Law Postgraduate Network Paper Series* 1. Available at: http://www.alpn.edu.au/publications/2007-alpn-paper-series [Online].
Fogel, A. (1993), *Development through Relationships: Origins of Communication, Self and Culture*. Chicago: University of Chicago Press.
Fukuyama, F. (1996), *Trust: The Social Virtues and the Creation of Prosperity*. London: Penguin.
Ginsburg, H. and Opper, S. (1979), *Piaget's Theory of Intellectual Development*. 2nd Ed. Englewood Cliffs NJ: Prentice-Hall.
Gladwell, M. (2008), *Outliers*. New York: Little: Brown & Co.

Greenspan, S. (1997), *The Growth of the Mind: And the Endangered Origins of Intelligence*. New York: Addison- Wesley.

Hare, J. (2011), 'Business takes a dim view of academe', *The Australian – Higher Education Supplement*, 29.

Jung, C.G. (1954), *The Development of the Personality (Volume 17 of the Collected Works), translated by R.F.C. Hull*. London: Routledge & Kegan Paul.

Kohlberg, L. (1981), *Essay on Moral Development, Vol. 1: The Philosophy of Moral Development*. New York. Harper & Row.

Kohlberg, L. (1984), *Essay on Moral Development, Vol. 2: The Psychology of Moral Development – The Nature and Validity of Moral Stages*. New York. Harper & Row.

Lemmings, D. (2003), 'Ritual, Majesty and Mystery: Collective Life and Culture among English barristers, serjeants and Judges, c. 1500 – c. 1830', in *Lawyers and Vampires: Cultural Histories of Legal Professions*, edited by W. Wesley Pue and D. Sugarmann. Oxford and Portland, Oregon: Hart Publishing.

Lobban, M. (1991), *The Common Law and English Jurisprudence 1760–1850*. Oxford: Clarendon Press.

Maharg, P. (2001), 'Negotiating the Web: Legal Skills Learning in a Virtual Community', *International Review of Law, Computers & Technology*, 15(3).

Maharg, P. (2007), *Transforming Legal Education: Learning and Teaching the Law in the Early Twenty-first Century*. Hampshire: Ashgate Publishing.

Maister, D. (1997), *True Professionalism: The courage to care about your people, your clients and your career*. New York: The Free Press.

Radding, C. (1985), *A World Made by Men: Cognition and Society, 400–1200*. Chapel Hill: University of North Carolina Press.

Reimer, J., Paolitto, D. and Hersh, R. (1990), *Promoting Moral Growth: From Piaget to Kohlberg*. Illinois: Waveland Press, Inc.

Robertson, G. (2006), *The Tyrannicide Brief: The story of the man who sent Charles I to the scaffold*. Australia: Vintage Books.

Ross, P. (24 July 2006), 'The Expert Mind' in *Scientific American*: [Online]. Available at: http://www.cerebyte.com/articles/Scientific%20American%20 Neuroplasticity.pdf.

Sells, B. (1994), *The Soul of the Law*. Rockport, MA: Element.

Steed, A. (2010), *Transactional Learning at a Distance: The ANU Legal Workshop Integrated Learning Environment Project*. Paper to the Association for Learning Technology conference, Nottingham, United Kingdom, 7–9 September 2010.

Sternberg, R. (2003), *Wisdom, Intelligence and Creativity Synthesized*. Cambridge: Cambridge University Press.

Stevenson, A. (2007), *Shorter Oxford Dictionary*. Oxford: Oxford University Press.

Teo, H. and White, R. (2003), *Cultural History in Australia*. Kensington: University of New South Wales Press.

Twining, W. (1994), *Blackstone's Tower: The English Law School*. Hamlyn Lectures. London: Sweet and Maxwell.

Vygotsky, L. (1978), *Mind in Society: The Development of Higher Psychological Processes*. Harvard: Harvard University Press.

Webbey, S. and Collins, C. (2010), *Facilitating Effective Learning for Legal Practice*. Paper to APLEC conference, Gold Coast, Australia, November 2010.

Westwood, F., Rowe, M. and Murray, M. (2011), *From Kilts to Kangaroos – Embedding Professionalism in Legal Education*. Paper to the Association of Law Teachers conference, Cardiff, United Kingdom, 15–17 April 2011.

White, J.B. (1994), *Justice as Translation*. Chicago: University of Chicago Press.

Wickes, F. (1988), *The Inner World of Man*. London: Sigo Press.

Chapter 8
Standardized Clients in Asia – University of Hong Kong's Experience

Wilson Chow and Michael Ng[1]

Introduction

Originating from the 'standardized patients' commonly used in American medical schools since the early 1960s,[2] 'standardized clients' (SCs) were first used in the Effective Lawyer-Client Communication (ELCC) project in 1998: four law school clinics, three from the United States and one from Australia, participated (Barton et al. 2006).[3] The ELCC project was designed to, through empirical research on client interviewing, look for ways to evaluate and enhance lawyer-client communication (Cunningham 1999).

The second phase of the ELCC began in 2005 when Cunningham, together with Professor Jean Ker of the Clinical Skills Centre, Medical Faculty (Dundee University), and Barton, Maharg and Westwood, conducted an international collaborative project in the Glasgow Graduate School of Law (Barton et al. 2006). Later in 2007, the interviewing of clients became a part of the assessment for the postgraduate Diploma in Legal Practice in Scotland (Cunningham 2011). The Solicitors Regulation Authority in England and Wales adapted the heuristic in its Qualifying Lawyers Transfer Scheme in 2011 (Fry, Crewe and Wakeford 2012). Also in 2011, the University of Northumbria Law School started using SCs in preparing their third level undergraduate students for their mandatory clinical work (Maharg 2011). The Law Society of Ireland joined in and made use of SCs in a part of their professional programs (Standardized Client Initiative Blog 2011).

Back to its homeland in the US, after the Grosberg's pilot at the New York Law School in 2001 (Grosberg 2001, 2006), the Daniel Webster Scholar Honors Program

---

1   The authors would like to thank Taki Chan for her assistance in collection and analysis of data for this chapter.

2   Those 'patients' are 'people with or without actual disease who have been trained to portray a medical case in a consistent fashion' to coach and to assess patient care and interviewing skills of medical students, for details see Barrows (1993).

3   The four law schools clinics included: Monash University School of Law (Melbourne, Australia); Brigham Young University Law School (Provo, Utah); New York University Law School (New York City); and Case Western Reserve University School of Law (Cleveland, Ohio).

provided by the University of New Hampshire School of Law added an additional assessment with SCs to enhance their training on students' communication skills in 2008, which has also been made a bar competency criteria since 2009 (Garvey and Zinkin 2009).

In Australia, the Graduate Diploma in Legal Practice of the Australian National University introduced the standardized client initiative to facilitate students' learning on interviewing skills with clients in 2011 (Rowe 2011) and, independently, the University of Adelaide's law school developed standardized clients on its programmes. Apart from Australia, SCs had not crossed to other parts of the other side of the Pacific. Hong Kong is its first stop in Asia.

The Clients at HKU

A former colony of the British Empire, Hong Kong inherited from England and Wales the common law system and the basic structure of legal education and training. Developed simultaneously with the deliberations of the Ormrod Committee, undergraduate legal education leading to the award of a Bachelor of Laws degree has been provided at the University of Hong Kong (HKU) since 1969. At the same time, a working party was formed to consider models for examinations leading to professional qualification in Hong Kong. Evans (1989) recalled that the working party, having first accepted the division of legal education into the three stages suggested in the Ormrod Report (1971), namely the academic stage, the professional stage and the training stage, recommended an expanded Department of Law both as an organizational vehicle for mounting and examining the professional courses and also as a guarantee of standards. Hence, the professional stage undertaken by a year of postgraduate study leading to the award of the Postgraduate Certificate in Laws (PCLL) had been provided exclusively by HKU until 1991 when City University of Hong Kong set up the second PCLL in Hong Kong.

For almost 30 years since its inception, the HKU PCLL comprised the same seven subjects. At all those times, it adopted a mix of learning methodologies including prescribed reading, lecturing, tutorials and for advocacy training, watching video demonstrations and scheduled court visits; the relative weight attached and hence time allocated to each of those methods, however, changed from time to time. Catalysed by the first ever review of legal education and training in Hong Kong in 2000, the HKU PCLL had undergone a major reform with an increasing emphasis to the training of lawyering skills, both oral and written. Despite a general level of satisfaction overall and high levels of satisfaction with some of the reformed courses, students still found it difficult to practically apply the legal knowledge which they learnt from their studies to solve real legal problems. Specifically, the graduate surveys conducted by the Law Society of Hong Kong, though with improving results over the years of reform, indicated that training in communication skill had not been sufficiently stressed.

Unlike medical students who have the benefit of training with real patients, skills training in interviewing, advising, negotiation, mediation and advocacy at the HKU PCLL has been relying on mostly full-time and part-time teachers who are professionally qualified, sometimes students and occasionally amateur actors who are friends of the teachers in charge, to play the role of a fictitious characters of a pre-set scenario on paper. While briefing before training is invariably conducted, review of the recordings of some of these performances suggests discrepancies in approaches. In all circumstances, student lawyers are being graded by the teachers and the teachers alone with reference to a skill guide of relevant criteria but without detailed and elaborative rubrics. As explained by Chow and Tiba (2013), the current circumstances of Hong Kong do not allow internships and a clinical course for even the majority of law students. The use of SCs can be considered a viable hybrid between, in the terms of Dale (1969), 'simulation' and 'doing the real thing' and useful for developing students' communicative competence.

Every new initiative requires additional resources to take off from the ground. It would not have been possible to bring the first group of SCs home in Hong Kong but for the funding support from HKU where the application for funding identified the Will, Trusts and Estate Planning elective (WTEP) as the base for the pilot project. Specifically, students would be interviewing SCs on two occasions, once as a practice and another for assessment purposes, and in both events followed by their drafting of a will. On the basis that the elective had been attracting 70 to 80 students each year, funding was asked for recruiting 10 SCs, each to be interviewed by seven to eight students on two half days. In addition, provision was requested for their attendance in a three-day intensive training workshop following the GGSL model. In figuring out how much SCs would be paid, reference was drawn to the daily rate adopted by the GGSL a few years ago. In any event, after the mark-up, the rate was still much lower than that for a part-time teacher. Given that this is ground-breaking and among the first of its kind in Asia, separate funding was applied for inviting overseas trainers to conduct the inaugural training at HKU. Both applications received approvals from the University committees making the decisions.

Standardizing Recruitment

Funding secured, time was taken to decide the main characters and backdrops against which the two scenarios were going to be built. In the preceding year, students had two wills-drafting exercises for the same fictitious wealthy young lady, first when she was set to be at the age of 30s and then at the age of 50s, based on different written instructions prepared by teachers. Students did the same first drafting exercise this year, but before they had the second one they met the SCs to take instructions. In another two weeks' time, each student met a different client on an unrelated scenario for the assessment. Once the basic scheme was laid out and agreed in December 2012, the recruitment process began.

The idea of open recruitment was considered not practicable. Additional resources would be required for even a simple advertisement and the selection process which could be time-consuming and ineffective. Instead, recruitment through personal connections was preferred. With the idea and the concrete plan of how the SCs would facilitate learning in the pilot project made known to them, three faculty members agreed to ask around among their inner circles of friends for suitable SCs, the target group being middle-aged housewives who were lay to the legal profession and could converse reasonably well in English.

It subsequently transpired that there were several challenges to those recruitment strategies. First, housewives in Hong Kong are no less busy than full-time office ladies even though most household chores nowadays are being taken care of by domestic helpers. Apart from devoting most of their time and energy to the upbringing and nurturing of their children, they have and enjoy their own personal lives. A three-day intensive workshop from nine to five each of those days, together with the commitment to come back half a day each for both the practice and the assessment, was too onerous for them. Second, the training days fell on the week following that of the Chinese New Year when some families might still be on vacations particularly if not all schools would be resumed by then. Hopefully these challenges would not be too much concern again next time round for another group of new SCs when training could be done in-house by faculty members at HKU who had participated and learnt from the inaugural one and by then the workshop could be scheduled at a different time with the three days being spread over at least two weeks.

Towards the end of January 2013, people not only confirmed their attendance, but they inquired if their friends could also join in. Amazingly, the idea had travelled fast through and by the first group of SCs. The final 10 SCs recruited all meet the standard criteria, sharing more or less the same background with only very minor variation. They come from quite well-off families, at least the middle class, and so should have little difficulty in understanding the concerns and hence playing the role of a lady with a number of valuable assets and family members. A few of them still have jobs but they can manage their time relatively easily. Although they came in as a few distinct groups of friends and each of them must have her own personality, they mingled well and quickly by the end of the first day. All of them were interested in the project and so they came well-prepared and participated fully and enthusiastically, which made the training most effective.

Standardizing Clienting

Taken from the GGSL model, the three-day training at HKU was divided into three parts, namely general role-playing training, familiarization and practice of scenarios and scripts and assessment training and standardization. These training activities were closely linked with the training outcomes that constituted key objective of the Scottish SCs: ensuring *validity* and *reliability* of using SCs for examining communicative competence of law students (Barton et al. 2006). The training of role-playing and familiarization of scenarios and scripts were aimed at enhancing the reliability of SCs' assessment by building up consistency in delivery of scripted response, articulation of scenarios and emotive expressions. Assessment training was aimed at allowing SCs to standardize their views and reach a common understanding of what should be identified as competent and non-competent responses of student lawyers so that the SCs' assessment results are as reliable and valid as teachers' assessment.

After being orientated to the background and development of the pedagogy, the SCs were introduced to the concept and objectives of standardization, as well as their role to act as both a client and an assessor in interviewing assessments of student lawyers. They were then divided into five pairs, with one being the interviewer and the other the interviewee. The interviewer was asked to gather enough personal information about her interviewee within ten minutes so that she is able to speak about the general background of the interviewee. The interviewee, on top of responding to questions asked by the interviewer, also offered additional information if she thought the information to be appropriate in forming a general personal description of her. This exercise not only served as an ice-breaking session but also enabled the SCs to familiarize themselves with the rapport of one-to-one interviewing. The SCs were also reminded of the importance of being able to clearly relay requisite information, listen carefully to the questioner, develop congruence with one's feelings and act appropriately (but not over-act) in the capacity of an interviewee and were trained to be so. This was the first step in standardizing SCs' ability to speak as a lay client, which we term as the process of standardizing clienting.

The second step to standardize clienting began when SCs were distributed with the initial set of facts and a scenario that they would later use for the practice session with student lawyers one week later. From the experience at HKU, a thorough discussion of the facts among the trainers and the SCs first, instead of rushing them into role-playing, has been found to be an important standardizing activity that gives an opportunity not only for the SCs to familiarize themselves with the facts and scripts and to empathize with a client's feelings under the given scenario, but also for them to go through as a group what would be the possible questions asked by a student lawyer and the most appropriate reaction to those questions. More importantly, the discussion could clear up any ambiguities or misunderstandings regarding the given facts. At the end of the discussion, SCs were clearer about the key facts regarding the client and her instructions to prepare the will, a list of anticipated questions from the student lawyers and a list of corresponding scripted responses.

After the deliberation on the facts and scenario scripts, a number of SCs were randomly chosen to role-play the scenario with HKU faculty members who acted as the interviewing lawyer. Trainers and other SCs observed the interviews and at the end of each interview commented on the performance of the client. The core areas for observation and comments were: (1) whether the client could accurately relay the information to the lawyer; (2) whether the client could act naturally and yet express appropriate emotive responses according to the given scenario; (3) whether the client could avoid proactively offering too much information to the lawyer without being first asked about the relevant questions. As mentioned above, the SCs considered the training seriously and had memorized the facts of the initial exercise, which were emailed to them a few days in advance, before they came for the first day. In such circumstances, most of them were able to act and deliver naturally most of the scripted information to the interviewing faculty members. Before the end of the first day's training, the trainers summarized and highlighted the common mistakes in acting and expression and helped refine the scenario scripts wherever necessary, with the input from the SCs from the client's perspective. They then further rehearsed with the SCs in groups all the important questions and scripted answers that could occur from the scenario so as to strengthen SCs' memorization. Through this practice and feedback session the SCs were able to build confidence, experience and consistency in interacting with our student lawyers. This marked the final step of this part of the standardization process, before the training moved on to standardizing assessment.

Standardizing Assessment

The validity and reliability of SCs' assessment also depends on how best their understanding and use of the assessment criteria and instrument to rate student lawyers' communicative competence can be standardized. Adopted basically from the refined GGSL assessment form which resembled that used in medical education by standardized patients in the United States (Barton et al. 2006), Part A of the HKU form dealt with the SCs' scores regarding the communicative competence demonstrated by the student lawyers. Among the eight items listed under Part A were:

1. The greeting and introduction by the student lawyer was appropriate;
2. I felt the student lawyer listened to me;
3. The student lawyer approach to questioning was helpful;
4. The student lawyer accurately summarised my situation;
5. I understood what the student lawyer was saying;
6. I felt comfortable with the student lawyer;
7. I would feel confident with the student lawyer dealing with my situation; and
8. If I had a new legal problem I would come back to this student lawyer.

Items 1, 6 and 7 relate to the general rapport of the interviewing session, items 2 to 5 concern the information exchange that took place during the interview and the last item represents an overall customer's satisfaction level. Generally speaking, items 1 to 7 can be rated based on the behaviour or verbal expression made by the student lawyers during the interview and hence a relatively more objective testing; whereas the last item entails relatively subjective feelings of the SCs. The SCs were required to assign a positive score (1–5) to each of these items, in ascending order corresponding to the level of competence, so that the higher the score achieved by the student means the higher level of communicative competence he/she has attained.

Part B is a case-specific checklist where SCs are required to confirm if the student lawyer has asked the SC-specific questions that were deemed by the designer-teacher of the scenario as necessary questions for completing a good first meeting for taking instructions to prepare the will. SCs are expected to check the boxes of the 'Yes' column if these questions were asked by the interviewing student lawyers. Part C is not to be assessed by the SCs but by the teacher from the file notes recorded by the student immediately after the interview.

Most of the training time was spent teaching the SCs how to apply ratings in Part A in a standardized way because this part is more vulnerable to influence of subjective impression, as compared to the checking of factual responses under the list of Part B. To standardize SCs' ratings on Part A and to minimize the influence of subjective impression on the assessment, a detailed rubric of scoring for all the eight items, originated from the GGSL design (Barton et al. 2006: 61–4) was provided to the SCs. This rubric, containing a total of 40 explanations (one for each of the eight items with five scores each), was explained in plain language, covering the kind of circumstances where SCs should assign a particular score in a particular item. Through a discussion led by the trainers over the meaning and implication of the content of each of the 40 boxes the SCs appreciated and understood that their ratings should be based on evidence and guidelines, and that the ratings should not resemble an expression of general customer satisfaction level. The trainers facilitated the discussion by giving examples of how particular responses and behaviour of a student lawyer would amount to the circumstances that each box described. After the discussion, the SCs went into the practice of standardizing assessment.

The practice session for standardizing assessment held at the GGSL in 2006 asked their SCs and tutors to practise assessing by watching the videotaped interview sessions previously held. Since it was the first time for HKU to run a project of this kind, no such recordings were available. It was decided to have HKU teachers play the role of the student lawyers and interview the SCs in turn. It had also been agreed among the trainers and the role-playing teachers, who had known the facts and instructions to SCs based on the scripted scenario, that some teachers would perform competently while others would deliberately be below standard by, for example, failing to summarize at the end of the meeting what the client said, lacking interest in the client's situation, asking questions aimlessly or interrupting a conversation frequently. While one of the SCs was being interviewed, the rest of the group and teachers assessed the interviewing lawyer and marked it on their own assessment form. After each practice interview, all observing SCs and teachers were asked to report their scores under Part A of the form. After noting all the scores awarded by SCs and teachers in an Excel spreadsheet shown on a projector screen, trainers began to compare the SCs' scores for each item, first among SCs themselves and then with the scores awarded by the teachers, which to an extent formed the 'HKU standard score'. Trainers and teachers then discussed the rationale behind teachers' scores and allowed SCs to share their views on, and feelings about, the divergence and variation. Those wide of the mark were particularly highlighted so as to allow further discussion. From the comparisons, explanations and further discussion over all 10 grounds of practice, the SCs were able to form a common understanding of how to apply Part A's ratings and came to know better how they would interpret the lawyers' responses and behaviour so that their future ratings would be brought back to the HKU-standard level.

These were witnessed by the much narrower margin both among the SCs' score and between the average SCs' scores and the teachers' scores. The assessment was getting *standardized* by and through the training sessions. Before the Day-2 training on assessment standardization ended, SCs were given a new set of facts and scenarios which would be used for the actual assessment of students. They needed to memorize the new facts and scripts at home and attend an interview by another group of teachers who *did not know* beforehand about the facts and scripts on the last day of training.

On the third day of training, two teachers with no idea about what instructions the SCs would give played the role of the student lawyers and interviewed two SCs respectively. As in the previous assessment training, the remaining SCs, together with the trainers and other HKU faculty members observed and rated the interviewers. Again, only little variation was found between the ratings of Part A on communicative competence applied by SCs and the teachers. The detailed scores of one of these final standardizing assessment training exercises were shown in Table 8.1. After more than 10 rounds of training, the total ratings of the interviewing lawyer made by the SCs in this session ranged from 21–7 (a mean aggregate score of 23.3), which indicates a moderate competent level, whereas the teachers also rated within the same range and gave a total score of 26. In items 1, 3, 6, 7 and 8, SCs' mean scores are very close to those of the teachers. More importantly, all SCs were able to notice the highly incompetent performance in one of the assessment items, that is item 4, and gave 1 in scoring, which converged with the teachers' ratings. It is also worth noting that out of the total 72 ratings given in the assessment (9 SCs x 8 items), only in 4 ratings the SCs gave a failing or non-competent score of 2, whereas the teachers gave a passing or competent score of 3. The results showed that after three days of intensive training, SCs were able to articulate information as a lay client in a relatively consistent way and able to assess an interviewer as validly and reliably as teachers do in examining the communicative competence of a student lawyer.

Table 8.1   Result of one of the final standardizing assessment training exercises

	Item 1	Item 2	Item 3	Item 4	Item 5	Item 6	Item 7	Item 8	Total
SC 1	4	4	4	1	4	4	3	3	27
SC 2	3	3	3	1	3	2	3	3	21
SC 3	4	3	2	1	3	3	3	3	22
SC 4	4	4	4	1	4	4	3	3	27
SC 5	3	3	3	1	3	3	3	3	22
SC 6	3	4	4	1	3	4	4	3	26
SC 7	4	3	3	1	3	3	2	3	22
SC 8	4	3	3	1	3	3	3	2	22
SC 9	4	3	3	1	3	3	2	2	21
Mean score given by SCs[1]	3.67	3.33	3.22	1.00	3.22	3.22	2.89	2.78	**23.33**
Score given by teachers[2]	4	5	3	1	4	3	3	3	**26**

Note: [1] One of the SCs recruited participated in all training except the standardizing practice for the assessment brief due to her family commitment; [2] Teachers' score represents consensus scores from two faculty members.

Assessment Results and Feedback

One week after the training, SCs returned to HKU on 26 February 2013 to conduct an interview practice session with the WTEP students. More than 60 students were graded by the SCs on a comment form which is the same as the assessment form as if they were assessed during the actual assessment. After the practice sessions, students were asked to self-evaluate their own performance using the same form with reference to the same rubric before attending a feedback workshop where the WTEP instructors provided the students with feedback of their practice performance reported by the SCs, highlighted common errors and shared what their instructors would have done in practice. The forms filled out by the SCs were also handed back to the students after the review. A comparison between students' self-evaluation and SCs' grading of the practice session shows that students tended to evaluate themselves more generously (mean item score from 2.75–3.26) than the SCs (mean item score from 2.25–2.89). Students also viewed differently from the SCs as to their strongest and weakest items. In students' self-evaluation, item 1 was graded with the highest mean score (3.26) while item 3 was graded with the lowest mean score (2.75). In SCs' ratings, item 2 was rated as the best item (2.89) and item 8 as the weakest (2.25). The variation in grading could be due to the fact that students, unlike the SCs, had not been standardized in understanding and applying the rating rubric. Further qualitative study such as focus group interviews with students is needed in order to understand the possible causes of this variation.

The actual assessment took place a week after, on 12 March 2013, when a student was assessed by a different SC based on another set of facts and scenario. Preliminary analysis of the assessment results (Table 8.2 to Table 8.4[D]) showed that students' communicative competence level on average rose from the non-competent level (mean item score from 2.25–2.89) in the practice session, to a competent level (mean item score from 2.91–3.31) at the actual assessment. It was probably because they improved after knowing SCs' feedback both from the feedback workshop and their comment forms. Substantial improvement was shown especially in the information exchange items (items 2 to 5) such as item 4 (The student lawyer accurately summarised my situation) where students' performance was boosted from a mean score of 2.44 during the practice interview to 3.31 during the actual assessment. In terms of overall passing rate of Part A on communicative competence, only 50 per cent of students attained the passing score of 20 or above in the practice session. At the actual assessment most of them (89 per cent) passed and were therefore assessed to be competent. Despite the overall improvement, when comparing the practice session results with that of the actual assessment, student lawyers improved less (17 per cent) in the soft skills (rapport and impression: items 1, 6, 7 and 8) than they did in hard skills (21 per cent) (Information exchange: items 2 to 5). In both the practice session and the actual assessment, item 8 (If I had a new legal problem I would come back to this student lawyer) stood out as the weakest, which shows that the student lawyers were yet to establish appropriate rapport and adequate trust with the SCs.

After the assessment, faculty members were invited to review and remark those videotaped interviews that had been graded by SCs as distinction (an overall score of 75 or above) and as failure (an overall score below 50). The purpose of this second marking exercise is to guard against the possibility that SCs failed students who were actually competent, or gave distinction to those who did not deserve. In addition, a selection of a few more recordings which were either near the two ends or in the middle were reviewed. The result of the second marking shows that reviewers graded by and large in the same way as the SCs had, which gave us more confidence as to the reliability and validity of SCs' ratings.

At the time of the submission of this chapter, we have not yet completed a full analysis of the assessment results and students' evaluation for the SC project run from February to April 2013. Suffice to say at the moment is that more than 75 per cent of students participating in this SC project agreed that SCs' interview enhanced their communicative competence, and over 70 per cent of them agreed that their ability to understand how clients feel and think was improved. More than 90 per cent of the responding students supported the extension of SC assessment in the core subjects of the PCLL program. From the aforementioned outcomes and feedback, it was proven that: (1) the SCs, with appropriate training, were able to assess students' communicative competence as validly and reliably as teachers do; (2) SCs' interview with students strengthened their ability in communicative competence, as shown in the improvement of their scores in the actual assessment compared with the practice session; and (3) most of the students felt SCs' interview was useful in enhancing their ability in communication and valuing what the clients think, and welcomed its expansion.

Table 8.2   Analysis of SCs' grading of practice session (26 February 2013)

	N	Range	Min	Max	Mean	Std. Deviation
Item 1: Greeting appropriate	64	3	1	4	2.73	.761
Item 2: Listening to me	64	3	2	5	2.89	.779
Item 3: Helpful questioning	64	4	1	5	2.56	.774
Item 4: Accurate summary	64	3	1	4	2.44	1.067
Item 5: Understood what lawyer said	64	3	1	4	2.73	.723
Item 6: Comfortable with lawyer	64	2	2	4	2.81	.664
Item 7: Felt confident with lawyer	64	3	1	4	2.41	.849
Item 8: Would come back again	64	3	1	4	2.25	.816

Table 8.3   Analysis of students' self-evaluation of practice session (26 February 2013)

	N	Range	Min	Max	Mean	Std. Deviation
Item 1: Greeting appropriate	62	4	1	5	3.26	.626
Item 2: Listening to me	62	3	2	5	3.25	.619
Item 3: Helpful questioning	62	4	1	5	2.75	.783
Item 4: Accurate summary	62	3	1	4	2.95	.858
Item 5: Understood what lawyer said	62	4	1	5	2.98	.659
Item 6: Comfortable with lawyer	62	3	2	5	3.07	.677
Item 7: Felt confident with lawyer	62	4	1	5	2.91	.733
Item 8: Would come back again	62	4	1	5	2.93	.712

Table 8.4   Analysis of SCs' grading of assessment session (12 March 2013)

	N	Range	Min	Max	Mean	Std. Deviation
Item 1: Greeting appropriate	65	3	1	4	3.02	.820
Item 2: Listening to me	65	3	2	5	3.25	.751
Item 3: Helpful questioning	65	3	2	5	3.23	.724
Item 4: Accurate summary	65	4	1	5	3.31	.809
Item 5: Understood what lawyer said	65	3	2	5	3.05	.571
Item 6: Comfortable with lawyer	65	2	2	4	3.00	.661
Item 7: Felt confident with lawyer	65	2	2	4	3.05	.623
Item 8: Would come back again	65	2	2	4	2.91	.678

De-standardizing Standardized Client in Asia? A Concluding Note on Culture

The above account shows that the SCs can smoothly travel across the globe and be adopted in the university education setting in Hong Kong. The statistics we have seen also tend to support that SCs in Hong Kong can, as per their counterparts in other parts of the world, examine the communicative competence of our future lawyers as *validly* and *reliably* as full-time faculty members do and help enhance students' learning experience. The use of SCs has another advantage of demanding less financial resources as compared to hiring part-time tutors/practitioners for examining a class of more than 200 PCLL students per year. After the close of this pilot project with reasonable initial success, application for additional funding to expand its use to other electives and certain core subjects of the HKU PCLL had just been lodged.

Yet, on the other hand, there exist potential challenges to adopting the pedagogy in this part of the world, owing to the cultural and institutional differences, as well as the professional background, which need to be addressed. *De-standardizing standardized clients* according to local contexts may be a way forward. A number of reflections can be drawn from the HKU experience in this first endeavour.

Communicative Competence

While communicative competence seems to be an issue common to contemporary legal educators globally, it remains a highly contextualized discourse that is inevitably shaped by cultural and jurisdictional particularities. The meaning and requirement of being communicatively competent differs from one society to another. Although there are a lot of commonalities between the legal profession, legal system and legal education in Hong Kong and the other common law systems, and although it is initially proven that SCs in Hong Kong were able to offer valid and reliable examination of communication skills of student lawyers, it remains to be tested if the 8-item assessment instrument used in the original SC project which stemmed from Scotland should represent the criteria which can fulfill the legal clients' expectation of a communicatively competent trainee lawyer in the context of Hong Kong. The scoring rubric for each of these assessment items posed another cultural challenge. What are meant to be appropriate greetings (way of greetings is the first item to be assessed in the assessment form) in one society may not be as welcomed in another. For example, it may look friendly for a lawyer in the US to start the initial meeting with a client by talking about baseball for five minutes before he or she goes into legal issues, the same conversation may not sound appropriate to legal clients in Hong Kong.[4] Item 5 of Part A of the assessment form asks if the SC can understand what the student lawyer says. One of the criteria in applying ratings under this item is to find if the student lawyer keeps using legal jargon in the conversation. However, a legal jargon in one jurisdiction can be a layman's term in another. When the SCs practised the scripted materials of the first case, they were divided as to whether the words 'estate', 'sibling' and 'executor' are legal jargon.

Therefore, the scoring rubric may also have to be de-standardized to fit the local culture and contexts of Hong Kong, an Asian city deeply hybrid in Chinese culture and Westernized lifestyle. The de-standardization can possibly be done by a local clients' survey to understand their experience of the legal service and their expectations for a communicatively competent lawyer.[5] A modified and more contextualized assessment form and scoring rubric can be formulated based upon the survey results.

Language

Owing to historical and cultural reasons, Hong Kong is a place with its particularities in the use of language. It is even more in legal education and practice. Chinese and English are both official languages under Hong Kong law. While they receive instructions in English at the law school, most of the law students spoke Cantonese as their first language in daily life or during outside-classroom discussion with classmates (unless English-speaking classmates are involved). In the professional context, lawyers in Hong Kong mostly use Cantonese in verbal communication with clients (who are mostly Cantonese-speaking Chinese). They sometimes speak in English and Mandarin when their clients are foreigners or mainland Chinese. Yet, most of the practitioners' written correspondence with law firms, counsel, regulators, law enforcement agencies, the courts and their clients are in

---

4   Thanks to the editors of this book for supplying this baseball example during the training workshop at HKU. The example was a real story that occurred in the SC training in the US.

5   It is the authors' plan to conduct such a survey in Hong Kong should application for further funding be approved.

English. Such reality leads us to reconsider the extent to which our SC assessment entirely conducted in English would help enhance our students' communicative competence in dealing with the typical clients in real life, such as a local Chinese client who more often than not gives verbal instructions in Cantonese. This issue, combined with the contextual issues of the assessment instruments mentioned above, call for a localized and indigenized scheme for Hong Kong, the experience of which may then be shared with other Asian countries in which English is not the mother tongue to fit any specific Asian socio-lingual context and make the SCs travel more comfortably and effectively to other parts of Asia and even further to other unexplored territories.

Institutional Setting

Legal profession and legal education systems do not particularly welcome change, especially when the regulations and market do not require so. In the Scottish legal education system, passing the assessment in communicative competence is a mandatory requirement for licensure of lawyers. In the US, the American Bar Association exerted substantial pressure on law schools by enacting rules and standards governing the availability of clinical legal education and experiential learning activities. In addition, fierce competition for students and financial resources drove the law schools in the US and the UK to look for innovative methods that can deliver experiential learning and assessment tools that are comparable to tutors' quality but at a lesser cost, such as the Standardized Clients. These conditions may exist in some other parts of Asia where law schools try to gain students by distinguishing themselves in offering innovative curriculum and pedagogical tools; such conditions do not exist in Hong Kong. Professional bodies and law schools in Hong Kong remain less enthusiastic than their overseas counterparts in the UK, US and Australia in endorsing clinical and experiential learning activities until fairly recently (Chow and Tiba 2013). Before any further step can be taken, it is envisaged that a substantial amount of effort and time is needed for legal educators to gain confidence and comfort in working with new learning and assessment methodologies such as the SCs. Furthermore, it would remain a challenge for the SCs in Hong Kong to continue to exist and more importantly to continue to improve if it is funded only through an ad hoc teaching grant that has to be applied annually, rather than from a regular faculty budget. Hopefully with the continuous positive feedback from students, both the law schools and the legal profession in Hong Kong are prepared to welcome and greet the SCs in a more extensive way so that majority of the law students can be trained to value what their clients feel before they meet the real clients in the office.

References

Barrows, H.S. (1993), 'An overview of standardized patients for teaching and evaluation clinical skills', *Academic Medicine*, 68(6): 443–53.

Barton, K., Cunningham, C., Jones, G.T. and Maharg, P. (2006), 'Valuing what clients think: standardized clients and the assessment of communicative competence', *Clinical Law Review*, 13(1): 1–65.

Chow, W.W.S. and Tiba, F. (2013), 'Too many 'what's, too few 'how's', *European Journal of Law and Technology*, 4(1). Available at http://ejlt.org//article/view/183/281 [accessed 23 April 2013].

Cunningham, C.D. (1999), 'Evaluating effective lawyer-client communication: as international project moving from research to reform', *Fordham Law Review*, 67(5): 1959–86.

Cunningham, C.D. (2011), 'Should American law schools continue to graduate lawyers whom clients consider worthless?' *Maryland Law Review*, 70: 499–512.

Dale, E. (1969), *Audiovisual Methods in Teaching*. 3rd edition. New York: The Dryden Press.

Evans, D.M.E. (1989), 'Taken at the flood: Hong Kong's first law school', in *The Future of Legal Education and the Legal Profession in Hong Kong*, edited by R. Wacks. Hong Kong: Faculty of Law, University of Hong Kong, 103–13.

Fry, E., Crewe, J. and Wakeford, R. (2012), 'The qualified lawyers transfer scheme: innovative assessment methodology and practice in a high stakes professional exam', *The Law Teacher*, 46(2): 132–45.

Garvey, J.B. and Zinkin, A.F. (2009), 'Making law students client-ready: a new model in legal education', *Duke Forum for Law & Social Change*, 1: 101–29.

Grosberg, L.M. (2001), 'Medical education again provides a model for law schools: the standardized patient becomes the standardized client', *Journal of Legal Education*, 51: 212–34.

Grosberg, L.M. (2006), 'How should we assess interviewing and counseling skills?' *International Journal of Clinical Legal Education*, 9: 57–72.

Maharg, P. (2011), 'Standardized clients @ Northumbria University Law School' [Online] available at: http://paulmaharg.com/2011/09/16/standardized-clients-northumbria-university-law-school/ [accessed 27 April 2013].

Ormrod Report (1971), *Report of the Committee on Legal Education*, Cmnd. 4595, HMSO. London, 1971.

Rowe, M. (2011), 'Standardized client initiative' [Online: Case studies of educational excellence, ANU]. Available at: http://edcasestudies.chelt.anu.edu.au/grants/margie-rowe [accessed 27 April 2013].

Standardized client in Ireland [Online: Standardized client initiative blog, 7 September 2011]. Available at: http://zeugma.typepad.com/sci/2011/09/standardized-clients-in-ireland.html [accessed 27 April 2013].

Chapter 9

Teaching Professionalism Online – An Australian Professional Legal Education Experience

Margie Rowe and Moira Murray

Introduction

Many legal educators have recognised the importance of integrating the teaching of concepts, practical skills and professionalism. This necessitates a common understanding of what is meant by the term 'professionalism' and a move to expressly articulating the attributes of legal professionalism as expected learning outcomes.

In 2010, the Australian National University Legal Workshop, in its post-graduate professional legal education course, launched an adaptation of the simulated transactional learning experience developed at the University of Strathclyde (Maharg 2007). The aim was to use the vehicle of the 'virtual firm' environment to teach and embed attributes of legal professionalism.

Maharg and colleagues in the Glasgow Graduate School of Law developed the concept of simulation-based transactional learning where students worked in 'virtual firms' to carry out legal transactions in a 'virtual office' (the SIMulated Professional Learning Environment: the SIMPLE project). The students worked with Senior Partners, clients and other 'characters' they would encounter in legal practice in a sophisticated role-play. A Practice Management course where the students learned, practiced and were assessed on their capacity for collaborative work and other professional attributes was a cornerstone of the course.

The way in which professionalism is taught, learned and assessed online has posed challenges and created opportunities including:

1. designing a program that fits within the educational and regulatory context applying to professional legal education courses;
2. arriving at a definition of legal professionalism that best describes the values and attributes that should be taught and embedded in the program;
3. how to teach and assess legal professionalism within the program;
4. teaching the program in a wholly online environment; and
5. using technology to create an educational experience more authentic to legal practice.

This chapter will explore those challenges and opportunities in the context of the Graduate Diploma in Legal Practice (GDLP) program, focusing on the Professional Practice Core course (PPC).

Legal Workshop and the Graduate Diploma of Legal Practice

Legal Workshop is part of the Australian National University College of Law, in Canberra, Australia, and offers the Graduate Diploma in Legal Practice (GDLP), a professional legal education course which is required for admission to practice in Australia. Approximately 1,000 students each year undertake the course, whilst living all over Australia and some overseas. The student body is diverse, some students having just recently graduated whilst others have significant life and work experience. Most students are already in full-time employment and many have legal jobs. The GDLP is a flexible online program that can be completed in six months or over a three-year period and comprises four components:

1. Becoming a Practitioner intensive
2. Legal Practice Experience
3. Elective Coursework
4. The Professional Practice Core.

It begins with the Becoming a Practitioner intensive, a five-day face-to-face course. This is an important foundation course and introduces the practical skills students will need to complete the GDLP and become a competent practitioner and is a compulsory prerequisite for beginning the other coursework.

Legal Practice Experience involves a 20-, 40-, 60- or 80-day placement in an approved legal environment. The length of time students spend doing Legal Practice Experience determines how many course electives they need to complete. Students must complete a reflective report on their placement. There are a number of different electives that students can study. With the exception of Criminal Law Practice, all are taught wholly online with the use of web-conferencing facilities for oral assessments. The electives cover:

- Administrative Law Practice
- Criminal Law Practice
- Family Law Practice
- Consumer Law Practice
- Employment and Industrial Relations Practice
- Planning and Environment Law Practice
- Wills Probate and Administration Practice
- Government Law Practice.

The PCC takes place over an 18-week period and is taught twice a year. During this time students work with other students online in a simulated legal practice environment to complete four practice areas:

1. Practice Management (including Accounts and Ethics)
2. Property Law Practice
3. Civil Litigation Practice
4. Commercial Law Practice.

The Professional Practice Core

The development of the was driven by a desire to better prepare students for legal practice by helping them to develop a professional identity, equipping them to deal with the uncertainties of practice and recognise the skills they have developed as an undergraduate or in their work are transferable to legal practice. This was also informed by:

- employers of newly admitted lawyers seeking graduates with good communication skills, good teamwork skills and an ability to apply the concepts and skills they learnt at university in a practical and professional manner,
- students seeking a relevant, flexible legal training experience that gave them the opportunity to develop and consolidate the skills needed to be a confident professional employee upon admission to practice, and
- Barton, McKellar and Maharg's work (2007) which indicated that authentic simulated transactional based learning within groups had the ability to create deeper, self-reflective and collaborative learning outcomes with relevant professional assessment and the promotion of ethical standards.

Staff on the Legal Workshop worked with Paul Maharg and the University of Strathclyde to adapt and develop the SIMPLE project into the PCC. The course is delivered entirely online and makes use of a simulated legal office and virtual legal firms to teach practical legal skills and to enable students to learn practical legal skills and begin to acquire and develop professional values before they enter the legal profession.

The course integrates property, commercial litigation, civil litigation, trust accounting, ethics and practice management into a single integrated learning environment. This engages students simultaneously on two levels, namely:

- the 'in role' simulation environment comprising a virtual office space where students work in groups with up to four other students to create a team of lawyers engaging in transactions in a virtual firm environment. In this space students undertake tasks with direction and support in the form of work, allocation, feed-forward and feedback from senior partners, associates, clients and other characters; and

- the 'out of role' support website where students engage with each other and teaching staff to access and process additional resources and information to support their work in the virtual office space. In this area, students are also required to complete individual assessment tasks.

The Challenges Faced by Legal Workshop

(a) Educational and Regulatory Context

The first challenge relates to the educational and regulatory context in which the GDLP program operates. The GDLP is effectively a capstone course at the end of a student's undergraduate legal education, and is required for admission to practice. It is a bridge between legal education and the working world. Externally prescribed competencies in content, skills and values must be achieved in a course that is generally taken by students over one semester. The challenge is to integrate the teaching of practical skills and professionalism to produce an entry-level lawyer who is ready to enter the working world.

The Legal Workshop must ensure that students attain competence in a number of skills, practice areas and values by the time they complete their GDLP. The skills, practice areas and values that must be taught and the standards of competence that students must attain were jointly developed by the Australasian Professional Legal Education Council (APLEC) and the Law Admissions Consultative Committee in 2000 and updated in 2002 (APLEC 2000).

The Competency Standards seek to describe the observable performance and set out a series of performance criteria required of entry-level lawyers at the point of admission to practice, in a number of key areas (see Table 9.1).

The performance criteria do not expressly refer to the development of the values and attributes of legal professionalism. However, they do refer in part to some values and attributes that can be considered elements of legal professionalism. For example, for Ethics and Professional Responsibility two of the criteria are:

- demonstrated professional courtesy in all dealings with others; and
- demonstrated awareness that mismanagement of living and work practices can impair the lawyer's skills, productivity, health and family life.

Included in those specified for Work Management and Business Skills is 'worked with support staff, colleagues, consultants and counsel in a professional and cost effective manner'.

Experience over the past three years indicates that as students master the skills and practice areas, they begin to develop their sense of professionalism. In other words, beginning to develop a professional identity is an implicit learning outcome

Table 9.1   Competency Standards (APLEC 2000)

Skills	Practice Areas	Values
• Lawyers Skills • Problem Solving • Work Management and Business Skills • Trust and Office Accounting	• Civil Litigation Practice • Commercial and Corporate Practice • Property Law Practice One of: • Administrative Law Practice • Criminal Law Practice • Family Law Practice And one of: • Consumer Law Practice • Employment and Industrial Relations Practice • Planning and Environmental Law Practice • Wills and Estate Practice	• Ethics and Professional Responsibility

of the Competency Standards. The regulatory requirements therefore support the educational decision to focus on developing professionalism, and the student's sense of their own professional identity.

(b) Defining Professionalism

In deciding to teach and embed professionalism in the PCC, the second challenge was defining what was meant by professionalism in a practical legal training context, and reframing this context to one of professional legal education. There is an ongoing debate about what professionalism means today. On the one hand there is the view that the traditional ideals of professionalism have all but disappeared as a result of market pressures, technology and the global economy, replaced by a narrow view of professionalism as technical competence and adherence to the written rules of the profession only (see for example Nicolson 2005: 601–26, Boon et al. 2005: 473–92).

On the other hand there is the view that 'traditional' values of professionalism such as autonomy, task variety competence, collegiality and public service orientation are still relevant to the legal profession (see for example Nelson and Trubeck 1992; Wallace and Kay 2008: 1021–4). Two additional elements of professionalism that apply to lawyers are a primary duty to the court and administration of justice and a fiduciary duty to the client (Foley et al. 2012).

The importance of congruence of professional and personal values is illustrated by a pilot study of students who had transitioned into legal practice undertaken in 2010 following 12 graduates through their first year of practice.

It involved a mix of survey, interview and observations to chart the early career lawyers' ethical and professional development (Foley et al. 2012) and found that the models of professionalism these graduates encountered in their new workplace had a significant impact on the construction of their own professional identity. The participants were 'honing their professional judgment by a process of trial and error, observation, imitation and repetition which was unique to each working environment' (Foley et al. 2012) and consistently described three influences or events as impacting on the development of their professional identity. These were:

- achieving a balance between working autonomously and being appropriately mentored and supervised,
- dealing with uncertainty about their role, about the law itself and the emotional aspect of lawyering, and
- finding a value convergence between their own values and those modelled by colleagues.

They consciously considered the values and ethical practices of their workplaces and colleagues, referring to both the espoused values of their workplace and the everyday practices and interactions within the firm and with other lawyers. Only one of the 12 participants had not found a value alignment and this led her to leave her firm and almost to leave law. None of the participants saw their professional identity purely in terms of technical competence, commercial success or mere adherence to professional conduct rules, but rather embraced the broader notion of professionalism.

In the PCC, the traditional understanding of legal professionalism, emphasising autonomy, collegiality and public service orientation informed the values and practices that students had to demonstrate to achieve competency in the course. The 'working in firms' model simulates legal practice and the work conditions in which professional identity formation usually takes place, providing an effective model for students to develop their professional identity.

Stuckey (2007: 82–3) talks about professionalism as represented by professional values. He lists the following descriptors of professionalism, which correspond with the definition of professionalism that underpins the PCC:

- Handling cases professionally:
  - recognising the broader implications of your work,
  - considering interests and values of clients and others,
  - providing high quality services at fair cost,
  - maintaining independence of judgment,
  - embodying honour, integrity and fair play,
  - being truthful and candid, exhibiting diligence and punctuality,
  - showing courtesy and respect towards others, and
  - complying with rules and expectations of the profession.
- Managing law practice effectively and efficiently
- Engaging in professional self-development

- Nurturing quality of life
- Supporting aims of legal profession by
  - providing access to justice,
  - upholding the vitality and effectiveness of the legal system,
  - promoting justice, fairness and morality, and
  - encouraging diversity (Stuckey 2007: 82–3).

In the Carnegie Report (Sullivan et al. 2007: 22) the authors argue that there are six tasks that legal education needs to tackle to prepare legal professionals. These are:

1. Developing in students the fundamental knowledge and skill, especially an academic knowledge base and research;
2. Providing students with the capacity to engage in complex practice;
3. Enabling students to learn to make judgments under conditions of uncertainty;
4. Teaching students how to learn from experience;
5. Introducing students to the disciplines of creating and participating in a responsible and effective professional community;
6. Forming students able and willing to join an enterprise of public service.

The use of the simulation model in the PCC enables students to develop the capacity to engage in complex practice, learn to make judgments under conditions of uncertainty, learn from experience and participate in a responsible and effective community. In addition, through assessment practices that reward these attributes and encourage the development of professional values, students are guided in the formation of their notion of professionalism. Students are required to develop and demonstrate their capacity for reflection throughout the course, by improving the quality of their substantive work in response to feedback on drafts and by participating in web-conferences with their firm members and Practice Mentor to discuss issues and scenarios relating to their ethical and professional development. The tasks and dilemmas students face help them to recognise and reflect on their emerging identities as legal practitioners, team members and professionals.

Teaching and Assessing Professionalism

(a) Teaching and Embedding Professional Values – 'learning by doing'

Throughout the PCC students are required to engage with the learning environment in an adaptable, professional, courteous and ethical manner as they complete rotations through Civil Litigation, Property and Accounts, Legal Ethics/ Professional Responsibility and Commercial Practice areas. Practice Management is the main practice area where students learn about the skills, attributes and values that characterise a legal professional.

These include:

- understanding professional obligations in context;
- developing a professional identity;
- developing effective practice management skills – such as time and file management and client service.
- voicing values/opinions/concerns in a manner that:
  a. creates effective team/group work relationships and procedures;
  b. supports and maintains ethical professional identity;
  c. supports and enhances individual wellbeing.

Practice Management draws on and supports the other practice areas in the PCC. The students will apply the skills, attributes and values they have learned to their 'in role' firm work in the other practice areas in which they work.

In July 2012, aspects of the 'Giving Voice to Values' curriculum (GVV) (Gentile 2010) were introduced into the PCC. The GVV is designed to help individuals learn to recognise, clarify, speak and act on their values when they encounter values conflicts in their careers and workplaces. The purpose of introducing this and working with the students to understand and practice it is to enhance their capacity for ethical conduct and to assist them to develop professional relationships, both in the simulation environment and in their working lives.

It facilitates students asking and answering the question: what would I say and do if I were going to act on my values? Students are encouraged to identify their own values (with an eye to professionally prescribed 'values') and practise the skills required to 'speak' those values. They are given a scenario and asked to pre-script what they would say or do, then role-play the scenario in web-conferences with their firm members and Practice Mentor. For example, students role-play raising the non-disclosure of documents to the opposing side with their senior partner, where they believe they should be disclosed, and raising concerns with their employer about the excessive amount of work they (or a colleague) are required to do.

(b) Modelling Professionalism

In addition to 'learning by doing', the PCC also presents an excellent opportunity to model professionalism, with staff leading by example. This necessitates a shared understanding amongst staff of what it means to be a legal professional.

The Legal Workshop employs around 140 practitioner teachers most of whom are full-time lawyers in practice, to teach in the PCC. These play the role of senior partners, associates and other characters in the virtual office space. They provide feedback on drafts of student work (based on the concept of 'feedforward' developed by Maharg (2007)) and assess the final version of the work. Legal Workshop staff and practitioner teachers also work as Practice Mentors (PMs) with the student firms. Each PM has between six to eight firms, or a maximum of 32 students.

The PMs promote and demonstrate professionalism in all their interactions with the firm. In doing so, they monitor and mentor students as they develop their professional identity during the course. They also provide support to firms to ensure that the firms function as productive teams to maximise their learning. They guide and coach firms to ensure work allocation occurs equitably, and firm members engage with one another, other firms, characters in the virtual office and staff in a professional manner. The considerable interaction that occurs between students and staff as a result of the simulation-based teaching means that there are many opportunities for professional behaviour to be both modelled and discussed.

Modelling professional behaviour is more difficult in the online environment and in a large course (500 students each semester) which relies heavily on practitioner teachers. Achieving a shared understanding of the attributes of professionalism and consistency in professional behaviour of all staff working in the program is an ongoing challenge, which has been partially met by improvements in the induction, training, briefing and de-briefing of staff.

The practitioner teachers in their roles of senior partners, associates and clients are the front-line teachers for their firms and have almost daily involvement with the students. It is vital that they consistently model the agreed attributes and values of legal professionalism. In earlier iterations of the program, some playing the role of 'senior partners' adopted a rude and aggressive demeanour, reflecting the partners they had come across when they were junior lawyers. Although students are sometimes surprised to find that 'courtesy' is one of the performance criteria for Ethics and Professional Responsibility and an attribute of professional behaviour, students in firms who interacted with these partners were quick to identify that this kind of behaviour was unprofessional and raised their partner's lack of professionalism with the program conveners.

Improved staff training has increased consistency in modelling professional behaviour. Underpinning this training was achieving a shared understanding of professionalism by reference to what was expected of both students and staff. These expectations focused on ethical behaviour, timeliness, good work management and recording, equitable and fair interactions with team members, honesty and courtesy to all. PMs led a series of web-conferences with their firms, discussing these attributes of professional behaviour in the context of the work they were undertaking as a firm. Additional training for both students and staff on giving and receiving feedback also assisted both groups.

One of the challenges in modelling professional behaviour is that those doing it need to be above reproach. This is particularly difficult when it comes to providing feedback and responses to student questions in a timely manner. Turnaround times for work in the PCC are tight – work is generally submitted each week and feedback needs to be returned to students within one to two days of receipt of the work. If feedback is not provided quickly, student learning and motivation is adversely affected. Slow turnaround times for feedback is one of the main complaints students make in the course.

The advantage of having a large number of practitioner teachers working in the course is that they have an authentic connection with current legal practice. However, that means that they are already dealing with the demands of their primary legal job and, as a result, their work on the PCC is undertaken at night and on weekends. Many of the student cohort also work in full-time positions during the day and work in the course after hours. It is at these times, when staff and students are tired, that professional communication skills can be compromised. Staff can become frustrated, short and abrupt when responding to student questions posted online or providing written feedback. When this occurs it is often reported by students to the Course Conveners, which in many ways is demonstrative of the student's growing awareness of what is and is not professional standard of communication.

(c) Assessing the Development of Professionalism

It is one thing to teach, or facilitate the learning of professionalism, another to devise an assessment scheme to assess that students have achieved competence in specified professional attributes. The assessment criteria used in the PCC were adapted in part from criteria developed by the Law Society of Scotland in their 2009 Professional Education and Training PEAT 1 Accreditation Guidelines for Applicants. (http://www.lawscot.org.uk/media/561669/peat%201%20guidelines.pdf).

The adapted criteria require students to:

- meet deadlines consistently and if cannot meet a deadline with good reason, proactively seek an extension of time before the deadline passes;
- help to generate an open, friendly work environment through demonstrating respect for others, and through supportive, professional and polite behaviour at all times;
- work cooperatively and willingly with others in their own and other's teams;
- accept responsibility for tasks within the firm;
- communicate effectively across all levels in the course using appropriate means of communication;
- volunteer to take on a leadership role within their firm, motivating the group and organising the delegation of tasks;
- modify their own practice in the context of feedback from tutors and peers;
- accept responsibility for their own learning and reflect on experiences and mistakes in order to improve future performance;
- produce high-quality work that is well written and researched;
- participate actively in web-conference discussions on Practice Management topics; and
- keep activity logs up to date.

Assessment rubrics have been developed and continue to be refined in order to assess students' capacity to work as part of a team and demonstrate reflective practice. Peer assessment was used in the first iteration of the course as a mechanism for students to comment on the quality and quantity of their own contributions and their firm members and to bring transparency to work allocation. However this was not continued with owing to a lack of understanding on the part of both staff and students about its value. However given this form of assessment is an important tool in the simulation, it will be reintroduced in 2013. Other aspects of professional working as set out above are assessed by the subject mentors, in relation to the quality of the work and its timeliness, and by the Practice Mentors' observations of and interactions with their firm.

Teaching in an Online Environment

Working in an online environment presents challenges and opportunities not found in traditional face-to-face teaching modes. Student engagement and the use of technology to facilitate learning are both the main positives in the online environment, and also the main challenge.

(a) Lack of Student Engagement and Dysfunctional Firms

Lack of engagement with the group and the course is arguably more problematic in an online environment where students are not meeting face-to-face but relying on technology to communicate with one another. One example of student feedback from the course illustrates this:

> It was way easy for people to drop off the face of the planet and not participate ... In an office environment you develop a rapport with each other and there is some guilt attached to not doing your own work. Whereas online it is just a faceless name requesting that you do something.

Virtual firms quickly experience difficulties if the individuals in the firms have varying levels of commitment to the course and to the group. The most common complaint from students concerns others who do not communicate and engage with their virtual firm or the course. Not all place the same importance on professional values such as diligence, respect for other firm members, clear and timely communication and time management.

In the six iterations of the PCC, between two and three virtual firms have become dysfunctional. In these cases failure of the firm to cohesively develop a shared set of professional values led to a complete breakdown in trust and the ability to work together as a team and the firms were dissolved. Intervention from PMs has also been needed in a handful of other virtual firms who display dysfunctional characteristics – the most common problem being a lack of communication and trust within the firm. Practically, this lack of trust is evidenced by students being unwilling to allow others to have input into a task, reacting negatively to feedback from other firm members and/or other firm members giving feedback that was not constructive and overly negative. Clearly, this presents a significant barrier to collaborative learning and working.

When first faced with these problems, the immediate concern was that the online delivery mode may have caused the failure of the firms to work well together or been an impediment to collaborative work. After consulting staff who had developed and worked with the virtual firms in the Glasgow Graduate School of Law (GGSL) at the University of Strathclyde, it became apparent that virtual firms in both courses were exhibiting many of the same problems. The GGSL also had the students working in an online virtual office; however there was significant face-to-face teaching and learning.

Fiona Westwood and Karen Barton, both of whom worked in the GGSL, researched the experience of students in the GGSL firms by analysing students' Individual Reflective Reports, a compulsory piece of assessment in the Practice Management Module. After analysing these reports in detail over a three year period, they developed a matrix to assess the trust and learning of individual firms. Their research (Barton and Westwood 2006: 5) identified four types of firms described as:

- Learning Communities (high trust and high learning)
- Legal Eagles (low trust and high learning)
- Happy Families (high trust and low learning)
- Dysfunctional (low trust and low learning)
- They reported that 12 per cent of the 51 firms they analysed were dysfunctional.

There was significant correspondence between the percentage of dysfunctional firms in the PCC, that is, those with low trust and low learning and those in GGSL. Barton and Westwood came to the conclusion that dysfunction is inevitable for a small number of firms working within the course. While these firms will develop competent legal skills, they are slower to develop shared professional values. This means that members of the firm will be behind their student cohort in developing their professional identity.

Staff mentoring of the students and their firms has proved crucial in meeting the challenges of lack of engagement and dysfunction, as has the simulation model of 'learning by doing'.

Lack of engagement and dysfunction in firms has been tackled by:

- ensuring, where possible, face-to-face interaction could occur (either in the five-day intensive preceding the online coursework or by the firm meeting up during the online coursework);
- undertaking a values exercise at the beginning of the course;
- early intervention from PMs who work with the firms during the course to emphasise the importance of adhering to professional standards, including

a first week web-conference to discuss firm working;
- better resources and guidance on giving and receiving feedback; and
- the newly introduced 'Giving Voice to Values' curriculum encouraging and giving students practice in speaking up effectively.

(b) Face-to-face Interaction

Legal Workshop realised early on the importance of firm members meeting face-to-face where possible, and the impact that this meeting has in accelerating the development of trust and mutual obligation between firm members in the online environment. It therefore created an initial five-day introductory intensive session not only to introduce the legal skills that will be developed during the online course, but also to give students the opportunity to work together as a firm in person.

Though logistically difficult, this session is run in eight different cities throughout Australia several times each year, every effort is made to ensure that students are placed in their firms on the first day of these intensives. Where this occurs, the firms generally work better as they move to their online work. As one piece of feedback put it: 'because we formed the group before the course – it was terrific. It would be impossible to establish the same rapport with somebody I did not know before'. While it is possible to develop professional values while learning in an online environment, the process of developing those shared values is enhanced by the springboard of initial face-to-face contact.

Students are also allowed to nominate who they want to work with in the course. One advantage of allowing students to choose their firm members is that they already share a set of values, formed when they worked together as undergraduates or in a workplace where they are all currently employed, that they can build upon in the course.

(c) Undertaking a Values Exercise

It is now regarded as crucial that students in the firm discuss their personal values as a group and then reach consensus about the values their firm will adopt as they work together through the course. Westwood (2001, 2004 and 2008) states that an essential part of establishing trust and community ethos is achieved by having values in common. As Nicholson (2000), McKenna and Maister (2002) and Ward and Smith (2003) identify, these values can be used in facilitating group working, for example in helping to clarify and address areas of tension.

The starting point in the course is for students in each firm to discuss and agree on a set of shared values which are of most importance to the firm and which will guide the way in which the firm operates. This discussion is facilitated by Practice Mentors. These values are included in a firm agreement and students are referred back to their agreed values as the first step in resolving any firm difficulties or issues. This is often the first time students have given thought to professional values, and, more particularly, to the values they associate with their emerging identity as a legal professional. The values exercise has been adapted in part from the values exercise used in the GGSL.

(d) Practice Mentor Intervention

PMs work with the firms as they progress through the course. They actively observe their firms throughout the course, monitoring firm work plans to ensure work allocation is equitable and monitoring activity logs to ensure that all students in the firm are actively contributing to work being submitted by the firm. They also discuss with their firms how each firm is progressing at web-conferences that occur at three points throughout the course and stage timely interventions when they see students who are not engaged with their firm or in other ways not acting professionally.

Because of the online delivery mode, they cannot deal with these issues by talking face-to-face with the students involved. However, they can speak with students by web-conference, Skype and telephone. They also work with the virtual firm as a whole to set in place good work allocation routines and communication procedures to reduce the risk of a recurrence of the problem. The values agreed by the firm at the beginning of the course can also be revisited by the PMs to reinforce the importance of commitment and active engagement with the firm, and of thinking and acting like a legal professional.

At the end of the first iteration of the PCC, a decision was taken to minimise dysfunction within firms by ensuring PMs worked closely with their firms to convey the importance of adopting a professional approach to work and interactions with each other and with staff. Early intervention was undertaken if firms showed signs of struggling with this approach and were slow to develop shared professional values.

Intervention took a number of forms. Sometimes it became necessary to move a student from one firm to another firm where the values and work practices were a better fit. Other firms benefited from a more intense relationship with their PM, working to develop skills and values that would enhance their experience – focusing on work allocation routines, establishing good and reliable communication between firm members, developing their ability to give and receive feedback and emphasising the importance of courtesy, reliability, collegiality and teamwork.

(e) Technology

Lastly, an exclusive challenge in the online environment is the technology required to facilitate communication, teaching and learning and to simulate a reasonably authentic legal office. Conversely, it is the technology that also provides many opportunities for innovative teaching practice and for embedding professionalism in the course.

The PCC runs on two online platforms. The first is the online learning environment known as Wattle (Web Access To Teaching and Learning Environments). Wattle is an online learning environment which uses Moodle as the underpinning platform. The Wattle site is used to support student learning by:

- providing access to course notes, readings and online resources;
- facilitating communication using discussion forums, messaging, web-conferencing and chat sessions; and
- providing information about individual assessment, details of assignments and online quizzes.

When students first enter the PCC, they can find the layout of the site overwhelming. This has been overcome to some extent by developing an online quiz that is designed to familiarise the students with the site. The full site is not released to students until they have completed the quiz. The students are stepped through setting up their computer, choice of internet browser and other applications that will ensure they can make best use of the site. They are also asked to locate course and assessment outlines, resources and other materials they will use throughout the course.

In an online course it is essential that staff can easily communicate with students. In the PCC, it is also very important that students can communicate with each other as they are required to work together in firms, with other firms and to collaborate on the work they undertake in each practice area.

One of the major advantages of the Wattle site is that students and staff can access web-conferencing facilities. Web-conferencing is an integral communication tool in the course as it allows students to communicate with each other and staff online. It is used for assessments: for example students conduct an interview in the property practice area and attend settlement of the conveyance via a web-conference. In the civil litigation and commercial practice areas students negotiate the resolution of a civil dispute and negotiate the inclusion of clauses in a sale of business agreement.

In Practice Management, PMs meet regularly via web-conference with the students. The students themselves use web-conferencing to discuss the work they are doing and work on documents together in real time. As the web-conferencing tool is new to students and staff, training and orientation sessions have been critical to ensuring that it can be properly used. These training sessions are also helpful in resolving issues that are specific to a student: for example the type of Internet connection they have may affect how the web-conferencing tool works. This is a tool that students are likely to utilise more and more in their legal practice careers, especially those working in global firms or on international legal issues, so familiarity with this platform before encountering it in practice is a useful skill.

The second online platform is the integrated learning environment (ILE) where the virtual office spaces are located. ILE is a development of the SIMPLE platform (the SIMPLE platform was developed by Strathclyde University and open sourced by ANU from the SIMPLE community) to create a Virtual Office Space (VOS) for students to interact with each other as junior lawyers and simulated characters in order to complete their transactions. This space includes email, discussion board, activity log and personal reflective log spaces to support student 'in role' learning. A new software platform is in development to provide students with a more authentic 'legal office'.

The VOS does not function exactly like the systems used in real legal offices. Students often comment that it is not what they are used to in a real legal office. As this is a simulated legal office, it will never be perfectly authentic and look and work like a real legal office system. Linser and Ip (2005) say that the most important factors that ensure good learning from a simulated environment are the need to identify with the character of the role students are playing and the sense that actions taken by students are taking some effect. Student feedback indicates that where they can interact with clients and senior partners and act on their instructions they get a sense that they are undertaking real legal work for real people. Some students even believe that the clients and partners are real people, rather than characters, despite clear explanations to the contrary at the start of the course.

Notwithstanding the substantial forms of communication students are able to access within the course, they have devised and adopted innovative and contemporary ways of communicating with each other. Some firms of students have set up Facebook groups where they meet online to discuss their work. Others have made use of 'Google docs' to work on and edit documents. One enterprising firm of students have made use of free Cloud technology and have created their own online portal within TeamLab (see http://www.teamlab.com/) to work on documents together and set project management plans.

Evaluation

Student evaluation surveys were conducted at the end of each iteration of the PCC. Staff evaluation surveys were also conducted, which covered both full-time academic staff and practitioner teachers. Informal feedback has come from administrative staff dealing with students over the past two years, and from former students of the course who are now practitioners, some of whom are now teaching on the course as well.

In January 2012, students starting the PCC were surveyed about their understanding of and approaches to professionalism and ethics at the beginning of the course.[1] At the end of the course students were asked whether their understanding and approaches to ethics and professionalism had changed or developed and, if so, in what ways. The number of students responding to the survey was so small that the data was not considered reliable. The survey has been

---

1   The survey was developed by Anneka Ferguson, a lecturer with ANU Legal Workshop and Stephen Tang, a research associate with the ANU College of Law.

repeated in mid-2012 with data evaluation in process to assess the extent to which the course promotes students to begin developing a professional identity.

It is likely that students will be better placed to reflect on their experiences in the PCC and assess the development of their professional identity when they have spent some time in the workforce. Informal reflections on the program by students who are now early career practitioners suggest that with hindsight they acknowledge a significant development of professional attributes and identity during the PCC. This includes students who did not enjoy the course at the time they undertook it, who had difficulties in their firms and who provided quite critical feedback. Some of those students are now working in the PCC as practitioner teachers.

(a) Development of Professionalism within the Virtual Firms – a Student Viewpoint

One of the most encouraging aspects of the PCC has been feedback from students that show the course has helped them begin to develop their own professional identity as lawyers. One student noted that 'the best part of the program was working as part of a team and growing professionally with each other. I cannot speak highly enough of my group as outstanding, compassionate and competent individuals'.

In the Semester 2 2011 course evaluation survey many students felt that the program was effective in encouraging professional conduct amongst colleagues. Many students spoke very positively about their experiences in establishing professional relationships with peers in the PCC. For example, 'there was an element of realism/professionalism of legal practice associated with the simulation'.

In the Semester 1 2012 course evaluation survey (the most recent available data) the development of professionalism was not directly addressed, this survey instead focusing on evaluating educational design changes, individual assessment and the use of technology. However in answer to the question 'What are the strengths of the PPC?' students commented on teamwork and the firm environment, the capacity to be autonomous in work allocation and time management, the development of good habits of receiving and completing work, gaining insights into their own development and understanding where they need to improve, gaining confidence in their ability to solve legal problems and 'to move from a learning environment into a practical professional space'.

This suggests that the development of professional culture and professional identity can be encouraged to start prior to admission to practice and can occur in a wholly online environment.

(b) Development of Professionalism within the Firms – Staff Viewpoint

Whilst academic staff working in the PCC have participated in formal evaluations, as with the student evaluations until 2012, these have focused largely on the mechanics of the course, the website design, workload issues and the like. At the end of 2012 the 80+ staff who have taught in the PCC will be asked to complete a survey about the students' development of professionalism and whether they consider the assessment criteria used in the Practice Management component of the course is useful in assessing the students and their developing professionalism.

During the introductory Becoming a Practitioner intensive, the professional attributes students are required to learn, practice, develop and demonstrate are explained and communicating courteously is emphasised. Students are advised that this expectation applies to all of their interactions, with staff and with each other, including those occurring outside the courses and which may relate to administrative matters. Administrative staff who often have significant dealings with students by phone and email, and are more frequently subjected to discourteous behaviour, are asked to alert the PCC Convener to this who will then take appropriate action. That action is couched in the expectation of courtesy as an attribute of professionalism, as well as being a requirement under the Ethics and Professional Responsibility competencies.

Courtesy is a useful indicium of a student's professionalism, as are capacity for organisation, to meet administrative as well as academic timelines and to be aware of their obligations as students. Papadakis et al. (2004: 249) found in their empirical study of medical students that 'Students who received comments regarding unprofessional behaviour were more than twice as likely to be disciplined ... when they became practicing physicians than were students without such comments ... We have, for the first time, demonstrated that unprofessional behavior in medical school is associated with unprofessional behavior in practice'.

Students who come to staff attention as a result of 'problematic behaviour' are observed to be fewer in number in 2012 than in 2011. Problematic behaviour encompasses discourtesy to academic or administrative staff and colleagues, lack of organisation with either administrative or academic tasks, or both, and an expectation that others should fix the student's problems, inability to adhere to deadlines and lack of resourcefulness often demonstrated by repeated and unnecessary contact with staff. Administrative staff report that students who have been problematic and are followed up by the PCC Convener generally have much more positive and constructive communications with them in the future. In addition, such students are watched more closely by PMs and coached more extensively if required.

Conclusion

The way in which professionalism is to be taught, learned and assessed online in the PCC has posed challenges and created opportunities. Both centre round the definition of legal professionalism so as to create a common understanding amongst staff and students of the values and attributes taught in the course;

teaching and assessing legal professionalism; and teaching legal professionalism in an online environment.

Having explored those challenges and opportunities in this chapter, the question was posed – has the PCC met its objective of teaching professionalism and fostering the development of professional identity? There are a number of indicia that suggest the course is on the right path to achieving this objective. Survey responses and feedback from students and staff gathered since 2010 suggest that students are beginning to develop their legal professional identity in the course environment.

Overall, staff and student responses to being immersed in a simulation with a heightened emphasis on professional behaviour have been positive with both groups reporting anecdotally a better learning experience. The more focused surveys that are currently being conducted and referred to above will enable this conclusion to be drawn with more confidence. Extending evaluation to both entry level lawyers in their first year of practice and their supervisors will provide even more rigorous data on which to evaluate the development of professionalism in this course.

References

APLEC. (2000), Australasian Professional Legal Education Council and Law Admissions Consultative Committee. Competency standards for entry level lawyers. Available at http://www.aplec.asn.au/Pdf/Competency_Standards_for_Entry_Level_Lawyers.pdf [accessed 12 August 2012].

Barton, K., McKellar, P. and Maharg, P. (2007), 'Authentic fictions: simulation, professionalism and legal learning', *Clinical Law Review*, 14(1): 143–93.

Barton, K. and Westwood, F. (2006), 'From student to trainee practitioner – a study of team working as a learning experience', *Web Journal of Current Legal Issues* 3 [Online]. Available at: http://webjcli.ncl.ac.uk/2006/issue3/barton-westwood3.html [accessed 15 September 2012].

Boon, A., Flood, J. and Webb, J. (2005), 'Postmodern professions? The fragmentation of legal education and the legal profession', *Journal of Law and Society*, 32(3): 473–92.

Foley, T., Holmes, V., Rowe, M. and Tang, S. (2012), 'Practising professionalism: observations from an empirical study of new Australian lawyers', *Legal Ethics*, 15(1): 29–56.

Gentile, M. (2010), *Giving Voice to Values – How to Speak your Mind When You Know What's Right*. New Haven: Yale University Press.

Linser, R. and Ip, A. (2005), 'Imagining the world: the case for non-rendered virtuality – the role play simulation model', *AusWeb05 The Eleventh Australasian World Wide Web Conference*, Southern Cross University, Queensland, Australia 2005. Available at: http://ausweb.scu.edu.au/aw05/papers/refereed/ip/index.html [accessed 1 September 2012].

Maharg, P. (2007), *Transforming Legal Education: Learning and Teaching the Law in the Early Twenty-first Century*. London: Ashgate Publishing.

McKenna, P.J. and Maister, D.H. (2002), *First Among Equals – how to Manage a Group of Professionals*. New York: Free Press.

Nelson, R.L. and Trubek, D.M. (1992), 'Arenas of professionalism – the professional ideologies of lawyers in context', in *Lawyers' Ideals/Lawyers' Practices – Transformations in the American Legal Profession*, edited by Nelson, R.L. et al. New York: Cornell University Press, 177–214.

Nicholson, N. (2000), *Managing the Human Animal*. London: Texere Publishing Limited.

Nicolson, D. (2005), 'Making lawyers moral? Ethical codes and moral character', *Legal Studies*, 25(4): 601–26.

Papadakis, M., Hodgson, S., Teherani, A. and Kohatsu, N. (2004), 'Unprofessional behaviour in medical school is associated with subsequent disciplinary action by a state medical board', *Academic Medicine*, 79: 244.

Stuckey, R. (2007), *Best Practices for Legal Education*. Clinical Legal Education Association, 82–3.

Sullivan, W.M. (2005), *Work and Integrity – the Crisis and Promise of Professionalism in America*. San Francisco: Jossey-Bass.

Sullivan, W.M., Colby, A., Wegner, J.W., Bond, L. and Shulman, L.S. (2007), *Educating Lawyers – Preparation for the Profession of Law*. San Francisco: Jossey-Bass.

Wallace, J.E. and Kay, F.M. (2008), 'The professionalism of practicing law: a comparison across two work contexts', *Journal of Organizational Behaviour*, 29: 1021–24.

Ward, A. and Smith, J. (2003), *Trust and Mistrust – Radical Risk Strategies in Business Relationships*. Chichester: Wiley.

Webb, J. (2002), 'Being a lawyer/being a human being', *Legal Studies*, 5(1 and 2): 130–151.

Westwood, F. (2001), *Achieving Best Practice – Shaping Professionals for Success*. Maidenhead: McGraw-Hill.

Westwood, F. (2004 and 2008), *Accelerated Best Practice – Implementing Success in Professional Firms*. Basingstoke: Palgrave Macmillan, Leicester: Troubador.

Chapter 10

We Must Make Law Students Client-ready

John Burwell Garvey and Anne F. Zinkin

Introduction

Law schools have a duty to their students and society to provide a legal education that adequately trains law students to represent clients (ABA 2002). Studies of current legal education consistently conclude that '(t)he dichotomy between doctrinal analysis and theoretical considerations on the one hand and practice on the other is unfortunate, since each has an important role to play in a sound legal education' (Barry et al. 2000: 33). This chapter provides a possible starting point for schools that have not yet begun the move toward integrative education, and an opportunity for further discussion among those schools already in transition.[1]

We have written in detail about the history and reform of legal education in the USA (Garvey and Zinkin 2009). For the purposes of this chapter, we focus on the Daniel Webster Scholar Honors Program, a unique program at the University of New Hampshire School of Law (formerly known as Franklin Pierce Law Center or Pierce Law referred to in this chapter as UNH Law). In Part I of the chapter we describe the two-year program in detail, demonstrating how it fully integrates the instruction of legal doctrine with legal skills and values. The program also provides comprehensive assessment of a student's ability to practice law, which constitutes an alternative, two-year bar exam. In Part II, we generally describe the process for replicating the program in other jurisdictions.

Of the numerous reports advocating the integration of legal skills and values as part of the standard legal education, one of the most comprehensive was the MacCrate Report (MacCrate 1992). It provided an exhaustive look at the legal profession, the skills and values new lawyers should seek to acquire, and the educational continuum through which lawyers acquire these skills and values. It set forth fundamental lawyering skills and professional values that it believed 'every lawyer should acquire before assuming responsibility for the handling of a legal matter' (MacCrate 1992: 7). The ten fundamental lawyering skills identified were: Problem Solving; Legal Analysis and Reasoning; Legal Research;

---

1 The background to this chapter and an earlier version of it can be found at Garvey, J.B. and Zinkin, A.F. (2009) 'Making Law Students Client Ready: A New Model in Legal Education', *I Duke F. for L. and Soc. Change*: 101–29.

Factual Investigation; Communication; Counselling; Negotiation; Litigation and Alternative Dispute Resolution Procedures; Organization and Management of Legal Work; and Recognizing and Resolving Ethical Dilemmas. The four fundamental values were: Provision of Competent Representation; Striving to Promote Justice, Fairness and Morality; Striving to Improve the Profession; and Professional Self-Development.

With respect to imparting these skills and values to law students, the Report recognized 'that students who expect to enter practice in a relatively unsupervised practice setting have a special need for opportunities to obtain skills instruction' (MacCrate 1992: 330). Because '[t]he transition from law school into individual practice or relatively unsupervised positions in small law offices ... presents special problems of lawyer competence [in] law schools' (MacCrate 1992: 334), it recommended a co-ordinated effort among law schools, the organized bar and licensing authorities to address these special problems, noting in particular that it was important for law schools to 'work with the organized bar to assure that the development of lawyering skills continues beyond law school' (260).

In 2007, the Carnegie Foundation for the Advancement of Teaching (Sullivan et al. 2007) released a report on legal education entitled *Educating Lawyers: Preparation for the Profession of Law*. It proposed an integrative strategy for legal education and identified three apprenticeships – the cognitive, the practical and the ethical-social – that should be integrated to marshal all three apprenticeships 'in support of the larger goal of training competent and committed practitioners' (Sullivan et al. 2007: 28–9, 191). The first apprenticeship, the cognitive, 'focuses the student on the knowledge and way of thinking of the profession'. The second apprenticeship, the practical, schools students in 'the forms of expert practice shared by competent practitioners'. The third apprenticeship, the ethical-social, 'introduces students to the purposes and attitudes that are guided by the values for which the professional community is responsible' (Sullivan et al. 2007: 28–9).

Around the same time the Carnegie Foundation issued its 2007 Report, Professor Roy T. Stuckey and others published the report of the Steering Committee for the Best Practices Project of the Clinical Legal Education Association, entitled *Best Practices for Legal Education* (Stuckey 2007). Similar to the MacCrate Report, it observed that while '[i]t may not be possible to prepare students fully for the practice of law in three years ... law schools can come much closer than they are doing today' (Stuckey 2007: 5). Its key recommendations were reminiscent of those in the MacCrate and Carnegie Reports and included: (1) the primary goal of legal education should be to develop competence defined as the ability to resolve legal problems effectively and responsibly; (2) law schools should integrate the teaching of theory, doctrine and practice, and teach professionalism pervasively throughout all three years of law school; (3) law schools should employ context-based instruction; and (4) law schools should assess student learning through various methods of assessment, including multiple formative and summative assessments.

The central message of both Sullivan et al. (2007) and Stuckey (2007) is that law schools should:

- broaden the range of lessons they teach, reducing doctrinal instruction that uses the Socratic dialogue and the case method;
- integrate the teaching of knowledge, skills and values, and not treat them as separate subjects addressed in separate courses; and
- give much greater attention to instruction in professionalism.

As demonstrated below, the Daniel Webster Scholar Honors Program achieves all three of these goals.

Part I: The Daniel Webster Scholar Honours Program[2]

The stated mission of the Daniel Webster Scholar Honors Program is 'Making Law Students Client-Ready'. Although the program does not presume to graduate new lawyers who are ready to take on all levels of complexity, and recognizes that legal education is a continuing process, it does seek to provide a practice-based, client-oriented education, which prepares law students for the awesome responsibility of representing others. As recommended by the MacCrate Report, the program is a collaborative effort, which includes the New Hampshire Supreme Court, the New Hampshire Board of Bar Examiners, the New Hampshire Bar Association and UNH Law.

To keep the program sufficiently small and flexible during the developmental phase, it was limited to 15 students per class. Based upon its early success, however, the program has been enlarged three times and the goal is to eventually allow all students to participate. Students apply to the program in March of their first year of law school and are selected in the June following their first year. Selection is based upon overall ability to succeed in the program, which includes evaluation of academic, professional and interpersonal skills.

Program participants must meet all of the law school's requirements for graduation, in addition to requirements that are specific to the Daniel Webster Scholar Honors Program. During each semester, in addition to electives, scholars must take specifically designed Daniel Webster Scholar (DWS) courses, which generally involve substantial simulation, including:

---

2 This section is based upon a presentation that co-author Garvey gave in 2012 as the TePoel Lecturer at Creighton University School of Law, entitled 'Changes in Legal Education and the Professional and Ethical Implications for Practicing Attorneys'. Detailed information about the Daniel Webster Scholar Honors Program can be found on the UNH Law website. See http://law.unh.edu/academics/jd-degree/daniel-webster-scholars (last visited 3 October 2012).

- Pretrial Advocacy;
- Trial Advocacy;
- Negotiations and ADR;
- a miniseries that exposes them to Family Law, Law Office Management, Commercial Paper (Articles 3 and 9) and Conflicts of Law;
- Business Transactions;
- and a capstone course, Advanced Problem Solving and Client Counselling, that integrates and builds upon the skills they have already learned through the program.

Each student must also take four additional courses that ordinarily would be elective:

1. Business Associations;
2. Evidence;
3. Wills, Trusts & Estates;
4. and Personal Taxation.

Moreover, each must have at least six credit hours of clinical and/or externship experience. Following the mini-series exposure to Family Law, each student is trained as a Domestic Violence Emergency (DOVE) attorney who can then provide *pro bono* service through the New Hampshire Bar Association. Students must obtain at least a B- in all DWS courses and at least a 3.0 cumulative school transcript grade point average on a 4.0 scale. Scholars who successfully complete the two-year program and who pass the Multi-State Professional Responsibility Exam and the character and fitness check are then certified by the board of bar examiners as having passed the New Hampshire bar exam and are admitted to the New Hampshire bar upon graduation.

1. Assessment

Formative, reflective and summative assessment is an integral part of the program, both as a critical aspect of the learning environment and as a means of measuring outcomes. Beginning with an all-day orientation workshop, new Webster Scholars are informed of the various goals for assessment and provided with the outcomes rubric for Pretrial Advocacy, their first DWS Course. The first page of the current Pretrial Advocacy rubric is shown below:

In addition to the MacCrate skills and values, the rubric uses information from a study conducted by University of California at Berkeley Professors Marjorie M. Shultz and Sheldon Zedeck, in which they identify 26 factors related to effective lawyering and the behaviours associated with each factor (Shultz and Zedeck 2009a, 2009b; see also Glater 2009).

A master document has also been created that lists all of the courses in the program and identifies the MacCrate skills and values each course is intended

Table 10.1   Retrial Advocacy: Summative Evaluation

Assessing Performance of Webster Scholars According to MacCrate Skills*

Fundamental Lawyering Skill (MacCrate)	Examples of Performances Showing that Student is 'Client Ready'	Project(s) Demonstrating Skill
1. Problem solving 1 Identifies and diagnoses legal problems 2 Generates alternative solutions and strategies 3 Develops a plan of action 4 Implements a plan of action 5 Keeps the planning process open to new information and ideas	Student demonstrates sufficient grounding in substantive law to enable him or her to recognize legal issues and potential courses of action Student is able to identify potential outcomes and consequences and develop contingency plans to handle various possibilities Student listens well, and tries to use the experience, knowledge and insight of others in dealing with a problem	Week 1: Interview of potential client by plaintiff's firm attorneys; oral report to partner by defense firm attorneys Week 2: Evaluative memo to partner by plaintiff's firm attorneys; conference call with HR person by defense firm attorneys Week 3: Letter to client Week 4: Discovery plan Week 5: Discovery requests Week 6: Discovery responses Week 7: Further discovery plans Weeks 8 & 9: Depositions Weeks 10 & 11: Summary judgment motion drafted by defense firm attorneys Week 12: Opposition to summary judgment motion drafted by plaintiff's firm attorneys Week 13: Oral argument Week 14: Post-discovery memorandum to partner Week 15: Reflective paper Summative Evaluation by Professor

Note: * Language primarily based upon other work performed on a grant to the principal investigators, Marjorie Shultz and Sheldon Zedeck from the Law Schools Admission Council.

to teach. Students also receive benchmarks for most of their portfolio items. Benchmarks describe various activities and indicate whether the students' approach, meet or exceed expectations. The students submit a benchmark with their work and the professors complete the same benchmark after reviewing the work in order to give the students feedback. This is part of the DWS learning cycle of preparation, performance, feedback, reflection and improvement:

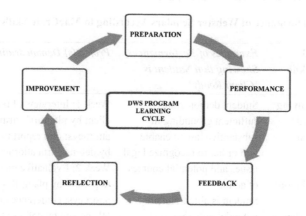

Figure 10.1   DWS program learning cycle

A sample benchmark for a draft evaluative memo followed by the benchmark for the final evaluative memo are shown below:

Table 10.2   Benchmark for Draft Evaluation Memo

Nature of Task and Performance Goal	Exceeds	Meets	Approaches
DRAFT Evaluation Memo to Partner Individual Work Goal – exposure, first attempt at receiving facts from client interview, researching law and providing coherent and concise written analysis for partner MacCrate 1, 2, 3, 4, 5, 6, 9	Memo includes facts and law and is well-organized, coherent, and concise. Supervising attorney would *be confident that writer understood and appropriately analyzed issues.*	Memo includes facts and law and is *generally* well-organized, coherent, and concise. Supervising attorney would *require some* additional *clarification, reorganization, and/ or analysis.*	Memo *lacks clear organization, coherence or conciseness.* Supervising attorney would require **significant** *clarification, reorganization, and/or analysis.*

Table 10.3   Benchmark for Final Evaluation Memo

Nature of Task and Performance Goal	Exceeds	Meets	Approaches
FINAL Evaluation Memo to Partner Review FINAL memo in conjunction with initial memo and comments Individual Work Goal – demonstration of adequate evaluative and writing skills for first year associate MacCrate 1, 2, 3, 4, 5, 6, 9	Memo includes facts and law and is well-organized, coherent, and concise. Supervising attorney would *be confident that writer understood and appropriately analyzed issues.* Incorporates feedback from initial memo and improves quality.	Memo includes facts and law and is *generally* well-organized, coherent, and concise. Supervising attorney would require *some* additional clarification, reorganization, and/ or analysis. *For the most part,* incorporates feedback from initial memo and improves quality.	Memo *lacks clear organization, coherence or conciseness.* Supervising attorney would require *significant* additional clarification, reorganization, and/or analysis. *Fails* to incorporate feedback from initial memo and improve quality.

DWS courses are graded based upon individual performance as measured against predetermined desirable outcomes rather than upon a curve. In keeping with all of the assessment recommendations discussed above, students are assessed by faculty, judges, lawyers, court reporters, lay people, bar examiners, peers and themselves. They keep a journal and, for each course, reflect upon their strengths and weaknesses, relating to and identifying the MacCrate skills and values in their work. At the conclusion of each DWS course, they also write a reflective paper, again using the MacCrate skills and values against which to evaluate themselves. They identify which MacCrate skills and values were implicated during the course, then discuss their own perceived strengths and weaknesses as they relate to these skills and values, and reflect upon how they intend to improve going forward. In addition to enabling students to develop the life-long skill of self-reflection, the reflective paper requires them to become familiar with the MacCrate skills and values, thus helping them understand the requirements for competent practice.

Consistent with the recommendations in the Carnegie Report (Sullivan et al. 2007: 174) and Best Practices (Stuckey 2007: 196–7), scholars have portfolios of their work compiled throughout their participation in the program. The portfolio includes papers, legal documents the scholar has drafted, exams, self-reflective analysis based upon the MacCrate skills and values, peer evaluations, teacher evaluations, various videos of student performances in simulated settings and the like. Every semester, each portfolio is evaluated by a bar examiner, who provides written comments to the student. In the spring semester of each year, every scholar meets with and is questioned by a bar examiner about the portfolio. This repeated review and reflection from multiple sources 'integrate[s] the teaching of knowledge, skills and values' (Stuckey 2007: vii), rather than as separate subjects addressed in separate courses.

In the summer of 2008, the program added an additional assessment component by training eight standardized clients. 'Standardized clients' are similar to standardized patients used in medical schools are actors trained to assess a student's skill in communicating with clients according to standardized criteria (Barton et al. 2006). Each actor is given a persona, using a carefully prepared simulation. Although the role is not 'scripted', the actors are trained to stay in character, based upon the detailed scenario that is provided to them. Each is then interviewed by a student, and acts like an authentic client during the interview. Each interview will vary depending upon how the student conducts it and what questions are asked. According to the standardized criteria, each client then evaluates the student's interviewing skills.

Standardized clients enable students to learn important client relationship skills, particularly those associated with client counselling, and allow the Program to assess student performance in those skills (see Barton et al. 2006). It has carried this work forward and expanded on it. Since May of 2009, standardized clients have been used for an empirical study comparing DWS students with newly admitted bar members (Barton et al. 2011). While the statistics have yet to be fully analysed, there appears to be a strong correlation in the initial data between DWS student training with standardized clients, and significant improvement in eliciting factual information in the case fact patterns.

Additionally, co-author Garvey is working with Professors Maharg, Barton and Cunningham to apply and integrate the Simulated Learning Environment (SIMPLE) software as a platform for running and assessing simulations. Developed by Maharg, Barton and others, and already operating in the United Kingdom, this transactional software is a vibrant learning opportunity and can provide an economy of scale for running simulations as the number of Webster Scholars increases (Maharg 2007, Barton et al. 2007). 'American law schools have yet to approach the ingenuity evident among some schools in Europe, most particularly the University of Strathclyde, under the leadership of Professor Paul Maharg, and other professional programs using stimulations to provide instruction in complex legal problem-solving' (Wegner 2009: 977).

2. A Two-year Bar Exam

The Daniel Webster Scholar program assesses the competencies of students to practice law over a two-year period. In this way it is like a two-year bar exam, instead of the traditional two-day bar exam. Upon graduating from the program, scholars are automatically eligible for admission to the New Hampshire State Bar, without having to take the traditional bar exam. While it is beyond the scope of this chapter to discuss in depth the need for alternatives to the traditional two-day bar examination[3] and the value of the Daniel Webster Scholar Honors Program as a viable alternative, it is worth noting that the assessment piece of the Program uses outcome measures recommended by Best Practices (Stuckey 2007: 175–96), the July 2008 Final Report of the Outcome Measures Committee of the ABA Section of Legal Education and Admissions to the Bar, and the Society of American Law Teachers (SALT 2008). Given these assessments, students that graduate from the program gain admission to the bar and are not required to take the traditional two-day state bar exam.

3. The Actual Experience

As noted above, the Daniel Webster Scholar Honors Program makes adjustments after each learning cycle. To provide a flavour for the actual experience, we will chronicle the program as it currently exists.

The scholars have an intensive first year in the program, which begins in the fall of their 2L year. In addition to their regular classes, they participate in simulations and have real client contact. They take Pretrial Advocacy, which divides them into two law firms to 'litigate' a Family and Medical Leave Act (FMLA) case in mock federal court. As in the actual case upon which the simulation is based, issues of ethics and professional behaviour are integrated into the fact pattern, meeting the third apprenticeship discussed in the Carnegie Report (Sullivan et al. 2007). Each firm has an experienced litigator/professor in the role of 'senior partner', and the 2L scholars are 'junior associates'. There are also two or three 3L scholars in each firm who serve as 'senior associates', providing the kind of assistance one would normally expect from a teaching assistant staying in role as a senior associate. Standardized clients play the roles of the parties and various witnesses. In the course of discovery, there are numerous issues which arise regarding professionalism such as continuances, working together to create a discovery plan, scheduling of witnesses.

In the course of responding to document requests, both firms have to make difficult production decisions about documents that may be responsive to the discovery requests. Also, both sides discover for the first time during a deposition that the witness did not produce all requested documents in advance of the deposition. Because this witness is under the control of the defendant corporation, this creates a real-time ethical dilemma for the defending attorneys and a professional decision for the deposing attorneys as to how they choose to behave

---

3   For sources discussing critiques of and alternatives to the bar exam, see Society of American Law Teachers [hereinafter SALT], *Potential Alternatives to the Existing Bar Exam* 6–7 (undated and unpublished manuscript), available at http://www.saltlaw.org/~salt2007/files/uploads/barexamalternatives.doc; see also Kristen Booth Glen, 'Thinking Out of the Bar Exam Box: A Proposal to 'MacCrate' Entry to the Profession', 23 Pace L. Rev. 343 (Spring 2003).

in light of the disclosure. These events are later debriefed by the firms when there is time to reflect.

Sometimes working in small groups and sometimes working alone, the junior associates carry out a range of tasks including:

- interviewing clients and witnesses;
- preparing or answering a complaint;
- preparing and answering interrogatories;
- taking and defending a deposition with a real court reporter who records it in real time and provides a transcript;
- preparing a motion or an objection to a motion for summary judgment which is then argued before a real judge in the judge's courtroom;
- and preparing a post-discovery evaluation of the case for the senior partner.

Throughout the semester, they also submit timesheets to their senior partners.

The junior associates receive constructive feedback from their senior partners, senior associates and from each other, as well as from court reporters, judges, attorneys, standardized clients and witnesses. They receive an added benefit by seeing practicing attorneys and sitting judges volunteer their time to the program, learning from their example the importance of giving back to the profession. They are also required to observe and critique their taped deposition and oral argument performances. At the end of the course, each scholar prepares a reflective paper in which, using the MacCrate skills and values as a guide, they identify those skills and values that were addressed in the course, reflect upon his or her own perceived strengths and weaknesses, and discuss how to cultivate strengths and improve weaknesses.

In the spring 2L semester, the scholars continue their FMLA case in Trial Advocacy. Using the interrogatories and deposition transcripts they obtained in the first semester, they try their hand at controlling the witnesses in the trial setting. They also participate in a simulated criminal trial from beginning to end, complete with a student jury that deliberates. Again, scholars are taped so that they can watch their performance, and receive feedback from peers, professors, lawyers, judges, jurors and witnesses. Their reflective papers are submitted when the course is completed.

Also during the spring 2L semester, the scholars take an intensive course on Negotiations and ADR, where they role-play in a variety of settings in cases involving issues including family law, criminal law, labour law and intellectual property. As with the Pretrial Advocacy and Trial Advocacy classes, student performances are sometimes taped so that scholars can observe and critique themselves. They also receive feedback from their peers and professors as well as from practitioners who observe these sessions. In addition to the negotiation problems that are designed by the professors, the scholars are asked to find and analyse two problems from current events and the class then chooses one of those problems to negotiate. As an example, the 2008 scholars negotiated a possible resolution to *Morse v. Frederick*, 127 S. Ct. 2618 (2007), the public school case where a student was suspended for displaying a sign which said, 'Bong Hits 4 Jesus'. At the time, the case was pending before the United States Supreme Court. A simulation was created, and the scholars were assigned to play various roles, including parents, student, principal and lawyer. Through negotiation, the parties arrived at a settlement, which included an apology by the student for his immature conduct and an apology and acknowledgement by the principal that she overreacted. Following the initial introduction to negotiation, students focus on mediation, collaborative law and arbitration and participate in simulations. As with all other DWS courses, the students submit a reflective paper at the conclusion of the course.

Additionally, in the second semester of their 2L year, the students receive four weeks of training in Family Law as part of a mini-series course – a number of short course modules that expose them to numerous areas of practice. They subsequently receive the DOVE training described above, which gives them an opportunity to meet clients in emergency domestic violence situations. This experience provides valuable client contact and integrates the concept of the lawyer as volunteer-citizen. At the conclusion of this experience, students again submit reflective papers. Finally, the mini-series exposes students to conflicts of laws, secured transactions and negotiable instruments.

In the fall of their 3L year, scholars take Business Transactions, which focuses upon the processes by which businesses are formed, financed, operated, altered and sold. Unlike a typical law school business course, the scholars are again involved in simulations. They create numerous documents and receive substantial feedback. They are asked individually to issue-spot in complex fact patterns, and then analyse the fact patterns as a group. As with the other courses, they receive review from their peers and from their professor. In addition, they integrate and build upon the negotiations experience of the previous semester, and negotiate various issues, including the formation of a limited liability company.

Then, in the spring of their 3L year, the scholars take the Capstone Course, called Advanced Problem Solving and Client Counseling. In this course, as in the real world, students are assigned roles in various factual situations that involve multiple areas of substantive law, without being first guided as to what issues are relevant. The course primarily focuses upon the client/lawyer relationship and developing the listening, analytical and counselling skills necessary to be a competent lawyer. Clients are then interviewed, necessary research is performed and advice is given. Students observe and provide feedback to each other using the same assessment forms that the standardized clients will later use. This familiarizes the students with what is being tested and makes them more conscious of the skills necessary to interview a client successfully.

In addition, some students have sometimes served as a focus group for practicing attorneys involved in a real pending case. The attorneys ask them for feedback about their theories of the case and the like. This experience allows students to view litigation from the eyes of a prospective juror or other decision-maker. Toward the end of the semester, students interview standardized clients, who provide written assessments based upon a standardized form. This form is nearly identical to the one used at Strathclyde Law School (Barton et al. 2006). A satisfactory score on the standardized client assessment is necessary to pass the alternative bar exam provided through the program. All interviews are taped. If a student does not receive a passing mark, the interview will be examined by the director and by the standardized client co-ordinator, who have the authority to overturn an adverse decision. Students who do not pass the interview the first time will have an opportunity to take it again.

Finally, during the last semester of the four-semester program, scholars participate in clinical courses and/or externships including court clerkships. These activities involve extensive feedback from supervising professors and outside attorneys. Students prepare reflective papers about these experiences.

At the conclusion of each semester, with the exception of the final semester, students meet with their assigned bar examiner who reviews the student's portfolio and asks questions about the work and the development of the student in general. The bar examiner provides written feedback on whether the bar examiner has any concerns.

4. Commentaries Evaluations on the Program

The program graduated its fifth class in May of 2012. We recognize that it is still in the early stages, but feedback has been positive. Experts in legal education agree that the Daniel Webster Scholar Honors Program is noteworthy. For example, The Society of American Law Teachers stated that '[UNH Law], through its Daniel Webster Scholar Program, is developing and testing assessment tools for a wide range of lawyering skills. That program, and others like it, should serve as a resource for this Committee'. Lloyd Bond, one of the authors of the Carnegie Report, has said:

> **[The Daniel Webster Scholar Honors Program]** fuses instruction and assessment in the most intimate and integrated way that I have ever seen. Two years of it. It's two years of what we actually recommended in [the Carnegie Report], integrated in such a way that truly instruction and assessment are indistinguishable (Bond 2008).

According to Professor Bond, 'The Daniel Webster Scholar Program ... exemplifies the sea change [the Carnegie Report authors] had in mind'.

Additionally, SALT encouraged replication of the program. We are gratified by this early success; we believe, however, that the program's ultimate contribution to broad-based reform will depend upon the extent to which it is expanded and replicated. Below, we provide a recipe for developing similar programs.

Part II: Moving Forward: Replicating the Program

We recognize that change can be a challenge in any institution, and we do not presume to tell schools exactly how to implement their own Daniel Webster Scholar Honors Program. As we described above, developing the synergy for creating the program was quite complex, and involved the buy-in of numerous stakeholders, including the New Hampshire Supreme Court, the New Hampshire Bar Examiners, the New Hampshire Bar, as well as UNH Law administration, faculty, staff and students. From that experience, we offer the following recommendations for creating a program like the Daniel Webster Scholar Honors Program:

1. Draft a mission statement. Using the MacCrate Report, the Carnegie Report and Best Practices as guides, identify the goals for students to reach before they graduate.

2. Review your school's current curriculum to assess the extent to which it addresses the goals identified above. If possible, survey the faculty and ask professors to describe their courses and the skills and values addressed in each course. At UNH Law, the curriculum committee prepared a survey accessible by computer to faculty members. A survey provides important information for the new program and helps to make all faculty members more mindful of what they are teaching and why.

3. Consider what you would like to teach in the new program, and how you would like to integrate it into the overall curriculum. Because the program attempts to integrate the educational experience in increasingly complex layers, it is important to be intentional about the educational sequencing. For example, the Webster Scholars must take Business Associations and Personal Tax in their 2L year because they need the information to take full advantage of the learning opportunities in the DWS Business Transactions course in their 3L year.

4. Identify all available resources in your law school, legal community and community at large. For example: (a) identify professors with substantial practice experience who are willing to participate, and catalogue that experience; (b) identify programs in the school which already exist, such as clinics, externship programs and moot courts, which can be integrated into an overall program; (c) announce the program in your alumni magazine and on the web, and seek alumni volunteers; (d) announce the program in the state and local bar publications, and seek volunteers; (e) use contacts to request volunteers personally. This includes judges, lawyers, court reporters, lay people and paralegals. You are only limited by your imagination and enthusiasm, and many people enjoy participating as volunteers in the law school setting.

5. Design your courses, intentionally weaving them together so that they create a seamless fabric. Carry simulations forward from one course to the

next, so that as the courses progress, you build additional complexity. This allows the students to develop their skills incrementally as they go from exposure, to competency, to mastery. For example, we carry the FMLA fact pattern forward from Pretrial Advocacy to Trial Advocacy so students see how the pieces fit together, and their skills and insights improve in the process through repetition. When they try the FMLA case in Trial Advocacy, students may discover how difficult it is to control a witness if they obtained only vague questions and answers from a deposition taken the prior semester in Pretrial Advocacy.

6. When designing courses, take advantage of resources that are already available. Visit our program. We have already created simulations that others may use. Some texts now offer electronic files with case documents. When the SIMPLE software simulations are developed they should be readily transferrable, and schools using the technology should be able to share programs that they create. Use the resources that are available on the ETL website and other materials that are now available without cost.[4]

7. Select your faculty. This is a critical task because not everyone has the energy, teaching skill and patience to run simulations and provide formative assessments. Experienced adjuncts can be very useful, but inexperienced adjuncts need substantial preparation and training. If possible, have a new adjunct co-teach the first time with a teacher who is experienced with the teaching method.

8. Communicate clearly and constantly with the faculty as you develop the program. Change can be threatening to some. Seek input and ideas, and show skeptics that the program provides added value. If they are not already familiar with the MacCrate Report, the Carnegie Report and Best Practices, educate them. You need faculty buy-in for the program to flourish. This should be easier now, with the publication of the ABA Section of Legal Education and Admissions to the Bar, Report of the Outcome Measures Committee, which makes it clear that outcomes assessment will be part of accreditation ABA (ABA 2008).

9. Communicate with the students. Explain the program on the web, in person and in writing. Get them involved in the planning process so that they have some ownership.

10. Create an application for students wanting to apply. Make it straightforward. You can effectively evaluate the applicants if you conduct personal interviews and obtain writing samples, references from 1L professors and access to student school files.

11. Have a selection committee – not just an individual. We use the director and four professors of 1Ls because they have personally observed the students in the learning environment.

---

4   See http://educatingtomorrowslawyers.du.edu/course-portfolios/submit-your-course/ (last visited 3 October 2012).

12. At least initially, limit enrolment. We found that 15 students per class were manageable in the beginning, and we have now expanded three times to the current enrolment of 24 per class. Our ultimate goal is to allow all students who wish to participate to do so.
13. As for the bar licensing part of this program, the school will need to approach the licensing entity in its state to see if there is any interest. We are happy to offer case-specific suggestions and guidance.

While this is only intended to serve as an overview, it does demonstrate that the program can be easily replicated on a modest budget and with a lot of energy. We have implemented the pilot phase with one full-time director, who also teaches at least nine credit hours during the year, supervises the other DWS courses and has continued a part-time practice as an arbitrator and mediator. Such mediations and arbitrations now take place at the school whenever the parties agree, which allows students to observe them. The judges, lawyers and court reporters have all been excited to participate as volunteers. The court reporters have donated eight 'real-time' depositions per year, at a value of many thousands of dollars, but we have more volunteers each year than we need. The judges use their own courtrooms, and court personnel consistently enjoy the experience. Lawyers consistently volunteer whenever available. The standardized clients are paid $15 per hour. Implementation on a larger scale will be more expensive and will require more faculty effort, but we believe that the SIMPLE simulation software will provide for an economy of scale. We are confident that the program can be replicated and expanded, and we encourage others to do so.

Conclusion

We are not naïve about the difficulty of creating real systemic change. We are familiar with the economies of legal education and the political power of 'standup' law professors. We recognize that '[m]ost faculty are drawn from a very small number of leading academic institutions, from among lawyers who have taken predictable career paths' (Sullivan et al. 2007: 89) and that law schools often 'pay scant attention to preparing their students for practice' (Sullivan et al. 2007: 90; see Segal 2011). We acknowledge that resistance to change is likely to continue.

But despite years of discussion without substantial action, the seeds of real reform are finally germinating throughout the legal community. Like the MacCrate Report before them, the Carnegie Report and Best Practices have led to a flurry of conferences that have considered the future of legal education.[5] This time, however, many law schools are taking a wholesale look at their curriculum, and

---

5 For a relatively complete list of such conferences, see Center for Excellence in Teaching (CELT), Conferences, Presentations and Events, http://www.albanylaw.edu/celt/events/Pages/default.aspx (last visited 3 October 2012).

many schools are working with Educating Tomorrow's Lawyers to collaborate and to implement lasting change (Glater 2007). With the ABA Section of Legal Education and Admissions to the Bar, Report of the Outcome Measures Committee (ABA 2008), outcome measurement has taken on increased credibility and priority, and cannot be ignored. Schools are freely exchanging ideas and documents. The Internet has become a vast and economical way of exchanging ideas and technology; many conference presentations and papers are available on it for free. As David I.C. Thomson, Professor and Director of the Lawyering Process Program at the University of Denver Sturm College of Law, has observed:

> [L]egal education has successfully resisted systemic change for many years. Given this dubious track record, the only way significant change can reasonably be predicted is if something is different this time. Fortunately, there is something different this time; the ubiquity of technology ... [T]he internet has achieved massive growth. A generation of students has grown up with the sophisticated and pervasive use of technology in nearly every facet of their lives. Computers are how today's law students communicate and learn. Fortunately, this same technology presents legal educators with a golden opportunity to reach students unlike any that have been available before (Thomas 2008: vii–viii).

Change is happening. Seeds long ago planted in the legal education community are showing signs of sprouting. We encourage the positive, and appreciate the signs of 'spring'. To those who would hesitate, we offer this final observation.

Most students attend law school with the intent of practicing law (NALP 2007: 1). They pay their law school tens of thousands of dollars and many take on tremendous debt, so that they can be properly prepared for the awesome fiduciary responsibility of representing clients (Wilder 2007). Law schools accept their money; in fact, 86 per cent of all law school income is from student tuition (MacCrate 1994). Given the source of their money and the reason for the expenditure, a primary purpose of law schools *must* be to produce competent lawyers.

We agree with those who opine that '[l]aw schools have a moral and ethical obligation to society and, to an even greater degree, to their students to adequately prepare the students to succeed as professionals' (Trujillo 2007: 70; see also Garvey[6]). Not only do law schools train students who will represent clients and become fiduciaries to their clients, but they also train students who will become 'the principal instrumentalities' for protecting individual rights, ensuring equal justice between persons and implementing policies to promote the common welfare (Gordon 2009: 1171). As such, *law schools are the fiduciaries of*

---

6   http://law.gsu.edu/FutureOfLegalEducationConference/Program(Final).php. Detailed information about the Daniel Webster Scholar Honors Program can be found on the UNH Law website. See Daniel Webster Scholar Honors Program, http://www.piercelaw.edu/websterscholar/ (last visited 21 February 2009).

these future public and private fiduciaries. Law schools, thus, have an obligation to make students client-ready, and to make legal education a means and not a bar to greater equality in the profession. This must be the standard of care, and the primary consideration of law schools and professors (Symposium 2008). Law schools must allocate their dollars *and* professors their time so that law students (and, in turn, their future clients) are the first priority. As Robert MacCrate has said, it is

> ... difficult to understand how a law school ... can derive 86 percent of its income from student tuition, send its graduates as a result out into practice with huge personal debt, and not be willing to assign equal priority in the law school, along with developing the law, to preparing its students to participate effectively in the legal profession (MacCrate 1994: 92).

After many thousands of hours of analysis from different interest groups, the overwhelming consensus is that law schools can and should do much better (Stuckey 2007: 7). Failing to change how we teach law students in light of so much evidence and so many advances is tantamount to professional malpractice (Symposium 2008). As Alice Thomas, Associate Professor at University of District of Columbia David A. Clarke School of Law, Visiting Professor at Howard University School of Law and former Carnegie Scholar for the Carnegie Foundation for the Advancement of Teaching, observed:

> Are we committing malpractice in the way we choose to design, deliver, and assess law school effectiveness in today's law schools? ... [Y]ou would not be surprised with my answer. It is an overwhelmingly resounding 'yes'. Yes, I think we are committing malpractice if we rely on presently held views and we ignore the findings of these reports and continue business as usual ...

I go back to Professor Wegner's earlier statement that all of this is a matter of conscience. Professor Stuckey, too, said and I paraphrase, if we, faculty, have no ethical centre and no sense of consciousness about what we are doing, we can easily sit back and watch others attempt to reform legal education and let the pursuit of tenure alone guide us. As the evidence in the reports emerges, one might be tempted to say that, 'I have been doing the same thing for a very long time, it seems to work, and I just do not want to change'. Or to say, 'I have my summers to myself so I have no time for new practice'. Well, I do not think we can say these things any more, in light of these reports, if we are going to meet the minimum standard of care and due diligence under the identity apprenticeship. I think we all need to enter the conversation. I also think that if you choose not to enter the conversation, then you are a part of the problem. The reform of legal education will take involvement from all of us (Symposium 2008: 868, 873).

We argue that the time for any serious debate about the need for substantial change in legal education has passed. The time to act is now. Change is not only necessary, but, as the Daniel Webster Scholar Honors Program and other initiatives around the country demonstrate, possible.

References

ABA Standards for Approval of Law Schools (2002).

ABA (2008), American Bar Association Section of Legal Education and Admissions to the Bar, Report of the Outcomes Measures Committee. Available at http://www.abanet.org/legaled/committees/subcomm/Outcome%20Measures%20Final%20Report.pdf.

Barry, M.M., Dubin, J.C., Peter, A. and Joy, P.A. (2002), 'Clinical Education for this Millennium: The Third Wave', *Clinical Law Review*, 7(1): 33.

Barton, K, Cunningham, C.C., Todd, G. and Maharg, P. (2006), 'Valuing What Clients Think: Standardized Clients and the Assessment of Communicative Competence', *Clinical Law Review*, 13(1): 3–5.

Barton, K., McKellar, P. and Maharg, P. (2007), 'Authentic Fictions: Simulation, Professionalism, and Legal Learning', *Clinical Law Review*, 14: 143.

Barton, K., Garvey, J. and Maharg, P. (2011), *Standardized Clients and SIMPLE (SIMulated Professional Learning Environment): Learning Professionalism Through Simulated Practice* at 4. Available at http://dotank.nyls.edu/futureed/2011proposals/05scas.pdf.

Bond, L. (2008), The Carnegie Foundation for the Advancement of Teaching, *Remarks Before the Carnegie Foundation/Legal Education Reform Project Assessment Workshop at New York University School of Law* (25 June 2008).

Garvey, J.B. and Zinkin, A.F. (2009), 'Making Law Students Client-Ready: A New Model in Legal Education', *Duke F for L. & Soc. Change*, 1: 101–29.

Glater, J.D. (2007), *Training Law Students for Real Life Careers*, NY TIMES, October 31, 2007, at B3. Available at http://www.nytimes.com/2007/10/31/education/31lawschool.html?_r=1&scp=1&sq=&st=nyt.

Glater, J.D. (2009), *Study Offers a New Test of Potential Lawyers*, NY TIMES, March 11, 2009, at A22. Available at http://www.nytimes.com/2009/03/11/education/11lsat.html?scp=1&sq=Sheldon%20Zedeck&st=cse (last visited 3 October 2012).

Gordon, R.W. (2009), 'The Citizen Lawyer: A Brief Informal History of a Myth with Some Basis in Reality', *Yale Law School Faculty Scholarship Series, Paper 1398*, 1171.

MacCrate, R. (1992), *American Bar Association Section of Legal Education and Admissions to the Bar, Legal Education and Professional Development: An Educational Continuum, Report of the Task Force on Law Schools and the Profession: Narrowing the Gap 106 (ABA 1992)*

MacCrate, R. (1994), 'Preparing Lawyers to Participate Effectively in the Legal Profession', *J. Legal Educ.*, 44: 89–92.

Maharg, P. (2007), *Transforming Legal Education: Learning and Teaching the Law in the Early Twenty-First Century*. London: Ashgate.

SALT (2008), Statement to ABA Outcome Measures Committee (1 Feb. 2008). Available at http://www.abanet.org/legaled/committees/subcomm/Outcome%20Measures_comments_SALT%20Feb%202008.pdf.

Segal, D. (2011), *What They Don't Teach Law Students: Lawyering*, NY TIMES, 19 Nov. 2011. Available at http://www.nytimes.com/2011/11/20/business/after-law-school-associates-learn-to-be-lawyers.html.

Shultz, M.M. and Zedeck, S. (2009a), *Final Report: Identification, Development and Validation of Predictors for Successful Lawyering* (30 Jan. 2009). Available at SSRN: http://ssrn.com/abstract=1353554).

Shultz, M.M. and Zedeck, S. (2009b), *Predicting Lawyer Effectiveness: A New Assessment for Use in Law School Admission Decisions*, CELS 2009 4th Annual Conference on Empirical Legal Studies Paper (31 July 2009). Available at SSRN: http://ssrn.com/abstract=1442118.

Stuckey, R. (2007), *Best Practice for Legal Education: A Vision and Road Map*. Columbia: Clinical Legal Education Organization. Available at http://law.sc.edu/faculty/stuckey/best_practices/best_practices-full.pdf.

Symposium (2008), 'The Opportunity for Legal Education', *Mercer L. Rev.*, 59: 821, 866–82.

Sullivan, W.M., Colby, A., Wegner, J.W., Bond, L. and Shulman, L.S. (2007), *Educating Lawyers: Preparation for the Profession of Law*. San Francisco: Jossey-Bass.

Thomas, D.I.C. (2008), 'Legal Education for a Digital Age. *The National Association for Law Placement, Class of 2007 National Summary Report* 1. Available at http://www.nalp.org/uploads/1229_natlsummary07revised.pdf.

Trujillo, L. (2007), 'The Relationship Between Law School and the Bar Exam: A Look at Assessment and Student Success', *Univ. of Colo. L Rev.*, 78: 69–83.

Wegner, J.W. (2009), *Symposium 2009: A Legal Education Prospectus: Law Schools & Emerging Frontiers; Reframing Legal Education's 'Wicked Problems'*, *Rutgers L. Rev.*, 61: 867, 925.

Wilder, G.Z. (2007), National Association for Law Placement Foundation for Law Career Research and Education, Law School Debt among new layers: an after the JD Monograph 3.

Index

For Product Safety Concerns and Information please contact our
EU representative GPSR@taylorandfrancis.com Taylor & Francis
Verlag GmbH, Kaufingerstraße 24, 80331 München, Germany